Autobiographical Essays by Native American Writers

I Tell

Edited by Brian Swann and Arnold Krupat

You

University of Nebraska Press: Lincoln & London

Now

∞

First Nebraska paperback printing: 2005

Library of Congress Cataloging-in-Publication Data
I tell you now: autobiographical essays by Native American writers / edited by Brian
Swann and Arnold Krupat.—Bison Books ed.
p.   cm.—(American Indian lives)
Includes bibliographical references.
ISBN 0-8032-9314-3 (pbk.: alk. paper)
1. Indians of North America—Biography.   2. Indian authors—Biography.
3. Authors, American—20th century—Biography.   4. Indians of North America—
Intellectual life.   I. Swann, Brian.   II. Krupat, Arnold.   III. Series.
E89.I24   2005
920'.009297073—dc22   2004030741

. . . Despite loss and disillusion, I count myself
rich, fertile, and magical.
I tell you now. You *can* go home again.

Mary TallMountain
"You *Can* Go Home Again: A Sequence"

These few things then,
I am telling you
because I do want you to know
and in that way
have you come to know me now.

Simon Ortiz
"I Tell You Now"

Contents

Introduction to the
Bison Books Edition

The broad genre of writing known to the West as *autobiography* had no oral equivalent among the cultures of the indigenous inhabitants of the Americas. Although tribal nations, like people the world over, kept material as well as mental records of collective and personal experience, the notion of telling the whole of any one individual's life or taking merely personal experience as of particular significance was, in the most literal way, foreign. And even though there is by now a large and interesting group of autobiographies by Indian people—David Brumble's *Annotated Bibliography of American Indian and Eskimo Autobiographies* (1981) and its "Supplement" (1982), for example, listed more than six hundred of these over twenty years ago—some Native Americans, as we shall have occasion to note, even today have a certain wariness in regard to autobiographical forms of writing.[1]

The first Native American autobiographies were written by Christianized Indians. So far as is known, the earliest was the work of the Reverend Samson Occom, a Mohegan, who wrote a brief autobiography in 1768. (Occom was the student of Eleazar Wheelock, founder of Moors Indian School and later of Dartmouth College.) In 1791 Hendrick Aupaumut, generally referred to as a Mahican, included a good deal of autobiographical material in his *Journal of a Mission to the Western Tribes of Indians* (1827). Neither of these early texts was published in its author's lifetime: Occom's manuscript reposed in the Dartmouth College Library until it finally appeared in its entirety in 1982; Aupaumut's saw print, somewhat obscurely, in 1827. Among Christian Indians, the first to produce a full-length autobiographical text, and one that was widely noticed, was the Reverend William Apess, a Pequot, a Methodist minister, and an activist on behalf of Indian rights. Apess's *A Son of the Forest: The Experience of William Apes, a Native of the Forest, Written by*

Himself appeared first in 1829 and went through several editions in the author's lifetime.[2]

Apess did not call his work an autobiography, and it is entirely possible that he did not know the word, which seems to have been invented (by the English poet Robert Southey) in 1827 to name works that had formerly been called memoirs, confessions, or, indeed, "experiences." But with the increased American awareness of the Native population occasioned by President Andrew Jackson's determination to make the removal of Indians east of the Mississippi to its western bank a national priority, it was not long before the autobiographical name and form was adopted for the use of Native Americans who, resisting the advances of the settlers, were called upon to tell their stories.[3] In 1833 J. B. Patterson, a young Illinois newspaper editor, published the *Life of Black Hawk*. Black Hawk was a traditional Sauk chief who knew little or no English, could write no language, and, left to himself, probably would not have enlisted the aid of a Euro-American to leave a record of his life and times. Black Hawk's particular incentive to tell his life story was, as Patterson noted in his "Advertisement" to the reader, "to make known to the world, the injuries his people have received from the whites—[and] the causes which brought on the war on the part of his nation." For it was indeed an Indian war—the last to be fought east of the Mississippi—that brought Black Hawk to national attention, as it would be Indian war that prompted the historical form of Indian autobiography for more than a century. There was Black Hawk and the Black Hawk War, Wooden Leg and the Custer fight on the Little Bighorn (1876), Yellow Wolf and the flight of the Nez Perces (1877), Geronimo and the Geronimo campaigns (until 1886): these are only some of the illustrious warriors—"resisting Indians"—whose association with a particular historical episode in the "winning of the West" led to autobiographical documents solicited by whites.

By the time of the so-called closing of the frontier in 1890, it was as if the Indian had dropped out of the American historical record. From this time forward, America's westward expansion would continue by "opening" China and Japan, by invading, as Richard Drinnon has argued, the Philippines, then Vietnam, and now outer space itself. (Recent American adventures in Iraq and elsewhere in the Middle East may call for a new or revised paradigm.)

Early in the twentieth century Native American autobiography was pursued by those interested not in the historical record but rather in the cultural or ethnographic record. It was, for the most part, the university-trained professional anthropologists, students of Franz Boas, who sought to record Indian lives in print as part of the great and urgent project of "ethnographic salvage" that sought to preserve, in the museum or the library, traces of lives and cultures that could not (so it was then believed) have a continuing existence anywhere else.

Of course Indians did not vanish, and before long a new generation of Native Americans came to maturity, respectful of traditional oral forms of expression but also competent in the various modes of Western literacy. These Indian writers, on those occasions when they turned their attention to autobiography, had no need of Euro-American assistance. In this regard we should at least mention the work of the Lakota (Sioux) authors Zitkala Ša (Gertrude Bonnin) and Charles Alexander Eastman (Ohiyesa) early in this century, and then, in the 1930s and 1940s, of such writers as Luther Standing Bear (Lakota) and John Joseph Matthews (Osage), among others. (The exception to this generalization is Black Elk, who told his story "through" John Neihardt, thereby contributing to what may still be the best-known Indian autobiography of them all, *Black Elk Speaks* [1932].) Zitkala Ša, Eastman, and the others we have mentioned were followed, in our own time, by Native American authors whose initial claim to national attention came not because of their world-historical deeds or their status as bearers of their culture but, instead, because of their contributions to art. We are referring particularly to N. Scott Momaday and Leslie Marmon Silko, both of whom published important works of poetry and fiction before composing autobiographical texts. Following upon his Pulitzer Prize–winning novel, *House Made of Dawn* (1968), Momaday published *The Way to Rainy Mountain* (1969) and *The Names* (1976). Silko's partly autobiographical text *Storyteller* (1979) comes just after her widely praised novel *Ceremony* (1977). The autobiographical texts of both these authors are important examples of autobiography as *literature* in every sense of this word.

I Tell You Now follows this line of literary autobiography in presenting the lives of Native Americans whom we know foremost as artists, writers of what Western culture distinguishes as literary prose and poetry. The degree to which each of these artists infuses the Western form with a particularly Native or tribal sensibility must be an ongoing subject of inquiry for critics and students.

To return to an issue raised above, although it may appear that this collection of autobiographies by contemporary Native American writers seems to testify to the congeniality of the autobiographical form to Indians today, the reality, as we have indicated, is a bit more complicated. Thus, when we first began to put this volume together around 1985, one writer whom we had invited to contribute wrote that after "months of agonizing over how to write an autobiographical essay," she thought she was ready to begin. Nonetheless, as she wrote in a moving letter, "You should realize that focusing so intently on oneself like that and blithering on about your own life and thoughts is very bad form for Indians. I have heard Indian critics say, referring to poetry, that it is best if there are no 'I's' in it. I grew up and continue to live among people who penalize you for talking about yourself and going on endlessly about your struggles."

Another of our invited contributors said she had been cautioned against writing her autobiography by a member of her tribe, and, in the end, did not produce an autobiographical text. Her sense was that not the autonomous individual but rather the individual in relation to relatives and other tribal persons—not an impossible relation for autobiographical writing to convey, but still a fairly uncommon one— was what most deeply counted for her. Another poet initially rejected the idea of what she called "speaking your own stories," although she later did find that she could write autobiography.

In soliciting pieces for this volume in 1985, we offered our contributors very broad guidelines regarding what they might do. We suggested that they write about their childhood and education, their relation to language, and the two cultures—the dominant culture of the United States and a particular tribal culture or cultures—that had formed them. We suggested, too, that they might choose to include pieces of their work as part of their autobiographies. As the reader will find, each contributor found her and his own way of handling the assignment. In the original publication of this volume in 1987, we provided very brief biographies of the authors, indicating their publications to that point. We are very pleased to say that since that time most of our contributors have gone on to publish many volumes of poetry and prose, and so we have updated the brief bibliographic information that appears before each essay. Nonetheless, it is important for the reader to be aware that the essays themselves have *not* been revised.[4]

Along with our editor, Gary Dunham at the University of Nebraska Press, we gave a good deal of thought to the possibility of asking the contributors to revise their texts if they so desired. In the end, however, we decided not to. Mary Tallmountain, the oldest of the original contributors, has passed on, and many of our contributors—Diane Glancy,

Joy Harjo, Linda Hogan, Simon Ortiz, Carter Revard, Wendy Rose, Gerald Vizenor, among many others—have, since 1987, published very substantial bodies of work, even further autobiographical work.[5] It is true, therefore, as one of the original contributors to this volume remarked wittily when told of its reissue, that *I Tell You Now* in 2004 might well be retitled, "I Told You Then." Indeed, it might—and we think that is all to the good.

To an extraordinary degree, we find that these essays read as powerfully and movingly now as they did then; they speak to their historical moment, and, we believe, they helped contribute to a burgeoning interest in Native American literary expression. It is our hope that this new edition will make apparent exactly how well the essays have endured in the way that good art in general endures. Readers unfamiliar with these writers can simply enjoy the texts for themselves; while readers familiar with these writers' subsequent works can use the texts comparatively to consider the relation between what these authors thought about their lives and works in the mid-1980s—when many of them were just beginning their careers or were at an early stage of their careers—and what they have said in the years that have passed. In these regards, we are very pleased that *I Tell You Now* may be read today as "I Told You Then!" Now, as then, we offer it as a tribute to the rich and richly developing body of Native American literature.

NOTES

1. Brumble's bibliographies and this book use "American Indian" or "Native American" to mean indigenous peoples of *the United States*, sometimes including Alaskan Natives although not those of Hawai'i. Although we have not included Canadian First Nations writers we offer here a few suggestions (complete references are given in the Works Cited) for readers wishing to learn more about their autobiographical work. Although not quite up-to-date, a good starting place is John Miska's *Ethnic and Native Canadian Literature: A Bibliography*. See also *Voices: Being Native in Canada*, edited by Linda Jaine and Drew Hayden Taylor, as well as *Crisp Blue Edges: Indigenous Creative Nonfiction*, edited by Rasunah Marsden. The novelist Thomas King, who holds dual Canadian and American citizenship, has edited *All My Relations: An Anthology of Contemporary Canadian Native Fiction*, and Daniel David Moses and Terry Goldie have edited *An Anthology of Canadian Native Literature in English*. For more personal or "autobiographical" statements, see *Contemporary Challenges: Conversations with Canadian Native Authors*, interviews conducted by Hart-

mut Lutz, and *(Ad)dressing Our Word: Aboriginal Perspectives on Aboriginal Literatures.*

2. William Apess published under the name of Apess, with a double "*s*" and also Apes, with a single "*s.*" Barry O'Connell's superb edition of Apess's complete works uses the spelling just given, and O'Connell explains the reasons for that choice in his introduction. Although not universally accepted, Apess has now become the standard spelling.

3. For a fuller account of these matters, as well as a representative selection of the life stories of "resisting Indians," as well as "the anthropologists' Indians" (see below) see Krupat, 1994.

4. We are thinking most particularly here of Linda Hogan's recent *The Woman Who Watches Over the World: A Native Memoir*, and Simon Ortiz's introduction to his collected poems in the volume *Woven Stone*. In an essay called "Autobiography in Fiction," Janet Campbell Hale briefly discusses her decision not to contribute to this volume originally. But she, along with many who did contribute, have spoken about themselves and their works in a number of interviews that they have granted over the years. We followed *I Tell You Now* with a second volume of autobiographies by Native writers called *Here First*, and the University of Nebraska Press followed *I Tell You Now* with Lawrence Abbott's *I Stand Here in the Center of the Good: Interviews with Contemporary Native American Artists.*

5. One of our contributors asked to correct some errors that appeared in his essay and we have, of course, allowed him to do so.

WORKS CITED

Abbott, Lawrence, ed. *I Stand Here in the Center of the Good: Interviews with Contemporary Native American Artists.* Lincoln: University of Nebraska Press, 1994.

Apess, William. *A Son of the Forest: The Experience of William Apes, a Native of the Forest, Written by Himself.* New York, 1829. Reprinted in O'Connell.

Aupaumut, Hendrick. *A Narrative of an Embassy to the Western Indians, from the Original Manuscript of Hendrick Aupaumut, with Prefatory Remarks by Dr. B. H Coates.* 1791. *Pennsylvania Historical Society Memoirs* 2, pt. 1 (1827): 61–131.

Black Elk. *Black Elk Speaks.* As told through John G. Neihardt. 1932. Reprint, Lincoln: University of Nebraska Press, 1977.

Black Hawk. *Black Hawk, an Autobiography.* Edited by J. B. Patterson. 1833. Reprinted and edited by Donald P. Jackson, Urbana: University of Illinois Press, 1955. Also reprinted and edited by Roger L. Nichols, Ames: Iowa State University Press, 1999.

Brumble, H. David, III. *An Annotated Bibliography of American Indian and Eskimo Autobiographies.* Lincoln: University of Nebraska Press, 1981.

———. "A Supplement to *An Annotated Bibliography of American Indian and Eskimo Autobiographies.*" *Western American Literature* 17 (1982): 243–60. Reprinted in *American Indian Autobiography*. Berkeley: University of California Press, 1988.

Drinnon, Richard. *Facing West: The Metaphysics of Indian-Hating and Empire Building*. Middletown CT: Wesleyan University Press, 1975.

Eastman, Charles Alexander. *From the Deep Woods to Civilization: Chapters in the Autobiography of an Indian*. 1916. Reprint, Lincoln: University of Nebraska Press, 1977.

———. *Indian Boyhood*. 1902. Reprint, Boston: Little Brown, 1922; New York: Dover, 1971.

Geronimo. *Geronimo's Story of His Life*. Edited by S. M. Barrett. 1906. Reprint, New York: Ballantine, 1970.

Hale, Janet Campbell. "Autobiography in Fiction." Chap. 1 in *Bloodlines: Odyssey of a Native Daughter*. New York: Random House, 1993, 1–16.

Hogan, Linda. *The Woman Who Watches Over the World: A Native Memoir*. New York: W. W. Norton, 2001.

Jaine, Linda, and Drew Hayden Taylor, eds. *Voices: Being Native in Canada*. Saskatoon: University of Saskatchewan, Extension Division, 1992.

King, Thomas, ed. *All My Relations: An Anthology of Contemporary Canadian Native Fiction*. Norman: University of Oklahoma Press, 1992.

Krupat, Arnold, ed. *Native American Autobiography: An Anthology*. Madison: University of Wisconsin Press, 1994.

Krupat, Arnold, and Brian Swann, eds. *Here First: Autobiographical Essays by Native American Writers*. New York: Modern Library, 2000.

Lutz, Hartmut, ed. *Contemporary Challenges: Conversations with Canadian Native Authors*. Sasakatoon, Saskatchewan: Fifth House Publishers, 1991.

Marsden, Rasunah, ed. *Crisp Blue Edges: Indigenous Creative Non-fiction*. Penticton, British Columbia: Theytus Books, 2000.

Miska, John. *Ethnic and Native Canadian Literature: A Bibliography*. Toronto: University of Toronto Press, 1990.

Moses, Daniel David, and Terry Goldie, eds. *An Anthology of Canadian Native Literature in English*. Toronto: Oxford University Press, 1998.

Matthews, John Joseph. *Talking to the Moon*. Chicago: University of Chicago Press, 1945.

Momaday, N. Scott. *The Names*. New York: Harper and Row, 1976.

———. *The Way to Rainy Mountain*. Albuquerque: University of New Mexico Press, 1969.

O'Connell, Barry, ed. *On Our Own Ground: The Complete Writings of William Apess, A Pequot*. Amherst: University of Massachusetts Press, 1992.

Occom, Samson. "A Short Narrative of My Life." 1768. In *The Elders Wrote: An Anthology of Early Prose by North American Indians*. Edited by Berndt Peyer. Berlin: Reimer, 1982.

Ortiz, Simon. introduction to *Woven Stone*. Tucson: University of Arizona Press, 1992, 3–33.

Ruffo, Armand Garnet, ed. *(Ad)dressing Our Words: Aboriginal Perspectives on Aboriginal Literatures*. Penticton, British Columbia: Theytus Books, 2001.

Silko, Leslie Marmon. *Storyteller*. New York: Seaver Books, 1981.

Standing Bear, Luther. *My People the Sioux*. 1928. Reprint, Lincoln: University of Nebraska Press, 1975.

Wooden Leg. *A Warrior Who Fought Custer*. Interpreted by Thomas B. Marquis. 1931. Reprint, Lincoln: University of Nebraska Press, 1962.

Yellow Wolf, His Own Story. Edited by Lucullus Virgil McWhorter. 1940. Reprint, Caldwell ID: Caxton Printers, 1983.

MARY TALLMOUNTAIN

You *Can* Go Home Again:

A Sequence

Born in 1918 in Nulato on the Yukon River in Alaska, Mary Tallmountain (Koyukon Athabaskan) lived most of her life in the Tenderloin District of San Francisco. Her book of poems *There is No Word for Goodbye* (Blue Cloud Quarterly Press, 1982) won a Pushcart Prize in 1982–83. Her fiction and poetry appeared in many anthologies, and she wrote a regular column, "Meditations for Wayfarers," in the Franciscan publication *The Way*. In 1989 Bill Moyers interviewed her for his PBS poetry series "The Power of the Word," for which she did a reading as well. She published two books, *The Light on the Tent Wall* (UCLA Press, 1990) and *A Quick Brush of Wings* (Freedom Voices Press 1991), and in 1995 posthumously published *Listen to the Night* (Freedom Voices Press). Mary Tallmountain died in 1994. Her will provided for the establishment of the Tallmountain Circle, which awards aid to struggling writers in San Francisco.

[handwritten: first person story]

[handwritten: curious, mysterious, no explanation]

The Yukon River lay below us like a bent brown arm. Its vast curves snaked back on themselves heavy with silt hurtling south across the face of Alaska. Suddenly the sight was unbearable. I closed my eyes. There it was again, that sound I had been hearing for fifty years. At last I knew what it was. The river was speaking to me.

The bushplane hovered, careened, tilted sidewise and down, rattling fiercely. Dizzy, I looked across the pilot's hands and saw Nulato. Its roofs crouched shining in a long bend of the river. The little two-seater growled and bounced past the whitewashed crosses of Graveyard Hill. Everything dimmed before my quick tears. I thought of the day in 1924 when I had left Nulato. Again I heard the hoarse cry of the steamboat whistle, the shouts of the men guiding the *Teddy T* into the current. The familiar faces on the riverbank grew smaller. The huddled cabins with their chalk-white caribou antlers faded into the distance. Finally it was all hidden, and there was nothing but the river and the land and the great cloud shadows racing.

Like the shadows, it was gone now. All except these rare quick clips of vision. Yet there was a knowledge in me that I had been close to this certain earth in another life, far beyond childhood, an existence as old as the river.

Through enormous stretches of time the Athabascan-speaking Indians of the Yukon had been nomads. They hunted and fished in the mountains and marshes of the Kaiyuh, west of Fairbanks, near where the brown arm of the Yukon elbows southwest to pour its silt into Norton Sound. It had been a good life for the natives, that ancient nomadic life.

Credit is due to Eliza Jones, linguist of the University of Alaska, Fairbanks, for review and assistance in the use of the Athabascan language.

My scenario reads this way:

One day two natives were fishing the river close to the bank downriver near Kaltag. "Hoh," one said. "What's that?" It was a piece of wood, floating. They scooped it up and stared at it. The flesh was fresh and white. How could a spruce tree break into pieces when it was young and healthy, they wondered. Look at the rough lines all along the heavier side. Maybe a bear. No, couldn't be. Those sure weren't tooth marks. Back at the fishcamp, they hung it where everybody could see it and wonder. Although they didn't know it then, the chip had been hewed for a fire by the axe of a white man.

Thus in the mid-1800s, Russians came down across the Diomedes and inland along the crooked brown arm. When they discovered the natives and found profit in trading furs, they build a redoubt. More Russians came, married native women, and built a *kashim,* a long log roundhouse where many families could live, sheltered against the violent sub-Arctic winters.

Another kind of violence came later when the redoubt was attacked from the north by Koyukuk Indians. The *kashim* was burned, and the people died within it. It was the beginning of the end of Russian trading at Nulato. The presence of traders had brought the nomads drifting in to live where they could barter. A cluster of log cabins had risen against the skyline of fir and spruce. They named it Nulato, "the place where we are tied together."

Today Nulato is one of three weathered villages collectively called the Koyukon, in honor of the nearby merging of the Koyukuk and Yukon Rivers. The people are called the Koyukon Band. They share the river, the language, and the past. They are so remote from the modern culture of cities that Anglos call them "Strangers of the North." That is not a misnomer.

After fifty years I was returning to this aboriginal and reticent people.

After the Russians departed, Jesuit missionaries came to the Yukon. The eminent sociolinguist, Father Julius Jetté, built a church and school, and the people learned to read and write English. Catechism was taught by the Sisters of St. Anne. The people concealed their medicine men and kept age-old beliefs, placating the "being who has no name," at the same time attending rituals of the Catholic liturgy.

In the twenties, the airplane diminished Alaska's immensities. Now, the journey from San Francisco to Nulato takes little more than a day by 727 jet to Anchorage, bushplane across the immense interior, and a smaller bushplane into the village. However, air travel is not an unmitigated blessing. Frequently, the natives charter a flight to buy liquor from a bootlegger and bring back a planeload. The violent oil conquest brought a reckless breed of people, and among them drug pushers, who penetrated the Koyukon. Death and addiction followed the new availability of liquor and drugs. The list of drownings, murders, and suicides is appalling.

Family life has been transformed, but the women try to keep the old customs. They are remarkably deft. For ceremonies such as Stick Dance they make beautiful garments beaded with Alaskan flowers, rich scarlet fireweed, delicate bluebell, orange paintbrush. As a child I watched Mary Joe beading by kerosene lamplight, and the brilliant gleam of beads still stirs in my brain the echo of soft woman-talk. Before it fell into tatters I treasured a little parka of fawnskin trimmed with beaver and wolverine furs from the animals she had trapped. A pair of mittens of black velvet was attached, and I remember each detail of the tightly sewn beads and how her hands moved against the velvet.

Mary Joe Demoski was Athabascan and Russian, and the soldier Clem Stroupe was my Irish and Scots father. They had ten years together and two children. The U.S. Army and the Catholic church would not let them marry. Mary Joe developed tuberculosis, as rampant and fatal as a plague. Doctor Randle ordered bed rest, and his wife Agnes took care of my little brother, Billy, and me. We were only two and three years old when we were told the Randles wanted us to be their children. Adoption of native children by Anglos was rare. Angrily, the village disputed the adoption, and the Anglos censured it. Relationships were embittered. Trying to yield to both factions, the village council said, "Girl go Outside with white doctor. Mary Joe keep Billy. Later he hunt and fish with his uncle." The separation would be the first of a series of calamities afflicting me during the coming years.

Billy and I didn't think about the coming years. We were as free and happy as the storybook children Agnes introduced to us. Fierce winds growled at the windowpanes as we tumbled off the attic trapeze. When minus-50° weather subsided, we rode behind Uncle's curly-tailed dogs, our noses buried in the frostproof wolverine ruffs of our parkas, slitting our eyes against the spray of sleet thrown by the scurrying paws of the malemutes. Around us always was the infinitely various land. We never imagined such joy would end. It was inevitable.

After my departure from Nulato, Billy went home to Mary Joe, and before she died he harbored the illness that would end his life at seventeen. We wrote to each other. Aunt had a big family. When hunting was poor, their life was hard. Some days he and Uncle trapped all day with only bread and tea to keep them going. Growing up with our cousins, he was a happy boy, in adversity as well as plenty. Reading was Billy's chief delight. Agnes had begun teaching us to read in primers, and Mary Joe took over from there. Letters from Billy and Mary Joe were my only consolation.

Being ripped out of my childhood had devastated me, and the devastation began in Oregon. I refused to go to school because my schoolmates mocked my Indianness. I hid away in closets and bit my hands in mute rage. The Randles took me back to Alaska, where Doctor was assigned to Unalaska on the Aleutians. The beautiful country lured me into a deep sense of the earth, its touch, smell, its spirit. The treeless volcanic islands were ringed by jutting mountains. Hidden meadows in the backcountry were lush with wild orchis, iris, violets. At ten I wrote my first story, about two polar bears I had seen in the Seattle zoo. *Child Life* printed it. Discipline came into my days, and at Agnes's urging I wrote regularly in a diary. My entries were always stories about people or about some simple philosophical discovery. That was the probable catalyst of the journal-keeping class I teach as part of spiritual search, a tool for personal growth and an asset for writers. My boxes of journals are piled high, each a chunk of my fragmented history.

Agnes was a teacher. My education lasted twelve hours a day. There was a lyric excellence in her that nurtured my early fascination with poems and stories. Literarily, I grew up with Shelley, Wordsworth, Keats; Dickens, Trollope, the Brontë sisters. A piercing memory returns. At Unalaska, Agnes and I walked along the narrow pebbled beach at night reciting poems to each other. Especially I loved Wordsworth.

> Waters on a starry night
> Are beautiful and fair . . .

We watched the moon, swimming in a sea of stars. We did not suspect how swiftly our brief respite from reality would pass.

For at that early age, my life was dreadfully harmed. Betrayal by a trusted friend nearly destroyed my spirit, and I arrived too soon at the edge of a turbulent maturity. The story is familiar in these times. In the 1920s no child dared to protest. I had turned twelve, and my blossoming creativity was crushed to fragments. Nothing came to me to write or think, beyond the anxiety of my days and nights.

Doctor was transferred to another hospital at Dillingham, just off the Bering Sea. A subtle beauty was hidden among the stunted trees and gentle mosses of a land apparently barren. In the two years we were there I tried to write a novel, *Tundra Country*. It was silly and premature, and I knew it, but I dreamed I would write a real novel some day. The story died ignominiously with other debris when we left the Territory.

I was fourteen then. Outside, I started high school, and my worry was relieved when I was able to cope with peers and make friends. I joined the glee club, and the old sense stirred again toward creation of beauty. It was short-lived. After my graduation at eighteen, Doctor died of a worn-out heart. Not long afterward I married Dal Roberts. In 1945 Agnes came down with Parkinson's and diabetes, and became a walking ghost. She went to the Willamette River and walked her little fleshless body out into the water. In that year my second marriage failed, and I left the Northwest. In Reno I learned to be a legal secretary, as an apprentice working on divorces.

Strangely, I never got my own divorce. It seemed safer to have a husband somewhere in the background. I met Reuel Lynch, a jazz musician. He was Catholic, and before I realized, I was studying his faith. I found that Mary Joe had had her children baptized at birth. My careless life began to change. This discovery led me to an intensive, continuing study of Catholicism. But my destructive behavior had not really begun. A little later I went to San Francisco, where I worked in law offices. Living alone, I started on the road of the silent, secret drinker.

Calamities that had begun so early I could scarcely remember their details, that had buried themselves so deeply that healing would take years of therapy, slowly and insidiously worked their aftermath. Therapy was hush-hush in those days. I kept on working, in a conservative, money-oriented business world. My private life was a harsh and painful rebellion. I began to drink, first socially and then compulsively, secretly. I left jobs without reason and while on a job was entirely undependable. Into my forties I stumbled along, my work suffering; but then the hideous hangovers took hold, blackouts added to my guilt, and I had to resort to temporary agencies. Alcoholism had seized me completely. My behavior sloped into periods of heavy depression.

One day I went out in a haze to the corner for my morning stinger at the Brown Dog Bar, and I suddenly realized everything was darker than usual. Why was traffic heavy? Why was it all going west? It looked more like 5:00 P.M. than the usual 9:00 A.M. Then I knew. It was evening, and I didn't know where the day had gone. Of course I had no job to go to. My latest agency had found out. Disgusted, I went back to the apartment and took a good look at myself and my situation. It was then that I made up my mind to quit drinking, cold turkey. No tapering off would do it. I suffered all the physical and mental agonies there were in the book. I tried to take the days one at a time. I sweated out the insomniac nights when I would formerly have been at some local bar. The nights were the worst, but they gave me the blessed time of peace to think and to bolster up my firm intention to make a substantially useful life. And it worked.

Long-ignored stresses had done their work constructively. I had dreamed up a public stenography business and was building a comfortable if not lavish living. I thought I had beaten it at last. The energy of building something, working free, for myself, gave me a tremendous boost. However, I had forgotten the series of calamities. Resentment, frustration, anger hidden for years exploded first in one radical cancer and ten years later in a second. I had inherited a strong survival instinct from my staunch mother and grandmother. Last year I came out of my latest surgical battle with a deep sense of new life and a surging spirit.

Shyly, tentatively, I had begun in the mid-1960s to make short poems. Small, but real. In 1962 the Friars Press editor, Franciscan Simon Scanlon, started printing them. Later he printed my stories. He still publishes my work. If he had not valued my ability, I might never have searched for help. I found a friend and tutor, Paula Gunn Allen, then teaching Indian Studies at San Francisco State University. She honed my unskilled talent into the great gift of wordsmithing. Together we worked for a year and a half. Every Tuesday night I took a week's writing to her, listened to her read it, then took it home and rewrote. Sometimes I worked a furious fifteen hours a day. She critiqued and guided in her gentle, perceptive way.

It became clear to me that this ability hadn't been given solely for my pleasure, and that I had an obligation to myself and my peers to use it constructively to rebuild, perhaps, some part of the world I live in. Paula and I never spoke these thoughts. They were conveyed to me in some subtle manner of our minds. In one of my quick clips of vision, Paula and I are caught changeless, sitting still and rapt, Indian women bound by the enduring thread of a common dream, a powerful purpose.

Everything came together, that summer. She told me, "This is all I can give you. The tools are in your hands. Go and write." She went home to Albuquerque, and I revisited Nulato for the first time in fifty years. Afterward I went to her in the desert, and we talked for days about my return to Nulato, dissecting my voluminous notes. When she took me to the airport, she asked, "What are you going to do about your father?" I had abandoned my dream of finding Clem after years of search and misinformation. I believed he was dead. Now I was going to Scottsdale, and Paula had remembered that the last rumor of Clem's whereabouts had placed him very close, in Phoenix. "Okay," I said.

At Scottsdale I attended a Catholic Charismatic Retreat and a healing service. When I reached Clem's name in my prayer, I felt a shuddering shock. Paula's voice came to me, "Find Clem!" I went to the phone booth, and there was his name in the book at the top of the page where I couldn't miss it. Clement C. Stroupe. He had kept his phone unlisted until that year.

My dad was eighty-five. I lived with him for two years until his death in 1978. I learned much from him about how to forgive, to sharpen my perceptions of human beings, to love. He helped me erase some of the lingering bitterness, for which there was no room in his gentle and tender world. For hours we talked and wrote together about Alaska. He played his fiddle, the beautiful old hands dancing on the strings as he jigged with joy like a mischievous elf.

He told me about his life with Mary Joe, about his visit with her during her last illness, and he gave me her message. She said this: "Tell my girl I always love her. I wanted her to have the best life she could. With me she would catch TB, and there would be nothing for her here. I had a feeling she would be all right."

NOVEL IN PROGRESS

Lidwynne's family camped on the river four miles north of Nulato. Mamma and Auntie Madeline's heads in bright bandannas bobbed. The glittering crescent blades of their *tlaamases* slashed straight along the bellies of immense fish. Pink strings of eggs slithered into squat tubs. Salmon dangled in crimson curtains between old silver-grey posts. Thin blue threads floated out of the smoke house. Away toward the meadow stood a row of brown weathered tents. West, where the land lifted toward the hills, bears came in summer to bumble in the bushes for ripe blueberries. When salmon were running, black bears lumbered down to the water and hooked them out with thick sharp claws. They were small but fast and dangerous. The elder persons warned the children never to go away from camp alone. Bears might get them. Woodsman might. They called him *nik'inli'een*. Nobody knew anything about him except he had an animal's head, paws as big as dishpans, teeth like a saw, and he'd carry you off and you'd never be seen again.

When she heard that, Lidwynne had run to the tent right away. Mamma was sitting on a wooden box. She passed her hand slowly over Lidwynne's cheek and she felt the coolness of Mamma's skin and the warmth of the sun. She almost forgot what she wanted to ask Mamma.

"Oh, *eenaa*, what's *nik'inli'een?*"

"Pretty girl!" Mamma cried, hugging Lidwynne and laughing with her happy sound. "There's no *nik'inli'een!* Go play!" She pushed Lidwynne's round stomach softly.

LETTER FROM CLEM, PHOENIX 1976

First time I saw your Mom was when I was practicing my fiddle for a dance there in Nulato. She dressed in nice little frocks she got from Sears, and wore her fine black hair bound around her forehead with bright bands of cloth.

It was the best part of my life. I was tough as a wet walrus hide. Outdoors most of the time. Some days on the trail and cold, the dogs and I were lost in the black, and my leader Moose always found the right trail no matter how deep buried. Then without warning that year when you were three, and as though a dark curtain dropped between us and reality, the beginning of your Mom's TB, the loss of you children, the animosity that bedeviled the village, slammed into our lives. Even the kids felt the mysterious spirits that hovered among us. The people talked of omens. I looked for meanings in the very shadows. All of it is written relentlessly in my memories.

TALLMOUNTAIN JOURNAL AND NOVEL IN PROGRESS, JUNE 1976

The river flowed past sometimes red, sometimes grey, and now, still getting rid of the glacial loess, was roily and full of silt. It pushed impatiently against the banks. Salmon have been seen at Holy Cross downriver, but still linger below till the river goes down. People are getting whitefish and sheefish. Summer coming on, they are friendly, and everybody laughs, sometimes self-consciously.

Across Mukluk Slough, Clem's old radio transmitter tower lies crooked after fifty years' decay, a black and rusty ruin.

Cousin Elmer: Shy, beautiful piercing eyes. He mourned about his drinking and angrily said he must stop it and go out to Anchorage and support his wife and little girls. But, he growled, it was so hard to leave Nulato. He didn't see how he could live out there. He said, "When I knew you were coming my heart got tight." He pounded his chest. Sometimes he wept, staring out over the river.

Grey clouds brought rain from the north. It is so gentle I walk down to the river. It speaks softly to me. Swallows dive and soar from the mud nests under the eaves of the convent of Our Lady of the Snows. Now about fifteen of them swoop down at once, fly in a perfect oval low above the river, dart to the sky again.

Rain drummed on the iron roof all night.

The island is closer than I remembered. It is overgrown with alder and willow and now a long sand spit has built over the years. Kids swim there in summer. I had seen it in my mind shadows far away and dusty blue. Mary Joe used to fish behind it. I wonder if she sometimes met Clem there . . .

Tassie Saunders made a picnic for us at Graveyard Hill. The old graves were peaceful in the hot sun. We forged our ways around and around through the scratching brush, reading the carved names on the white crosses, visiting people gone, and felt the loving, kind presences. We ate Spam and graham crackers high above the river beside the Demoski grave houses, and she said long ago, Koyukuk warriors attacked the Russian fort at Kaltag and massacred all but a little boy who escaped on snowshoes. In his old age, he was buried just across the river under a lonely spruce tree.

We knocked mosquitoes off each other and talked for several hours in the shadows of swaying rosebushes. In front of us a wild rose in full bloom trembled in the wind.

We didn't find Mary Joe's grave.

I grieved awhile, then she said, "Your Mom is in there," and tapped a finger against my chest. At last I realized. It didn't matter where my mother was laid. I would have her always, in there.

Tassie has the blues. Her husband died last year; this is her first fish season without him. She hasn't been fishing or cut fish. Her mind dwells on death; she rushed to find her baby hawk, fearing he was dead somehow. I can't remember how many deaths she told: drowning of a little girl by two teenage boys; stabbing of an eighteen-year-old girl by an older boy; a man caught in a motor and chewed up by it, his body lost in the river; more stabbings; the death of a boy from sulfa pills with whiskey; her grandpa's death by falling with a thud while driving dogs. He hit a hollow and–"I guess his heart drop down," she adds. Then just a week ago, the GI drowned near Galena, found by my cousin Freddie Ben while setting nets 100 miles south at Kaltag, the GI swollen to the size of a log. All this within the space of just a few months.

Cousin Edna had a potlatch and brought out a skin scraper my Mom had used until her death; my grandpa had made it. The handle was a warm smooth brown wood, silky with years of use. I held it in my hand and felt it. I knew it was designed exactly to her grip, my mother. She had used it, and now my hand held it. The only article I have touched that she used.

It didn't occur to Edna to offer it to me, though she must have seen the longing in my face. And I would not ask for it. I said secretly: Let it stay here. It belongs here and it will be here when I have joined Mom. I have far more than a scraper. I have her, I have Mom, her blood and her spirit.

I am immensely weary. Due to the constant daylight of the time of the Midnight Sun we go to bed at 2 or 2:30 in the morning, no earlier, and are up nevertheless by 7:00 A.M. So many people, so much talk, so many conflicting stories. My brain is exhausted.

Their language is atrocious. They talk very fast. Each has terrible discrepancies. And I suspect lies, to mollify me, because they know I'm searching for Mom and Billy's graves. They peer out the windows of the cabins. Nothing is hidden. (The Honey Bucket is the greatest leveler in the world!) The only relaxed people appear to be the Anglo teachers. The natives and their kids are easily hyped. It's culture shock.

Paula and Sister Anne Eveline say I've idealized the people too much. I agree. They aren't poor; they have too much, and they suffer from it. They drink and lie and steal, and they have lost my mother's grave.

Cannot write, need aloneness, have got these notes together with tremendous difficulty. Weariness, disillusion, communication breakdowns. I think they resent my staying with Sister Anne. And probably they're saying that I'm a white woman.

Now I feel that I have done some strange unknown thing I came here to do and it's done and I must go on.

A gale is blowing and the river is filled with whitecaps. The trees back by the playfield are boiling with wind, and the three spruce trees by the greenhouse are bent nearly double by the lashing wind. Water dances on the tops of the brilliant blue oil-drums. Rows of young cabbages inside the fenced convent garden are whipping tender new leaves. Hunched-over people hurry by on the river road. I hear the wind mourning where the swallows nest; and I remember the sound.

Mosquitoes are so sluggish they cloak our shoulders and heads. The river is like glass and there is no wind. The people look at me with eyes of the past. They watch every move of my hands on the china, the fork, the food. The rain is starting (the mosquitoes knew it would) and there is no sound but a dog far off stirring his mates into a wild wail in the half-night.

The cold pierces the walls, and the heat from the brittle iron stove does not last. The lovely chime of Father Baud's handwrought grandfather clock doesn't overcome the howling gale. The flung velvet of the island can't outweigh the dirt that blows in the road. The spirits in the graveyard can't show me where my mother lies, and I will not let them persuade me to return here. But I know who I am. Marginal person, misfit, mutant; nevertheless I am of this country, these people. I have used their strengths. I have wrestled to the earth their weaknesses that have echoed in me.

My roots are here, I feel them deep in my memories, in the hidden spaces of my blood. It doesn't matter where I live; I will see the rounded cabins set together. I will see the hill where my mother lies clean and shining under the roots of this ground.

Across the river a streak of red dirt turns copper all along the bank of the island, and the river burns with the lowering sun in bronze flames. A seagull wheels above, looking for salmon. I will fly out over Graveyard Hill at morning on one of Harold's bushplanes.

I recall with startling clarity and longing every detail of the land, the river, the people. I know now why my mother wanted to let me leave them. It was contained in her message to me. I understood; sometimes I almost agree with her. Yet Alaska mesmerizes my spirit, and I finger the thoughts like beads of prayer. I still feel the crush of the lost bed of wild violets in the Aleutian hills where one day I flung myself down in a rapture, knowing who I was, what the wild violets meant. Alaska is my talisman, my strength, my spirit's home. Despite loss and disillusion, I count myself rich, fertile, and magical.

I tell you now. You *can* go home again.

RALPH SALISBURY

Between Lightning and Thunder

Ralph Salisbury (Cherokee), who was born in 1926 on a farm in northeastern Iowa, is professor emeritus of English at the University of Oregon. His volumes of poetry include *Ghost Grapefruit and Other Poems* (Ithaca House, 1972), *Going to the Water: Poems of a Cherokee Heritage* (Pacific House Books, 1983), *A White Rainbow: Poems of a Cherokee Heritage* (Blue Cloud Quarterly Press, 1985), and most recently *Rainbows of Stone* (University of Arizona Press, 2000). *The Last Rattlesnake Throw and Other Stories* (University of Oklahoma Press, 1998) is his most recent fiction collection. Salisbury has traveled widely in the United States and in Europe. He worked in Norway with Lars Nordtrom to translate the late Sami (indigenous Norwegian) poet Nils-Aslak Valkeapaa's *Trekways of the Wind* (1994) as well as Valkeapaa's *The Sun, My Father* (1998). Salisbury's autobiographical essay "Some of the Life and Times of Wise-Wolf Salt-Town" appears in *Returning the Gift: Poetry and Prose from the First North American Native Writers' Festival* (University of Arizona Press, 1994).

When I was asked to write this autobiographical sketch, it occurred to me that I had already written it—in five books of poems, in several short stories, and in an autobiographical novel, "Lightning Boy and the War against Time," which I am now near completing. Perhaps by inserting some examples of my autobiographical poetry and fiction, together with comment, I can say something about myself as a Native American writer and about the people I come from.

WITH THE WIND AND THE SUN

When the squadron I was in
bombed a Navajo hogan, killing,
by mistake, some sheep—
just like that flipped-
out ancient Greek Ajax did—
and blinded an elderly man,
my White buddies thought it was funny—
all those old kids' war-movies again
against the savages, and,
ironically, near where
the Atom bit the dust, White Sands; but

the Jew navigator,
who'd thought World War Two
had been won,
didn't laugh, and I,
hidden under a quite light complexion,
with the wind and the sun waging Indian war
to reconquer my skin,
defended myself
with a weak grin.

This poem, from the "Every Damned Day" section of my 1983 book *Going to the Water: Poems of a Cherokee Heritage,* suggests my situation, part white and sometimes finding it wise to pass as white but intensely aware of my Cherokee heritage and able to relate the pariahhood of my conquered Native American people to the pariahhood of others—in this poem, to the pariahhood of Jews, of many people oppressed by the ancient Greeks, and of the Japanese, for whom the atomic bomb, tested at White Sands, was to inflict the ultimate pariahhood: obliteration.

I have written often about my family's desire to pass as white in the racist southern United States and referred to this as a kind of murder—a kind of genocide—against one's own people. N. Scott Momaday has eloquently put it that the oral tradition in literature is always one generation from extinction. This is also true for the survival of one's tribe; if the impulse to "fit in"—to become a part of the American "melting-pot"—causes one generation to fail to acknowledge their heritage, tribal identity will pass from the earth forever, obliterated from the minds of the people for whom it should have been a sustaining source of pride.

My father's family's oral history has the English side of our people leaving the Carolinas and invading Kentucky with the second expedition of Daniel Boone. My Cherokee people were those allowed to stay scattered among the clay hills when most of the Cherokees were dispossessed of their prosperous farms and driven west, in the Death March called "The Trail of Tears," to Oklahoma. I knew my father's mother, who was half-blood Cherokee or more, and have published several poems about her, as I knew her, alive, and as one of our dead denied "the Cherokee grave your children were / too Christian to bury you in, as you'd pleaded—" (from *Spawning the Medicine River 7,* Institute of American Indian Art, 1981).

My father's father was a healer, with a wide reputation throughout the Kentucky hill country where our people lived, and I experienced some of my grandfather's healing formulas—the ceremonial blowing of tobacco smoke into the ears, for earache, for example—as they had come to be passed on to my father, but that is perhaps my only deeply felt knowledge of the man. My grandfather was probably part Native American—Shawano? Cherokee?—but my most important awareness of him is that he abandoned my grandmother and twelve children, and I have written of him as a betrayer. When I was a small boy back visiting the home ground with my parents, someone told my grandfather that I was in a group of children playing a few yards from where he was standing and would he like to see his grandson from Iowa? His response, as told to me, was simple and eloquent: "Naw, I don't think I care to." We cannot escape remembering the important things that have happened, and we cannot escape the awareness of the important things that have not happened. I have written a great deal about both.

"Our Irish mother's tongue would stitch / wool glowing needles of the wood-stove wove, / and there was bread-and-milk hunger / made us / lovingly recite . . ." is the opening of "Family Stories and the One Not Told" from my second book of poems, *Pointing at the Rainbow* (Blue Cloud Quarterly Press, 1980), and the poem is one of many I have written about my mother and her Irish heritage—in many ways similar to my father's Cherokee heritage, the Irish also suffering pariahhood in the United States and also keeping alive an oral literary tradition, still a part of everyday life when I visited County Kerry in 1967, ordinary working people reciting long poems from memory in the pub where I stayed. Although my mother's people were Christians, she had been kicked out of the congregation "for asking too many questions." Her religious feeling was rooted in an awareness of Creation (or Nature) and was harmonious with the Cherokee Spirit Life—which I try to live, to this day. An Iowan, my mother learned to cook the cornmeal Indian dishes to which my father was accustomed, dishes which had by now also become a part of southern white cuisine. I grew up aware of when we were eating southern and when we were eating northern. At age twelve, my mother lost her mother; her first husband died in World War One, while my mother was still pregnant with my half brother; from meager diet and harsh winter, my brother, my mother and father's first child, became ill and died in infancy. All of us came close to dying of hunger or freezing; the winter prices were so low we couldn't sell any crops, and we were weak and always ill. My mother had grown up in town in a family that lived rather comfortably, but she endured the harsh, primitive life we all knew on the farm, working in the fields as well as in the house. She was a heroic person, and I would not neglect her memory, though I will deal more with my father in this essay intended to describe my situation as a Native American writer.

Afflicted by claustrophobia, which kept him out of the coal mines, and by an impressive imagination, my father made his living as a wandering minstrel, singing and accompanying himself on a five-string banjo, one he had fashioned out of a tree limb and a wooden cigar box and taught himself to play. This was the first musical instrument I saw and heard. Singing at community events and providing music for square-dancing enabled him to travel. He also worked as a logger and harvest hand, among other things. Perhaps the most lucrative of these was boot-legging. He had a still at home in Kentucky, and he sold the corn whiskey he made all during Prohibition. Caught with a suitcase of whiskey in each hand, he was held at gunpoint by a revenuer or business rival until a friend rescued him, disarming the gunman. I am named for that friend. One of my dad's songs went "God bless them moonshiners. I wish them all well. / Those United States Marshals—I wish them in hell." I have a hard time not telling stories even when I'm supposed to be trying to be a literary historian of sorts.

On his bootlegging run from Kentucky to Minneapolis, my father stopped off in Iowa—having lost his merchandise to the law, or for what-ever reason—and one of the harvest-hand jobs he worked at to finance his further travels was working for my mother's father. Dad's traveling had ended. And mine had begun.

I was born—the middle child in what was to be a family of four boys and one girl, including my half brother—in the midst of a thirty-below-zero January blizzard. My father brought a doctor six miles to the farm, with a horse-drawn sled. A slick, fast-moving runner wrecked against something hidden under snow, and the doctor had to doctor his own broken ribs before he went to work on me, an eight-and-a-half-pound poet-and-fiction-writer-to-be, arriving, reluctantly, butt first. My father told and retold this and other stories, some funny, some grim. He'd had only two years of schooling, deep in the hills of Kentucky, but he had listened to story-tellers from his earliest days, and he carried on the cen-turies-old tradition of Cherokee storytelling.

My father told hunting stories, in which animals were real characters. You understood that he'd thought a lot about the animals in order to be able to hunt them successfully, and you understood that what the animals *were* had become a part of my father's life—not just their meat becoming a part of his body.

"White as a field-sacked deer, in winter underwear / he'd wake me to pant-legs cold as rifle-barrels / and shoes stiff as mules' hoofs . . ." In "A Hunt" (from *Going to the Water*), which the lines above begin, and in many other poems and stories, I have tried to get some sense of my father's spirit life as a hunter—and my own—onto the page.

When the Oral-Literary-Tradition Revival reached the University of Iowa, where I was studying with "the man who re-invented the couplet,"

Robert Lowell, I was too young to realize that Charles Olson, Robert Creeley, Allen Ginsberg, Lawrence Ferlinghetti, and the other poets in the revival were talking about me and my people. An art instructor had suggested that I go to Black Mountain College to combine my painting with poetry study with Olson, but I was too short of money to travel that far. I made it to Iowa U., sixty miles from home.

For me the oral tradition needed no revival. From Sequoyah, half German, half Cherokee, our tribe had the first written North American Indian language, but my people knew only English. As a child, I read whatever books were scattered around home and the one-room school I attended for seven years—*Ivanhoe,* the *World Book, Oliver Twist* . . . whatever was there—but my most important literary experience came from my father's stories and ballads. We had no electricity, no radio—once an old battery-powered, hand-me-down set had expired, early in my life—and television was many years from becoming the glib, falsifying, evil coeval of the nuclear bomb; my father was nearly all of our evening, after-work entertainment, our literature. How this has affected my writing I cannot say, but perhaps one example may give some idea:

CHEROKEE GHOST STORY: MY FATHER'S

What was it so pale astride its mount white
as moonlight on the stream
they rode thirsty horses toward,

their whisky, their women, the dancing
fading with words robed in breath's
warmth on wind, greeting. The figure

sped through them,
their gun echoes
arrows of enemies decades dead

pulling back into quiver
deeper than valley the young men ride,
these decades, toward the son of one of them.

That poem grew out of one of my father's ghost stories—this story something he'd actually experienced as a young man. I will tell you how the poem came about.

Learning that I'd been invited to teach a seminar in contemporary Native American literature at Goethe University in Frankfurt, West

Germany, Bo Scholer–a young scholar specializing in Native American studies–invited me to lecture at Aarhus University. The lecture had to be arranged very shortly after my arrival in Germany; with little time for interchange to learn what might be expected of me, I decided to do the one thing none of my unknown Danish colleagues could do–that is, to speak as a Native American writer and from my single situation to speculate on what seems to be true of other writers in the contemporary Native American literary movement and on why the things we stand for seem to be important, not just to Native Americans but to serious readers in general.

Without explanation, I began telling the ghost story and, at its conclusion, said, "Those young men were Cherokee, and one of them was my father." As it often happens, with me, telling a story or retelling one at just the right moment starts my creative processes–inspires me, I suppose I should say. About a month after I'd returned from an intensely meaningful few days of talking with Scholer and others in Denmark, I spent a long afternoon exchanging knowledge with Bernd Peyer, the German-Swiss scholar who had set in motion the correspondence which culminated in Dr. Martin Christadler's inviting me to teach in Germany. Talking with Bernd brought back the intense feelings I'd had in Denmark; and before I left my desk at the university that day, my father's story had migrated through Time and Space, from his youth in Kentucky, through my childhood in Iowa, by way of Denmark and Germany, onto a sheet of paper, and after some months of revision the poem made its way back to the southeastern U.S., where it–and my father–had originated, the poem published in *A Negative Capability*, printed in Alabama in 1984.

Something of my audience of three or four hundred Danes is in my poem, I am convinced–something of what we were, together, an hour in Aarhus, those people were my tribe during the telling. It was a big audience that day, and it is a big-audience poem–more formed, more akin to oratory than would be the case if I were quietly sharing a telling with a few friends.

Many dimensions of voice constitute the Oral Tradition, but its essence is its sense of a person speaking a certain way to certain people; thus the sense of those people, the hearers, is mingled with the speaker's lyric voice. There is a sense of an occasion, the moment and the situation of the telling; and, whatever is being presented, the reader of a poem or other written work deriving out of the Oral Tradition should get a sense of being located in an occasion – an occasion of utterance and hearing and feeling shared.

Sometimes I think I write as some other people say they write, "to an imagined ideal reader, perhaps someone like my best self," but I think my essential stance as a writer was formed while sitting with my brothers, my sister, my aunt, my mother, and sometimes a neighbor family, the small room dimly lit by the flickering grate of the wood stove and a kerosene lamp turned low to conserve fuel, my father's voice telling the old stories of the family, the People, and the new stories, which he had lived.

" 'A good man that had to kill' . . . one prison the stares of children . . ."

"One Prison" (from *Going to the Water*) and other poems have grown out of my father's battle stories. The man he'd shot had attacked him with a knife. My father had been imprisoned; then, after a year, pardoned. "Direction of Storm" (also from *Going to the Water*) deals with the killing and relates it to my own life: "Resin blood run down from dawn, / that bullet-hole in a blue / policeman's coat, this turn- / of-the-century-planted tree / was felled the same spring my / fifteen year old body, also, was struck, / by lightning, which bleached my world / white like hospital sheets . . ."

My father had wounded at least one other man, who'd tried to rob him. Several times each year he would have to go out into the darkness and shoot at thieves come to steal grain or livestock – or gasoline, once we had progressed from horse-farming to tractor-farming. A nighttime marauder shot out the window under which I lay sleeping, only a few months old, and the broken glass fell on me in my baby bed. I have very early memories of being frightened by gunshots. From some age, I remember whining to my mother, asking why couldn't Dad stay inside the lighted farmhouse with her, my sister, my aunt, my brothers, and me and be safe, and she told me a man had to do what my father was doing.

"Part of him does not want to kill anyone. A part of him does want to kill someone. To be like his father. Equal to him. And like his brother, off killing in the war. . . . 'Shoot to kill,' his father told him." This passage from my novel, "Lightning Boy and the War against Time," comes directly out of my experience.

"Old Kentucky, dark and bloody. Kentucky, the dark and bloody ground." These folk phrases are supposed to refer back to the years of battle between the Cherokee and the Shawano – so bloody that both tribes agreed to forsake the land because it was crowded with the spirits of the dead. But along with stories of Indian fighting Indian and Indian fighting white, and the stories of the American Civil War—our people divided, some fighting with the North, some with the South—I heard enough battle stories to know that my father's time in Kentucky was also a bloody time.

By now, you know that the northeast Iowa of my growing-up time wasn't any peaceful, law-abiding territory.

Somewhere, on paper and, vaguely, in my mind, I have a poem about the time a white former harvest hand came back, with a Sioux companion, to try to kidnap and rob my father. Sensing danger—he was amazingly alert, beyond my comprehension, even after all my soldier training— Dad was ready and drew his pistol at the same time they drew theirs. They left, pretending they had only meant to show him what kinds of guns they had. That same night they kidnapped a neighbor, left him on the icy ground, tied with barbed wire, and stole his money and car. Dad was a witness against them after they were caught. My teenage sister got a strange letter the white man wrote from prison. I was worried they would seek revenge once they were free. There was always violence and danger where I grew up, and that's why I've written so much about terror and battle, even though I'm a dedicated pacifist and refused to return to active duty in the Korean War after having been a volunteer in World War Two. I believe that an overwhelming movement against the killing of one's own kind is the only possible salvation for humanity, but that doesn't mean that I can't see the world as it really is.

I was blooded at four years of age, my father helping me shoot a chicken, but my real blooding came at age twelve, when I first hunted alone and brought back meat, two pheasants, just like the main character in my novel.

Wings battering up through corn blades, Seek angled the gun, and as a rooster pheasant rose, brown wings chop-chopping air to bring coppery body up against the blue sky, the shotgun moved steadily into track, safety catch already off, and Seek squeezed the trigger, knowing that the bird would fall—the glittering front sight round like the invisible pellets hurtling toward flesh and round like the pheasant's small eye, glittering golden in a red mask in the brilliant light of the round, midday sun.

At fifteen, I first shot at another human being. My father was off coon hunting that night. My half brother was a prisoner of war in Italy.

I was the nearest thing to an adult male; I had to defend my home. I suppose I was afraid, but I didn't question my duty. This was only one of several similar events in my teenage life.

He shoots, at the last instant pulling the rifle up to aim above his dark target.
Glass shatters behind him. He feels splinters slash his nape, he hears the shot, like a louder echo of his .22 shot, and he drops onto the porch, works the rifle bolt and, with trembling fingers, carefully thrusts another cartridge into the chamber.

That's part of my fifteen-year-old's experience as rendered in my novel. I don't mean to go too deeply into the violent times I've written about in fiction and poems, but I do want to suggest that my early years were what some people call "primitive."

I was constantly aware of life and death concerns. I felt in harmony with the patterns of creation and destruction in Nature, and, like everybody else in my family, I based my spirit life on Nature.

Years later, when I was in the Air Force, at age eighteen, I went to a Christian church—a military chapel, actually—for the first time, accompanying a friend, but the experience made no deep impression on me.

I had enlisted in the Air Force when I was seventeen. My oldest brother was already a prisoner of war, captured by a Nazi armored unit while fighting as a rifleman in Algeria. The presence of his father, dead in World War One, was always in our family—in my brother's last name and striking resemblance, in the wildflowers my mother sent me to pick for Decoration Day, in my parents' quarrels, in a large, oval-framed photograph—"and I / saluted my mother's first husband's / uniformed and flag-backed solemnity" (*Going to the Water*).

The day after my eighteenth birthday, I was on a train for the first time in my life, called to active duty, with the prospect of becoming an aviation cadet—a fighter pilot, I thought, though I had had no mathematics beyond algebra in the small high school I'd attended and had only piloted horses, tractor, and car. My innate intelligence showed high on the entrance exams, but nothing had prepared me for modern air warfare except my years of experience with guns. Like the pheasants and wild ducks I'd killed, I flew—but not as a pilot, as an aerial gunner.

A lot of people I knew were killed, and quite horribly, many burned alive, and some of this right before my eyes. "The red of blood dried by the burning of a bomber" begins "Then and Still" (in *Going to the Water*), one of several poems I've written about the violent deaths of people I knew. I did some praying. I also read the military pocket Bible all of us were issued—read it twice, in my simplemindedness, because the first reading hadn't reached me as I'd thought it should. I read from the Koran, which I'd found in a town library near one air base where I was stationed.

After the war, in college, I read from the Vedic holy books. "Learning imparts beauty to a homely face"—that meant a lot to me; I knew I looked different from most people; I assumed, therefore, I was ugly; I'd always read as much as I could, and now I had a new motivation.

A reviewer of my first book of poems, *Ghost Grapefruit* (Ithaca House, 1972), found it to have some of the qualities of Zen Buddhism, and one of my well-loved former students, Olga Broumas, has referred to me as a Zen-like teacher, but it has to be a natural affinity because I know virtually nothing about Zen.

Though I gain much from reading, still, today, I mostly find my spirit-awareness in Nature. I say my morning prayers to the Spirits of the Four Directions of Our Sacred Earth and to the God Who Can Not Be Named. I read over and over the Sacred Formulas of the Cherokees and try to learn from them. That is how it is with me.

Ha Yi Yu

Hear Great Spirit of the River.
My kind spawned in your blood
not so long ago.
Like you I have lived in the clouds,
have fallen
and crawled—my length many times broken—home,
have seethed with lightning
and have inflicted lightning.

I would rise and would have my people rise
and fall
like the rain
and rise again.

The linden leaf fell,
brown wave broken by boulder
and thrown into air,
and, in this spring's sun, in one bud,
new veins, like glowing rivulets of lava, flare.

This poem, which begins *Going to the Water,* is my own—one of several prayer poems I have published—but it grows directly out of the Sacred Formula for the Going to the Water Ceremony, a ceremony which itself grows out of my tribe's most important Life-and-Death needs. My conviction is that I must write from my own experience and from my own awareness—Camus's writing means a great deal to me, and I've been called an existentialist—and I've no impulse to become a museum-artifact-reproducing Indian writer; but Cherokee history, tradition, and myth are a part of my awareness, and I try to be faithful to them in all I do.

World War Two took me from a life of hunting and farming—with horses and a few old rusty machines—and put me into the Twentieth Century. The Air Force taught me electronic weaponry and some Japanese. The war ended while I was training to take part in the B-29 fire-bomb raids on Tokyo.

MY BROTHER'S POEM: VIETNAMESE WAR 1969

You tell me you can not write it
yesterday's pretty village splinters and in
your aircraft's cargo compartment ammunition/rations/med-
icines gone an American lies wrapped in his rain-coat
strapped to the floor of that machine generations struggled
to invent and thousands of hours of lives went to create
the boy's belongings all he could bear
on his back packaged beside him
sunset a shimmer like cathedral-glass
a memory the instrument-panel glow
as low as devotional candles showing
in plexiglass monsoon screams past your face
above the controls your own American face

(from *Going to the Water*)

For me, World War Two went on—in my mind—and other wars went on—in fact—for too many people, including my brother, as the poem above says.

The Korean War started while I was studying at the University of Iowa. In the Air Force Reserve—having been brainwashed, at age twenty, into believing the U.S. would be at war with Russia in a matter of months—I was subject to call-up and was notified to put my civilian affairs in order and prepare for active duty. Like many others, I was convinced—by a *New York Times* article—that the war was an immoral war, begun by the South Koreans, and I resisted call-up. Conscientious Objector status was narrowly defined, not nearly so just as standards adopted during the Vietnam War; another student was sentenced to twenty or thirty years in prison. I had secretly decided to go if I had to, rather than endure prison, but I would go as a medic, not in my old specialty as an aerial gunner—in this case machine-gunning ground troops. Through some computer goof, my honorable discharge—supposed to be frozen for the duration of the war—arrived a couple of weeks before my call-up. Not all were so lucky, and, as I've written in "Feeling Out of It," "some would spill, / blood 'Integrated / with Black comrades' blood / in Korea (*Going to the Water*). Seven years—seven a Cherokee sacred number: I was twenty-four years old when the Korean War began—not so innocent or "primitive" as the seventeen-year-old volunteer I had been.

Though my novel will seem to many to depict Vietnam, because there are helicopters involved, the main character's progression from criminal innocence to some kind of moral awareness is my own. "You asked for this, he accused himself—you volunteered—just like your uncle before you—just like a lot of Indians—to get out of poverty. You asked for it, he told the unconscious boy. If you hadn't tried to kill me, I wouldn't even have seen you."

There was no higher-education reward for military service when I volunteered, but the GI college-training legislation was put into law not long after I went into uniform. I remember buddies talking about it, and I suppose it must have interested me or I wouldn't remember it, but I don't think "after the war" meant anything to me at age eighteen. I was eating three big meals a day; no doubt it was lousy food, as most of my buddies said, but starvation changes you; "enough" is the definitive word; "delicious"—that's just a sometimes word. In "Four Men of Distinction at a Party in Honor of Three of Them" I've written about my hunger: "quite young I could make a bite of meat / flavor the maximum mouthful of potatoes / and fill my belly."

There was plenty of meat in the mess halls. We could fill our bellies; we were the machines of war, and we got our fuel. Since the war had helped farm prices somewhat, I'd been eating pretty well at home before going into the Air Force, and I was strong from working hard on our own farm, with my half brother gone into the army and more required of the rest of us—usually a twelve-hour workday, sometimes as much as a seventeen-hour workday—and I hired out to work for other farmers, once earning twenty-five cents for a twelve-hour workday, I remember. I've written about one of the bosses whose work regimen toughened me for my military life: "The bombers really his, / his tax-receipts would say, / and history—not mine, / though I'd labor in them, / loading, unloading" (*Spawning the Medicine River* 7).

If crops were ready to harvest, I missed school. Except for the war, I'd have had the twelve years of study required by state law—ten years more than my father had in his entire life—and then, I would have gone on laboring in my home region, probably, like my brother "Ray, who was always / two years older, and strong— / a loser pariah ditch digger 'nigger' part / Cherokee and me . . ." (my brother dead, from poor health care and hard work, at age fifty) "worked hard 'not / an ounce of fat' the undertaker's helper / simple said to comfort our sister—my brother his heart quit the job." That's probably the only way I could have quit laboring to just barely break even, if war hadn't caused the government to reach down to my level of society to recruit talented, potentially capable killers. Because of my military service, I got almost seven years of university training.

I'd always loved to read, and while I was a bomber crewman, I would read novels during slack periods in the six- to ten-hour flights. On the ground, when I wasn't learning new modern warfare skills, I read fiction, history, and Freud in the tiny base libraries. At night, I drank beer and went dancing with girls in town, as long as my $117 a month lasted.

One night, when I was on guard duty, I propped my rifle up against the same wall I was leaning against and, by the light of a fire-exit bulb behind a huge warehouse, I read all of Stephen Crane's novel *The Red Badge of Courage*—not knowing that Crane was a great writer and not knowing how much the main character's situation resembled my own. The muskets and cannons of the American Civil War would have seemed no weapons at all compared to what I was guarding—some millions of dollars of B-25 bombers, the plane that became famous in *Catch-22*—these planes secret weapons, armed with 75-millimeter cannons, big enough to be effective against Japanese warships—but, as it turned out, so big their powerful recoil jolted the airplanes' rivets loose: catch 22. Eighteen, that night on guard duty, I was still a gung ho, idealist soldier, but before I was nineteen I had begun to notice some ironies.

Dust from helicopter blades settling through palm camouflage, Seek looked down and saw a fine cloud of earth settling onto the boy's clenched face. Blood was thick in nostrils, not bubbled by breath. Seek remembered the convulsive jerk when the boy heard his sister's anguished cry, and Seek thought that now there were five dead, and, whatever crazy, compassionate thoughts he'd been having, the brutal truth was that he had killed five strangers, for some reason he couldn't even begin to guess.

Seek owes something of his literary existence to Stephen Crane, I feel—and am bound to acknowledge my debt—but his experience throughout my novel is my own youthful experience in essence, though differing at times in particulars.

Though some of my spirit visions and dreams give "Lightning Boy" a dimension some people would call "surrealistic," it is essentially a realistic novel, based on events I have lived through or closely observed. I try to base my writing on things I know well and feel strongly about—either hate or love. Even a fantasy short story like "The Sonofabitch and the Dog" is almost always based on something I have lived. "I love your strange and beautiful fiction," Simon Ortiz wrote, in accepting the story for his anthology, *Earth Power Coming* (Navajo Community College Press, 1983). " 'This sonofabitch remembers everything. . . .' That really blows me away." It's exactly what a soldier from New York City said of me when I remembered the exact route from the train station to Buckley Field outside Denver from just one fast truck ride. The dog who learns to catch bus rides from army base to town and back is the dog I knew in Mountain Home, Idaho.

University people seem generally to assume that the mode of fantasy generally labeled "surrealism" was invented by early twentieth-century French writers such as André Breton, but visions and dreams are nearly always important in tribal life, and I think the French writers did not discover "*surrealisme*"—they rediscovered it in much the same way the visual artists were rediscovering fantastic "primitive" African art. I think it's a fair assumption that contemporary Native American writers—particularly the ones who grew up in primitive ways, as I did—derive their "surrealist impulse" from the ways of their own people rather than from the educated French writers, splendid though some of those writers are. I remember being quite proud, as a young writer in my early twenties, when some work of mine was published next to translations of surrealist poems of the French poet Paul Eluard. By now, I'm more proud of coming from a people who acknowledge and value the dream world—perhaps one-third of most lives, even looking at it mathematically—and I'm glad for having grown up in a context that let me value dreams and carry them with me into my waking day.

By the end of my military service—age eighteen through age twenty—I'd moved from a primitive existence to somewhat informed knowledge of a world that was far from primitive. The University of Wisconsin administered tests for military personnel, and by passing these tests I received credit for two years of college, though I'd never taken a college class, not even the correspondence courses for soldiers. Air crews were mostly made up of people who had had at least some college work, and some of these people had been kind enough to steer me toward meaningful reading. I'd seen some death, I had come close to being killed, and I wanted to understand my life; I read urgently with a sense of personal stake in what I was reading.

Like the main character in my novel, I was, I am sure, reading what I could to help me find sanity—in the world, in myself. I remember throwing a heavily built six-footer down the stairs. I was five-foot-seven and weighed one hundred and forty pounds. I had to fight fast and violently or I'd lose. But the fight hadn't been a real fight based on hatred—just a big guy I'd been more or less friends with pushing what he probably thought of as "horseplay" too far when I was worn out and irritable from flying ten hours, and from recently having lost my girlfriend. It worried me that I might have badly hurt or killed someone I thought of as a friend. From Stephen Crane and Sigmund Freud, among others, I was learning something of the complexity of human emotions and intentions and learning that what was true of me was true of others. The military world was rough and raw; I saw a lot, I lived a lot, and I learned. I felt an instant affinity for Duane Niatum's fine story "Crow's Sun" when considering submissions for my anthology *A Nation Within,* recognizing my own eighteen-year-old soldier self in Duane's young sailor. After I accepted the story, Duane phoned me long distance—we've never met—and in the course of a long conversation and comparing of lives, he told me his own life incident on which the story is based. He's a real storyteller in the oral tradition, and his telling, over the miles of telephone wire, was as fine as the story printed on the page.

During my last year of military service, I started trying to write fiction and poetry but didn't show my work to anybody. I went on writing, and when I was twenty-one and a junior at the University of Iowa's

Writers' Workshop, I first published a story with a New York magazine, *Tomorrow*. The magazine was holding a nationwide fiction competition. Both Flannery O'Connor and I had our stories accepted for publication but didn't win a prize. She was a graduate student, and I was two years from graduate study; I never saw her, but by now I know her writing very well and know her to have been one of the finest talents of our age.

"Why is it that all the great artists of the world have been Caucasian males?" one of my art professors asked. Though I was a militant egalitarian, with some battle experience in controversial journalism, I didn't dare answer back to the man who held the grade book, and none of my women classmates said anything.

The Writers' Workshop was egalitarian and supportive. One of my classmates was Herb Nipson, a black writer, who went on to edit for *Ebony* magazine. Throughout my schooling a lot of people helped me, and I am grateful to them all, but, to be brief, I can mention only a few: James Hearst ("You are one of two people in this class who can go on to be writers"); Robie Macauley, my first instructor at Iowa and one who gave me perceptive criticism as well as the example of his own superb writing; Paul Engle, who had selected me for the Workshop and who went on to help me in every way possible; Robert Lowell, who told me, "Your essay style is not so brilliant as your poetic style" and gave me A's in Poetry Workshop; and R. V. Cassill, surely one of the best fiction writers and best teachers of this or any other day.

It was a white writer, William Faulkner, who first gave me a sense of the sanctity of my Indian heritage. Faulkner's character Sam Fathers, "son of a slave and a Chickasaw chief," became my spirit father.

Because my actual father's people lived in the South, they tried to pass for white as much as possible. I recall that one of my darker relatives was nicknamed "Nigger." The most Indian-looking of my father's brothers told me about the ways of our Cherokee people. Some people tell me I look like that uncle and like the medicine man Jukiah, photographed by Franz Olbrechts. Because of this resemblance and because I survived being struck by lightning, some Cherokees have spoken of me as a medicine man. I should like to think that this is so in some sense, for I believe in medicine, in the spirit destiny of each individual in a spirit order that is beyond human comprehension, but if I am in any sense a medicine man, my ceremonies are my fiction and poems.

Clearly, "Lightning Boy and the War against Time" relates to my having been struck by a lightning bolt. In real life my scientist younger brother explained to me that sometimes extremely high-voltage electricity, such as lightning, travels over the surface of a conductor instead of through it.

In the novel, I present the moment, the experience, not the years-later explanation.

He would recall the stench of burning flesh and would recall seeing a charred shape propped against a charred fence brace, head thrust between barbed wire strands, burned-black teeth clamped onto a few smoking wisps of clover. . . .

At another gate, he stopped, seeing lightning flash in every raindrop lengthening to fiery, pointed teeth under each wire.

In a poem, "A Midnight Dawn," I've put it this way: "the flame / in my quaking mirror is Red Man Thunderer God / myself fifteen / my older brothers   dry under oat-bundles propped / like Ioway teepees watch me turn / to unsnag soaked jeans the fence blazes / I've shaved / thirty years / of smoke."

Speaking of that poem and others in *Pointing at the Rainbow* (Blue Cloud Quarterly Press, 1980), Wendy Rose wrote me:

It is happenstance and foundation that Ralph is Cherokee; the poems come from this source, but they are not, themselves, identical with it. This is not specifically with your work; this is my general concept of poets and poetry. I do not write Hopi poems, Peter Blue Cloud does not write Mohawk poems, Simon Ortiz does not write Acoma poems—yet these works are all infused with our Hopiness, Mohawkness, and Acomaness—one from another place could not have written them. So also with your own.

I think Wendy's points are important and ones all of us who write from an Amerindian perspective should keep in mind. That Red Man, Spirit of Thunder and Lightning, is an important part of my religion infuses my awareness, but I write out of the experience of having been struck by lightning myself.

Hearing a Native American brother writer tell a university audience, "I want to be judged not as an Indian writer but as a writer," I thought I hope he means not *just* as an Indian writer, but I'm afraid he didn't; I'm afraid he was accepting the white assumption that whatever comes from an Indian is second rate and subject to acceptance only on the basis of compassion—"best a poor savage can do, and since we're so liberal and kind to our inferiors, etc. . . ."

"American Indian writing is among the most important literature being written in the United States," Bo Scholer said to me in Denmark, and he has devoted years of study to that belief. Needless to say, I agree with him. "Victory in war is good for a nation, defeat in war is good for the individual," writes the heroic, persecuted Soviet writer Andre Solzhenitsyn. Like Faulkner and other southern white writers, Native American writers write from a conquered people's awareness, and since the United States' shattering defeat by tiny Vietnam, Amerindian writers have taken on a new importance to contemporary readers. "Much of United States history is falsified because the professional historians' careers are best advanced by their taking an optimistic view. The truest contemporary history is in contemporary literature," the noted American historian Lawrence C. Goodwyn said in a lecture I attended in Germany, and he agreed with me that Faulkner and many Native American literary writers are good examples of what he was talking about. Social significance is one measure of great writing, and spirit significance is another. Amerindian writing has both. I would say to my people: "No apologies. Don't accept the conqueror's version of your worth. Be proud."

When I first started teaching, in Texas, I read about a mixed-blood who was sentenced to a long term in prison for miscegenation and realized that I, too, was subject to imprisonment for being married to a white woman. The same year, an Oklahoma Cherokee killed in the Korean War was denied burial in the graveyard of his white wife's family. My students were dominantly racist; one class threatened to lynch me; one night a Molotov cocktail was thrown against my door but fizzled. Through three years of teaching I won my students' respect, by patiently hearing their views but not backing down on my own, but one of the liberal students was beaten and driven off campus, and the college administration sided with the attackers. I managed to write and publish three stories during this time, but it was a dangerous place for me, and I moved on to a job in the North as soon as one was offered.

I first published poems referring directly to being Indian in 1959, a few years before the tremendous resurgence of Native American writing. Because of my outspokenness I've had some lonely, fearful, and discouraging times. Not long ago a drunken colleague said to me what others obviously feel: "You're an Indian, and I hate Indians; that's just the way it is." I've experienced a lot of harassment and salary discrimination on the job, and whenever someone worries, on my behalf, that the easy, unreal, ivory-tower life of the university may affect my writing, I say to them, "You just don't know what universities are like."

I've said often that the university is a battleground where the struggle for Native American survival must be won. As a university professor, it has been my good fortune to instruct some talented young Native Americans destined for high achievement—Paula Gunn Allen among them. The young writers keep me reminded that each of us is a part of the future, not just somebody defined by this year's applauding audiences and book reviewers, as some white establishment writers are inclined to think.

All of us who share Native American blood and commitment to the survival of Native American culture make up a far-flung and scattered nation. Wendy Rose has phrased it well for all of us, saying that we are a Nation Within—a cohesive nation within the more discernible nation, the United States.

Last year, I taught Native American literature in West Germany. This year, I am back on what will probably continue to be my home ground, Oregon, teaching at the state university in Eugene.

Another collection of my poems, *A White Rainbow: Poems of a Cherokee Heritage,* was released by Blue Cloud Quarterly Press in March 1985. I am writing new poems and stories as well as continuing to revise and polish the final draft of my novel. I am carrying on in the Oral Tradition by presenting my poems and fiction and by telling my own and my family's stories to audiences. *New Letters on the Air* is broadcasting over National Public Radio a half-hour program in which I am interviewed by Joseph Bruchac and in which I read my poetry and a section of my novel.

With my wife, poet Ingrid Wendt, and our daughter Erin, I do a lot of hiking and camping in the Oregon mountains and at the ocean. We grow as much of our own food as possible and try to stay in harmony with the land. That's how it is with us, now, and I hope it will be for a long time.

MAURICE KENNY

Waiting at the Edge:

Words toward a Life

Maurice Kenny (Mohawk) was born in 1929 in northern New York State and raised near the St. Lawrence River and the foothills of the Adirondacks. He taught for many years at Saranac Lake College and is currently a visiting professor at the State University of New York at Potsdam. He is the author of many volumes of poetry, fiction, and essays including *Blackrobe* (North Country Community College Press, 1982), which was nominated for the Pulitzer Prize and received a National Public Radio Award. His *Mama Poems* (White Pine Press, 1984) won the Before Columbus Foundation's American Book Award in 1984. In 2002 he was recognized with a Lifetime Achievement Award from the Native Writers' Circle of the Americas. He edits poetry and fiction anthologies and is founding editor of the Strawberry Press, which publishes poetry and art by Native Americans.

Kenny's most recent works include *Backward to Forward: Prose Pieces* (White Pine Press, 1997) in which he writes, among other things, about gay issues; the book-length poem *Tekonwatonti: Molly Brant* (White Pine Press, 1992); *In the Time of the Present: New Poems* (Michigan State University Press, 2000); *Tortured Skins and Other Fictions* (Michigan State University Press, 2000); and *Carving Hawk, New and Selected Poems, 1953–2000* (White Pine Press, 2002).

.,:;"

poem and explanation
(personal)

"SOMETIMES . . . INJUSTICE"

The day I was born my father bought me a .22.
A year later my mother
traded it for a violin
Ten years later my big sister traded that
for a guitar, and gave it to her boy-friend . . .
who sold it.

Now you know why I never learned to hunt,
or learned how to play a musical instrument,
or became a Wall St. broker.

The Mama Poems (White Pine Press, 1984)

I could easily have commenced this essay with any number of poems; however, I decided the one above was more apt than others dealing directly
with either home in northern New York state and the Adirondacks or
directly with Iroquois (Mohawk) ancestry or culture, which I have written
about over many years. "Sometimes . . . Injustice" says for me, at least,
where I was, where I was going, and pretty much how I was to get there.
There is also a touch of humor—which is in short supply in my work, and
it is a poem my father would enjoy were he alive to read it, though to this
hour "my big sister" denies the guitar swap. It is a poem that leads me back
in time to birth, childhood, and young manhood when I sporadically
published feeble efforts in local newspapers.

Yet at this very moment the poem strikes me as an odd choice because
I am sitting in a window staring out at the high peaks of the Adirondacks while "writer in residence" in Saranac Lake during the deer-hunting

season. Bear season has just nicely closed, and deer opened this very morning. I am obliged to remember the mornings I would steal out and board
my father's Chevy, snuggle behind the back seat, and hope my dad would
not discover me until he reached the hunting woods. He was a fine hunter
and rarely returned to my mother's kitchen without having bagged at
least a "supper" rabbit if not a deer, grouse, or pheasant. I don't remember
him coming home with either a bear or moose. At that time moose still
roamed the northern woods.

My father would have been proudly overjoyed had I, too, become
a skilled hunter, though confidentially, I think he'd be satisfied to know
that I have been a hunter of words and my game has been abundant.
I have hunted not only words and images, metaphors, but, to my
mother's relish, also song. I have heard the cedar sing, I have listened
to the white pine, I have imitated white-tail deer and hawk and cocked
an ear even to the more plain song of robin, a running brook, chicory
weaving on summer winds. I have sung the round dance of the Long-
house—feet stomping the wooden floor, drum beating, singers' throats
throbbing. I have sung the *adowe,* I have wailed at death, I have chortled
at weddings, I have attempted to lyric all the sounds of the earth not
only of us two-legged but of the four-legged, the winged, and those of
the waters. In good mind I have laid open my complete self to all those
sounds, those musical notes of birth and death and all that happens
between, whether it be the sighting of woodchucks sunning on the edges
of the Mohawk River, the bend of a mullein, the trot of wolf across cold
winter hills, the four winds and directions themselves, the fruit hanging
on my sister's sour cherry tree, my niece Martha's apple orchard, my
ever-so-great grandfather Joshua Clark's entry into the bowels of northern New York where he sponsored, founded the first Baptist Church and
where his loins eventually produced my mother, who also came from
good Seneca (Parker) stock. I have sung the Adirondacks . . . the death
of its rivers and blue lakes from acid rain. How odd when creative rain
kills what it first helped create . . . like in Greek tragedy. I have sung
the mountains with their rising peaks, packs of coy-dogs, bear, the mountains' history and future. Yes, I have been a hunter of song. My father
taught me well, how to hold my .22, to aim, when to pull the trigger,
and, last, how to skin out my game.

This mid-October I sit here in the window staring out at birch, white
pine, sugar maple rather drenched this morning from last night's rain
. . . unsullied, one hopes, by the midwestern industrial acids that are

killing the mountains and all the life upon these mountains. A grey
squirrel rushes up and down a beech tree; his mouth is crammed with
a large hickory nut. He stops, flicks his tail at the sound of this typewriter's racket, and scuttles up the trunk. I sit in this window, the lake
a brief walk down the hill. I sit in this window within a house called
"Tamarack House"–not exactly a tree house but it houses, temporarily
homes, students of the community college where I am resident. Some
of the students from Tamarack House are in the wet woods now tracking
the white-tail deer, hoping for a venison feast, a venison which probably
none of them have the faintest inkling of how to prepare and cook. They
are mainly from big cities and being freshmen, and fresh to these magical
mountain woods, have never hunted before–not bear, not white-tails,
and especially not word-songs.

I was a shy child, the youngest of three and an only male. My sisters
were not only pretty but rather smart and certainly talented. They both
sang with quite lovely voices and played the piano with some small gift,
having been taught by an elderly neighbor whom we called "Aunt Flo,"
though she was no relation. A former schoolmarm and spinster who loved
children, she thoroughly enjoyed seeing that some art–book reading and
piano playing–entered their lives. Aunt Flo was instrumental in opening many doors for me and especially for my older sister–the big sister
who traded my violin for a guitar–who to this day sings professionally
in a chorus in St. Louis. Aunt Flo gave me respect for the written word
where father gave me respect for the hunt, the game itself, the woods.
   My mother did not actually place such instruments in my young
palms; she did, however, give me a prophecy, a tea reading. When I was a
mere slip, my mother went to a fortuneteller and had her tea leaves read.
I stood near the gypsy, or what I took to be a gypsy; she stared blankly at
me probably sucking my thumb and wailing to go home. She ignored my
mother's future and exposed mine. I remember her saying, "I see him,
that little fellow there, I see him holding books or rocks. But I think it is
books. He holds many of them. Things are spilling out of them. Pictures.
Will he be a painter? He will be verrrrry famouuuuuuse." Well, I didn't
actually become a painter but a painter of word pictures, though as a
teenager I did dabble with oils but not successfully. I had no sense of
draftsmanship. I couldn't draw the straight side of a barn, let alone the
flight of an eagle or the head of a horse. My paintings were quite remi-
niscent of Grandma Moses. I had seen many reproductions of her paint-

ings and enjoyed them. I duplicated, and it wasn't difficult, but was certain I had no talent, even though my father encouraged this painting, neighbors bought a canvas or two, and I was offered the opportunity to take drawing classes. The prediction had been made. I was to hold books or rocks. Naturally, the preference became books.

It is only fair that I mention here that my sister next was a good story-teller of ghost tales on a summer eve when bats flew low and fireflies lit the darkness. I recognized fairly soon that I should never become a teller of tales. I possessed neither the knack nor the memory to record let alone invent them. Traditionally, stories are told in the depths of winter when the village is safe from ambush and the work of both men and women is completed for the long cold. Game is stored with dried corn and fruit. Then there is time to relax, to sit back and listen to stories, to be entertained and to be instructed, as traditional stories are teaching instruments, educational, for sharing knowledge and practical know-how. My sister's stories were merely told to scare the beans out of us. No teaching was ever intended. I have asked her many times to tell those stories she told when we were children, but she claims she long ago forgot them.

As I said, I was a shy boy. My sister's talents did not help me to get over my inadequacies. I knew I was a hunter. I knew also that the songs my father sang on Friday night, particularly when encouraged by a few bottles of beer or a pint of Christian Brothers brandy, were greatly to my liking. One song from Friday nights I remember, as he sang it continually, went thus: "If I had the wings of a turtle, over these prison walls I would fly." Turtles don't have wings. And turtles weren't incarcerated—or not to my young impressionable mind. Was he speaking of turtle doves? No, he meant turtles. Mud turtles. Turtles in the pond at my Aunt Jennie's farm. Turtles in the minute lake where I used to go play on "Witches' Hill" in the foothills of the Adirondacks where I grew up. These many years later I think my father felt he was jailed, imprisoned, even though—to the best of my knowledge—he was literally jailed briefly only once on a drunk charge and for recklessly driving the old Chevy. There were things he desired to do, accomplish, and places he fervently desired to go, to see—such as the blossomed cherry trees in Washington, D.C., and Alaska—though he constantly instructed that there was no place more beautiful than northern New York state. (That was a lesson which took some years for me to learn, digest, and agree with.) He died before he saw the cherry trees, or Alaska. Though he had had the opportunity of only the first two grades of school, my father was a clever, sharp, and, in a homespun fashion, intelligent man—though he did have a hard time understanding his children, as did my mother. He rose from being the water boy on a ditchdigging crew to be foreman, and eventually gave up a comfortable job working for the city to open and operate his own business, a restaurant and a small chain of three gas stations. When he died in 1958 he was comfortably solvent. But all those years he felt imprisoned. I'd suppose that only when he tracked the woods or boated the lake fishing did he feel free, unfettered, alive.

> My father wades the morning river
> tangled in the colors of the dawn.
>
> (from "My Sixth August" in
> *The Smell of Slaughter,*
> Blue Cloud Quarterly Press, 1982)

Surely, because my father found so much beauty and joy in the woods and the lakes and rivers, I too found this same beauty and freedom. And because Aunt Flo was never able to coordinate my fingers to the keys of her piano, and because my older sisters teased my singing voice (I was, naturally, a boy soprano), I too took to walking lone and free near those same rivers and creeks, through those meadows and fields, and within those dark but green woods that my father trailed. It was there I could sing, sing to wrens and larks, maples and cedars, fox and rabbits. I learned, walking these meadows edging the woods, crossed by the various streams, that I could make up songs not merely of my loneness but of the loneness and the beauty of these other creatures, and could actually write these songs down on paper. My first poems were composed.

I was born on the hottest night of August, so hot my mother always claimed she could not remember the hour, though I have a strong feeling that it was late. I was born a blue baby two months early, already confronting the vicissitudes of life; eczema blemished my skin. I suffered this horrific rash most of my childhood and painfully remember too well going to bed with my hands tied in mittens to prevent my scratching open the skin. And I was not only found to be allergic to eggs, which to this moment disturb some of the joys of living; I also had a weak chest and was prone to hay fever. I loved the haying in the summer fields and playing in the high haylofts. Adults who came and went in our house sneered at these allergies: I was making them up as little boys are often wont, seeking attention. They played games by tempting me to down an egg and offered me a nickel if I could keep a hard-boiled egg in my stomach. (It proved impossible.) They would give me a pudding or a slice of cake pretending it was eggless, yet I retched the moment the sweet reached the stomach's lining and acids. Of course, these allergies helped make me feel different, an outlaw. Neither my sisters nor my friends seemed to have these physical problems. It helped make me the "loner."

I spent my summers at one of three places: either my Aunt Jennie's farm (my mother's old homestead) on Fox Creek Road in the township of Cape Vincent; or my father's lakeside cabin on Chaumont Bay; or my Uncle Eugene's farm in Canada near Verona and Enterprise, a strongly Catholic community of heavy Irish drinkers. I intensely disliked my uncle's house. He was a prankster and thoroughly enjoyed seeing me stew, lose my temper, cry for my father to come retrieve me from his—as I thought—fiendish clutches. He once made my life there so miserable that I physically struck him. He whipped me in the field with my two cousins, his sons, watching. My father arrived shortly, whipped me a second time for disrespecting my uncle, his half brother, and took me back to the States, where I was shipped to my aunt's farm in Cape Vincent. I remember it vividly. It was my birthday when I arrived, and her neighbor baked me a surprise cake with pink frosting. I took a bite and became instantly ill. That was probably my worst summer. I sang out my heart and made good friends with my aunt's old mongrel dog, his pedigree being most apt for the occasion. I felt bedraggled, outlawed, imprisoned.

It is quite unusual for Indian parents to whip children. It is thought the child learns better by example—hence the teaching stories. My father rarely whipped his children, but when he did it was almost with a vengeance and that usually on beer-night Fridays.

All this summer traveling, shifting-about, farming us to various family members, helped develop my wanderlust, my own discord with settling, my varied and sometimes erratic travel, my impatient need to be on the go, to settle back in the seat of either a Greyhound bus or an Amtrak rail car. My father never suspected that my desire to roam was partially due to his shifting us about. He could not come to grips with my wanderings.

Obviously, my father and his life-style influenced my life. It's odd because early in my youth I figured it was my mother who so strongly affected me. It was perhaps only twenty years ago that I came to this astounding realization. I thought I was running away from my father's influence, and the opposite was the truth. I was running toward it, deeply into it. Though from time to time I have lived in large metropolitan cities or in foreign countries, I was seeking the blossoming cherry trees and Alaska that he never got to see, even though as yet I have not seen those trees or visited Alaska. I have always been running home – my father's thought – which I fully recognize now as being that warm fireside or bosom of "home." "Place" is an extremely important theme in my poetry, and I have been questioned many times where that "place," that "home" is. Is it northern New York with mountains and rivers, woods and fields; is it the reservation, the town in which I grew up; or is it Brooklyn, where I currently live? (I'm only passing through Saranac Lake.) Is it Albuquerque, which I deeply enjoy visiting; Berkeley, where my life's best friend lives? Is it Mexico, which I love most next to northern New York? Or is it on the Greyhound bus passing through this land that has been called "America" which I prefer calling, if it must be named, the earth on turtle's back? My father never spoke of this beautiful land as being "America" but as being "home," and said that there was no "place" like it and that one day I would come to that truth, that realization, that positive fact. I would accept "home" and "place," and be content. Save the cherry trees for dreaming, for wishes to be fulfilled.

So where is this place that I write of? Is it the foothills of the Adirondacks, the Lake Ontario summer cabin, my aunt's farm on Fox Creek Road, the reservation on the St. Lawrence River; is it the woods or the fields growing wild strawberries so sweet to the tongue? Is it where I was born, where my first cry rent the night of that hot August; is it the Brooklyn apartment I share with my cat, Sula; is it Kaherawaks, my surrogate granddaughter at Akwesasne; or is it a stuffy bus traveling the night highways across turtle's back? It is all of these places and things. It is even, yes, even the poems themselves, the persons I have created of wolf or berry, my ancestors such as Molly Brant or Ely Parker; my Aunt Jennie, old and now slightly feeble, but still driving the northern roads selling Avon products because when she stops she knows her life ends; my mother, whose own life-pain is with me still; my father's dreams and victories; my sisters and their lives; and my first tricycle that a cousin wrecked for me on the railroad track, my first red fire engine; the first pencil Aunt Flo placed in my hand when the piano intimidated those fingers of that hand. The "place" is within me and all around – whoever I touch, wherever I travel. It is not the personal "I" but the collective, because I wish all peoples to relate to that "I," become that "I" and find their place now that I have mine.

I was born on the hottest night of August in 1929 in a small town nesting in the foothills of the Adirondacks on the shores of Black River, which flows out of the mountains and into the great Lake Ontario. The day I was born my father bought me a .22 and gave me a hound dog. Happy was his name. My mother traded the gun for a violin which I never learned to play, and my sister traded the violin for a guitar and gave it to her boy friend—who later became her husband. I never became a Wall Street broker but a hunter of words, of songs. I am still hunting.

§2

"WILD STRAWBERRY

FOR HELENE

And I rode the Greyhound down to Brooklyn
where I sit now eating woody strawberries
grown on the backs of Mexican farmers
imported from the fields of their hands,
juices without color or sweetness.

    my wild blood berries of spring meadows
    sucked by June bees and protected by hawks
    have stained my face and honeyed
    my tongue . . . healed the sorrow in my flesh

    vines crawl across the grassy floor
    of the north, scatter to the world
    seeking the light of the sun and innocent
    tap of the rain to feed the roots
    and bud small white flowers that in June
    will burst fruit and announce spring
    when wolf will drop winter fur
    and wrens will break the egg

    my blood, blood berries that brought laughter
    and the ache in the stooped back that vied
    with dandelions for the plucking,
    and the wines nourished our youth and heralded
    iris, corn and summer melon

we fought bluebirds for the seeds
armed against garter snakes, field mice;
won the battle with the burning sun
which blinded our eyes and froze our hands
to the vines and the earth where knees knelt
and we laughed in the morning dew like worms
and grubs; we scented age and wisdom

my mother wrapped the wounds of the world
with a sassafras poultice and we ate
wild berries with their juices running
down the roots of our mouths and our joy

I sit here in Brooklyn eating Mexican
berries which I did not pick, nor do
I know the hands which did, nor their stories . . .
January snow falls, listen . . .

Dancing Back Strong the Nation
(Blue Cloud Quarterly Press, 1979;
White Pine Press, 1981)

I began this poem in the winter of 1978. January to be exact, living
in Brooklyn Heights in New York City; I was ill. A close friend and nearby
neighbor had the goodness of heart and thought to bring to my sick bed
a basket of cultivated strawberries. Helene knew my fondness for the
fruit and just how important the strawberry is to me and my poetry.
The wild strawberry is not only the first natural fruit of the eastern spring,
but it is the symbol of life to Iroquois people. The strawberry holds strong
significance for all the people of the Six Nations and for me as a person,
as a Mohawk writer, and as both editor and publisher. In 1976 I estab-
lished Strawberry Press to be an exclusively Native American press to
publish the poetry and art of Native People. There were, and remain
still today, other Native Americans who publish Indian writing, but not
exclusively. Joseph Bruchac of the *Greenfield Review* and Press, of Abnaki
descent himself, indeed publishes many Native American writers, and
it may well be the press's thrust; but he also publishes Black, Chicano,
Asian, Anglo, and African writers. William Oandasan, Yuki/Filipino, of
"*A*" *Magazine* and Press, likewise prints the works of a multicultural
group of authors. Brother Benet Tvedten, deserving high praise for his
Blue Cloud Quarterly and Press, has published more Native American
writers, and others on related subjects, than anyone. Yet Brother Benet
is of Swedish abstraction.

As I rallied from the illness, and while biting into those cultivated berries, sucking juices, I began to realize, to remember the many mornings of my childhood at home in northern New York state when I would follow my mother and two older sisters into the flowering fields where the wild strawberry vines crawled under the sun.

STRAWBERRYING

morning
broods
    in the wide river
Mama bends
    light
    bleeds
    always
in her day of
    picking
(our fields are stained)
the moon, bats
    tell us
    to go
in the scent of
    berries
fox
    awaken
    in stars

(from *Kneading the Blood*,
Strawberry Press, 1981)

With their children, other women, often my mother's friends, would be there picking and filling their baskets. It was a good time. Burning hot as it was in those open meadows, breezes did rush the grasses and flowers from off either Lake Ontario or the St. Lawrence River. It was a time of laughter, jokes and teasing, cries and tears from children bored with the labor and eager for a river swim, and certainly not only a time of filling the belly with the deliciously honeysweet fruit, dripping in ripeness, but a time when the women exchanged what I thought were stories, gossip. I am convinced that was the reason they came to the fields. Even then, in 1934–35, those many years back, cultivated berries could be bought at roadside stands or in the village markets.

Also while eating the berries in my sick bed I recalled a strong senti- ment of the Lakota Holy Man, Black Elk:

When the ceremony was over, everybody felt a great deal better, for it had been a day of fun. They were better able now to see the greenness of the world, the wideness of the sacred day, the colors of the earth, and to set these in their minds. (*Black Elk Speaks,* University of Nebraska Press, 1979)

There is no doubt in my mind that picking wild strawberries was a ceremony, and to this day it has offered me a better look at the grasses of the world, the width of a sacred day, and certainly the "colors of the earth." Picking those berries enriched not only our everyday lives and bellies but our imaginations and spirits as well. We all, even the children, truly felt better later. I wanted to write of this good feeling, this betterment and enrichment.

This year, winter 1983, strawberries were shipped air freight to the United States from Chile, in South America—a long way from the home meadows of the north. Obviously, air-freighted fruit must be harvested rather green and needs to complete the cycle en route. And, so, too, the berries in the basket that Helene had brought to me in January of 1978. The straw basket was stamped with purple ink: "Hecho En Mexico" —meaning, made in Mexico. The peaches, watermelons, cantaloupe, and berries are raised in the Mexican state of Sonora. I have spent large chunks of time in Mexico. I also knew that these fruits, and especially the strawberries, were grown with the aid of chemical fertilizers, chemicals that could and surely would cause great pain to the people working those fields with bare hands. So as I am in my bed popping berries into my dry mouth, I recognize the horrendous fact that people were possibly dying, people I did not personally know, nor ever would; people were dying so that I could eat those terrible berries in a winter city, an unnatural time to be eating strawberries. And they were terrible. Large though they were, at least an inch in circumference, they were tasteless. Below the bright red skin the flesh was colorless, pale white. I did thank my friend profusely, but once she had left, I not only threw the wretched fruit out but vowed I'd never eat Mexican strawberries again unless I personally knew the hands that raised and picked them for the table, and especially those harvested in Sonora.

Directly, I was not the cause of this pain to the workers in Sonora. I'm sufficiently realistic to comprehend this. But my purchasing these fruits decidedly encouraged the use of not only the chemical fertilizers but the deaths of men and women, probably children as well. I was acutely aware that they, the harvesters, could not enjoy the labors as we had when I was a child of those northern meadows, meadows etched by blackeyed susan, purple clover, dandelion; meadows sung to by wrens, larks, bluejays; meadows that in the continuum not only supported our desires for fresh fruit but supported our strengths as a people and as a Nation, for the wild strawberry was given to us by the "little people" who live in a quarry, for the pleasure of eating and to be used in a healing ceremony.

DECEMBER

Set up the drum.

Winter's on the creek.

Dark men sit in dark kitchens.
Words move the air
A neighbor is sick.
Needs prayer.

Women thaw frozen
strawberries.

In the dark . . . a drum.

> Kids hang out
> eating burgers
> at McDonalds.
> The Williams boy
> is drunk.

Set up the drum.

Berries thaw,
are crushed,
    fingers stained, and tongues.

Set up the drum.
A neighbor is sick.
Say a prayer.
Dark men sit in dark kitchens.

Wind rattles the moon.

(from *The Mama Poems,* White Pine Press, 1984)

While nibbling those horrible cultivated berries I became enraged with the conglomerate fruit companies, as Pablo Neruda had years ago, which control the lives of those Mexican farmers who scratch out a meager livelihood from the sands, and I was discouraged with my own self.

§3

Travel has fallen to me easily, I'm sure, as a result of all those early childhood shiftings, and also because at the age of eleven years I was taken by my mother–then legally separated from my father–to live in Bayonne, New Jersey. I stayed in that oil-refining town better than a year. I had many troubles there but the major problem centered at school. I despised every aspect of it. I was, indeed, made to feel I was not only different from the other students but inferior on all accounts. Because of this I refused to attend school/classes and spent my time either in the local park hiding away or at a candy store that was then called "Jelly Bean," or took flight by bus to Manhattan across the Hudson River with the monies my mother gave me to buy lunch. I can't recall precisely how many days now, but I skipped school a sufficient number, a number dangerously high, enough to bring me before a judge who recommended a reform school for truant boys. My father saved me from that fate and brought me back to northern New York. From high school I returned as often as finances would allow to New York City, much to my father's chagrin. Finally I hitchhiked to North Carolina, at eighteen or nineteen, to pilgrimage to the Thomas Wolfe shrine in Asheville. From there I hitched farther, to New Orleans, with Mexico as my destination. Money prevented this, and I wandered tired and starving along the Mississippi River up to St. Louis where my eldest sister and her husband lived. I stayed there a few months and then came east to Indianapolis, where I entered Butler University.

This was perhaps the wisest move I have ever made. Fortunately, I came under the spell of an instructor, a Keats scholar, took numerous courses in both literature and creative writing from him, and at last was blessed by his hands and sent adrift to sink or swim as a writer/poet. Werner Beyer has continued to be a very strong influence on my life and writing. I dare not to this moment type a period to the blank page without wondering if Werner would challenge the punctuation. I also worked at Butler with Roy Marz, who was enjoying some national reputation as a poet. He published frequently in *Poetry Magazine*—then most prestigious. Roy did not hold as high a degree of respect for my creative efforts as did Werner Beyer, though he did suggest I try my hand at fiction. He felt I struggled under enormous difficulties with poetry . . . as did John Crowe Ransom, then editor of the famous *Kenyon Review*. Ransom felt I lacked a sense of rhythm. Roy felt my poems lacked not only depth but a classical stance. Little did either poets or teachers ever suspect that European classical poetry might not be my forte.

Under erratic conditions I left Indianapolis, with my father's aid, and returned once more to northern New York, where eventually I enrolled in St. Lawrence University, which had an extension in Watertown. I worked there with Douglas Angus, the novelist, who encouraged me back to poetry and away from fiction. How the young are shifted by whatever prevailing winds! I then made a decision to enter Columbia University in New York City—much to my father's pleasure. I took the entrance exam, which proved extremely difficult, passed and was admitted to the university. However, that was in April of 1957. I never registered. That winter next I enrolled in New York University, deciding it was more important to me to study with Louise Bogan, who taught there then. It proved another wise choice. Louise encouraged my poetry. Her tragic spirit and advice stay with me still. Her suggestions remain constant at my pencil's movement across a blank notebook. At this time my first collection, *Dead Letters Sent* (1958), was published. I remained in New York for approximately six years and then traveled south to Mexico for a brief time. A year later I returned and worked for a great length of time with Willard Motley, the black novelist, author of the very famous best seller *Knock on Any Door*. Willard, a most undisciplined writer, oddly taught me discipline. Rise in the morning, accept the challenge of the blank sheet of paper, and write. Finish the day with a composition: a poem, an essay, a story, or at least a book review or an entry into a journal.

Willard died in 1965, at which time I was living in the U.S. Virgin Islands—St. Thomas, to be exact—not exactly beachcombing but close to it. I drank heavily there, nightly, and wrote practically nothing, though I did complete one poem and proudly saw it appear in the *New York Times*—a major publication for me at that time. Eventually I was rescued from the beach bars of St. Thomas by friends who flew down to the island to boldly retrieve me bodily. I stayed briefly in New York. I appeared on a cold December morning off an airplane in Chicago, where I took a job with the *Chicago Sun* which I held exactly one year. I made my return to New York City in 1967, found an apartment in Brooklyn, and have remained nesting there since. Needing employment, I was fortunate through friends to land a job as a French waiter in a chic discoteque on Park Avenue, where I worked for some six years. I began writing prolifically while in Chicago and continued this, for me, prodigious output. It was not until seventeen years after the publication of *Dead Letters Sent* that my next chapbook was printed: *I Am the Sun*. It originally appeared in *Akwesasne Notes*.

I commenced publishing poems regularly in the *Notes*, which led to my first appearance in an anthology (edited by Walter Lowenfels), *From the Belly of the Shark*. Since then I have been very active as writer, editor and coordinator, even a college professor. I'm sure Werner Beyer would blanch were he to learn of that fate—my being a teacher. Werner counseled that I should stay as far away from academia as possible, that it was no place for a writer, that it was suicide. I have concurred with him for thirty years. But so, too, is alcohol suicide for the writer—or for this writer, at least. I gave up booze in 1974 when I suffered a heart attack.

Since then I have continued to travel across "turtle's back," perhaps looking for the cherry blossoms or Alaska, still hunting song and words, up to this morning sitting here in the window looking out at the birch, the yellowing tamarack, looking toward Mt. Baker rising outside the village of Saranac Lake, a town in which nearly a hundred years ago another poet/novelist made his home. Robert Louis Stevenson composed his novel *The Master of Ballantrae* and a few short fictions here. Perhaps because his "cottage" is a short walk along the edge of the hill and because I feel his presence, I'm able to sit here at this machine and type out these few facts and figures of my life.

Writing in the north country, either in the mountains or at Akwesasne, has been difficult for me—to write well. There has been little need. The mountains are here. I live amongst them and with the birch outside my door, the white pine, and my friend Ray Fadden's "bears." I can hear the loons, the Canadian geese flying south to winter; I see mallards and lilies on "Turtle Pond"; I smell the clarity of air, and await the snow surely to come. All the elements important to my poems, to my life, surround me presently—even the knowledge that wild strawberry vines are deeply embedded in the earth sleeping until spring and June sun. Akwesasne is a mere seventy miles north: Akwesasne where my granddaughter lives with her mother and father/poet Rokwaho, where my ties remain strong, and where my summers are savored.

is summer this bear
    home this tamarack
are these wild berries song

    . . .

is summer this wolf

    . . .

is summer this turtle

    . . .

is summer this tongue
    home this cedar

(from *Is Summer This Bear*,
Chauncey Press, 1985)

ELIZABETH COOK-LYNN

"You May Consider

Speaking about Your Art . . .

Elizabeth Cook-Lynn (Crow Creek Sioux) was born in 1930 in Fort Thompson, South Dakota, and raised on the reservation. She is professor emerita of English and Native American Studies at Eastern Washington University in Cheney, Washington. With Beatrice Medicine, Roger Buffalohead, and William Willard, she was one of the founding editors of *Wicazō Sa Review: A Journal of Native American Studies* (Red Pencil Review). In 1978 she was awarded a National Endowment for the Humanities Fellowship, which she spent at Stanford University. She has received many awards for her work and has appeared in many journals. Her many books include *Anti-Indianism in Modern America: A Voice from Tatekeya's Earth* (University of Illinois Press, 2001), *Aurelia: A Crow Creek Trilogy* (University Press of Colorado, 2002), *I Remember the Fallen Trees: New and Selected Poems* (Eastern Washington University Press, 1999), *The Politics of Hallowed Ground: Wounded Knee and the Struggle for Indian Sovereignty* (University of Illinois Press, 1999), and *Why I Can't Read Wallace Stegner and Other Essays: A Tribal Voice* (University of Wisconsin Press, 1996).

.,;"

[handwritten: statement then background (optomistic)]

Ever since I learned to read, I have wanted to be a writer.

I was born in the Government Hospital at Fort Thompson, South Dakota, in 1930, and when I was a "child of prairie hawks" (*Seek the House of Relatives*), I lived out on the Crow Creek (a tributary of the James and the Missouri) in what anthropologists like to call "an extended family." And I loved to read.

Reading, if it is not too obvious to say so, precedes writing, though I teach college students today who are examples of an apparently opposing point of view. They have read nothing.

On the contrary, I read everything: the Sears catalog, *Faust,* Dick and Jane, *Tarzan of the Apes, The Scarlet Letter,* the First Letter to the Corinthians, *David Copperfield,* "The Ancient Mariner," Dick Tracy, "Very Like a Whale," *Paradise Lost, True Confessions,* and much more. I went to whatever libraries were available as often as I went anywhere.

But I read nothing about the Dakotapi. Much later I took a history course at South Dakota State College called "The Westward Movement," and there was not one mention of Indian Nations! I keep the text for that course on my own library shelf as a marvelous example of scholarly ineptitude and/or racism.

Wanting to write comes out of that deprivation, though, for we eventually have to ask, what happens to a reasonably intelligent child who sees him or herself excluded from a world which is created and recreated with the obvious intent to declare him or her *persona non grata?* Silence is the first reaction. Then there comes the development of a mistrust of that world. And, eventually, anger.

That anger is what started me writing. Writing, for me, then, is an act of defiance born of the need to survive. I am me. I exist. I am a Dakotah. I write. It is the quintessential act of optimism born of frustration. It is an act of courage, I think. And, in the end, as Simon Ortiz says, it is an act that defies oppression.

In those early days, even though I had a need to write – that is, survive – I lived in a world in which the need to write was not primary. The need "to tell," however, was. And so I listened and heard about a world that existed in the flesh and in the imagination, too, and in the hearts and minds of real people. In those days I thought the world was made up of "Siouxs" and "Wasichus."

It is this dichotomous nature of the real world and the literary world and, yes, the present world that accounts for the work I do. It is the reason I call myself a Dakotah poet, however hesitantly I accept the label, however unclear the responsibilities that come with that label.

The best way to begin a philosophical discussion concerning the nature and substance of the work of a contemporary Dakotah poet is to admit, oddly enough, to a certain kind of timidity and lack of confidence and to conclude by saying that I do not speak for my people.

First of all, one must be timid because there is the consideration that poets have a tendency to think too much of themselves. It is quite possible that we poets think we are more significant, more important than we are; that the events we choose to signal as important for one reason or another are, after all, something else; that the statements and interpretations we have given to these events are mistaken and/or irrelevant.

Second, the idea that poets can speak for others, the idea that we can speak for the dispossessed, the weak, the voiceless, is indeed one of the great burdens of contemporary American Indian poets today, for it is widely believed that we "speak for our tribes." The frank truth is that I don't know very many poets who say, "I speak for my people." It is not only unwise; it is probably impossible, and it is very surely arrogant, for *We Are Self-Appointed* and the self-appointedness of what we do indicates that the responsibility is ours and ours alone.

Therein lies another dichotomy: I claim to be a Dakotah poet by disclaiming that I speak for my people.

I am not greatly surprised that this dichotomy does not exist for the "real" poets of our tribes, the men and women who sit at the drum and sing the old songs and create new ones. That is an entirely different matter, for it remains communal. Thus, when I hear the poetry of the Crown Butte Singers, the Porcupine Travelers, and the Wahpekute Singers, I have every confidence that they speak in our own language for the tribes, Oyate.

"A Poet's Lament: Concerning the Massacre of American Indians at Wounded Knee" is a good example to use to discuss and illustrate the problems that I see involved in the matter of responsibility for a poet like me, one who writes English, using contemporary forms.

This poem describes what was and is a very public event. Yet as a self-appointed poet I bring my own perceptions into this tribal event even as I am aware of the public nature of the event and the history that surrounds it. The private histories which do not rely upon the written word, research, and text are a part of that perception.

All things considered, they said,
Crow Dog should be removed.
With Sitting Bull dead
It was easier said.

And so the sadly shrouded songs of poets,
Ash-yellowed, crisp with age
arise from drums to mark in fours
three times the sacred ways
that prayers are listened for; an infant girl stares
past the night, her beaded cap of buckskin brightens
Stars and Stripes that pierce
her mother's breast; Hokshina, innocent
as snow birds, tells of Ate's blood as red as plumes
that later decorate the posts of death.

"Avenge the slaughtered saints," beg mad-eyed
poets everywhere as if the bloody Piemontese are real
and really care for liberty of creed; the blind
who lead the blind will consecrate the Deed, indeed!

All things considered, they said,
Crow Dog should be removed.
With Sitting Bull dead
It was easier said.

In this specific case I mean to suggest that it is the responsibility of a poet like me to "consecrate" history and event, survival and joy and sorrow, the significance of ancestors and the unborn; and I use one of the most infamous crimes in all of human history, which took place against a people who did not deserve to be butchered, to make that responsibility concrete. Only recently has the mainstream of American society been confronted with the monstrous nature of this historical act and others like it, but Indians have always known it.

The ceremony I describe in the second stanza really did occur, I'm told; the people and the warriors gathered within hours after the dreadful killing, and they swept into the grounds and guarded their dead, placing twelve red-draped markers at the perimeters of the site. I don't know if this is "true." I wasn't a witness. I have not read any account of it. Surely, though, in the memories of the people, this ceremony took place in order to consecrate the event. And the poem that I write in English and in contemporary form, and the songs that continue to rise from drums in Dakota and in traditional forms a century later, recreate that consecration. That is what I mean to hold on to when I talk of responsibility in the creative process.

It is no accident that I refer to the number "twelve" to record this event in sacred terms, for that number figures prominently in sacred ritual. It is no accident that I begin and end with the names of Sitting Bull and Crow Dog, both religious leaders of the people, because I mean to deliberately place this event which is usually described in military terms into the religious context to which it speaks.

Ceremony, in literary terms, can be said to be that body of creative expression which accounts for the continued survival and development of a people, a nation. In this instance, it relies upon ancient symbols which are utilized spontaneously in a communal effort to speak with the givers of prayers, to recall the knowledge about life and death that has its origins in mythology and imagination.

The people who gathered to perform this ceremony a hundred years ago did so at risk of their lives. It was then and remains now an important commitment to nationhood and culture. They imagined the grief of the Unktechies who arose from the water, hundreds, perhaps thousands of years ago, to give the people a religion and then went deep into the Earth to listen for the sounds of our drums, songs, poetry, and prayers. The people wept and sang of their own grief and sorrow.

Years ago when I was twenty and I first started sending out my poems, an editor wrote on an acceptance letter a question that has haunted me for the rest of my so-called career as a poet. She asked, "WHY is Native American poetry so incredibly sad?"

Now I recognize it as a tactless question asked out of astounding ignorance. It reflects the general American attitude that American Indians should have been happy to have been robbed of their lands and murdered. I am no longer intimidated, as I once was, by that question, and I make no excuses for the sorrow I feel in my heart concerning recent history. I do not apologize for returning to those historical themes, for that is part of the ceremonial aspect of being a Dakotah poet.

Attending to ceremonial matters as a writer does not mean, however, that I am not writing about myself. Quite the opposite is true. There is a self-absorption in my work which is inherent in my survival as a person, and my identity as a Dakotah. This self-absorption has always been a part of tradition, I think, for Dakotahs, in spite of the pervasive articulation in recent times of the idea that the Indian "self" was somehow unimportant; that Indians have been absorbed in the contemplation of the natural world, readily giving themselves up to it, mastered by it philosophically as well as physically; that submission to environment dominates American Indian life and belief.

This overstatement has been handy for the perpetuation of the longed-for nineteenth-century idea concerning the ultimate and expected disappearance of Natives and Native America from this continent. It is convenient to suggest from this imagined obsession with the natural world that the American Indian would become an artifact, too unreal and obsolete for survival in the modern world. The Indian's "journey," then, as a race of people, would be concluded.

The function of contemporary American poetry is to disavow that false notion.

One of what I consider my best poems is entitled, "Journey," and it is an attempt to express that disavowal:

I. DREAM

Wet, sickly
smells of cattle yard silage fill the prairie air
far beyond the timber; the nightmare only just
begun, a blackened cloud moves past the sun
to dim the river's glare, a malady of modern times.
We prayed
to the giver of prayers and traveled to the spirit
mounds we thought were forever; awake, we feared that
hollow trees no longer hid the venerable ones we were taught
to believe in.

II. MEMORY

Dancers with cane whistles,
the prairie's wise and knowing kinsmen
They trimmed their deer skins
in red down feathers,
made drum sticks from the gray grouse,
metaphorically speaking, and knocked on doors
which faced the East.
Dancers with cane whistles,
born under the sign of hollow stems,
after earth and air and fire and water
you conjure faith to clear the day.
Stunningly, blessedly you pierce the sky
with sound so clear each winged creature soars.

In my mind Grandmothers, those old partisans of faith
who long for shrill and glowing rituals of the past,
recall the times they went on long communal
buffalo hunts; because of this they tell the
lithe and lissome daughters:

> look for men who know the sacred ways
> look for men who wear the white-striped quill
> look for dancers with cane whistles
> and seek the house of relatives to stay the night.

III. SACRISTANS

This journey through another world, beyond bad dreams
beyond the memories of a murdered generation,
cartographed in captivity by bare survivors
makes sacristans of us all.

The old ones go our bail, we oblate preachers of our tribes.
Be careful, they say, don't hock the beads of
kinship agonies; the moire-effect of unfamiliar hymns
upon our own, a change in pitch or shrillness of the voice
transforms the ways of song to words of poetry or prose
and makes distinctions
no one recognizes.
Surrounded and absorbed, we tread like Etruscans
on the edge of useless law; we pray
to the giver of prayer, we give the cane whistle

in ceremony, we swing the heavy silver chain
of incense burners. Migration makes
new citizens of Rome.

The journey theme is pervasive in contemporary Native American poetry. The oral traditions from which these expressions emerge indicate a self-absorption essential to our lives. They follow the traditions of native literatures which express as a foremost consideration the survival of the individual, thus the tribe, thus the species, a journey of continuing life and human expectancy.

The final responsibility of a writer like me, and an essential reason to move on from "wanting to be a writer" to actually writing, is to commit something to paper in the modern world which supports this inexhaustible legacy left us by our ancestors. Grey Cohoe, the Navajo poet and artist, once said to a group of Native American students we were working with: "Have confidence in what you know."

That is difficult when we ordinarily see ourselves omitted from the pages of written histories. but not impossible.

CARTER REVARD

Walking among the Stars

Born in 1931 in Pawhuska, Oklahoma, Carter Revard's Osage tribal name is Nompehwahthe. A "quiz kid" in his youth, Revard went on to become a Rhodes Scholar at Oxford. In 1997 he retired from teaching in the English department of Washington University in St. Louis, where he had specialized in medieval literature. He continues to live in St. Louis where he is actively engaged in both scholarly and poetic work.

Revard's many books include *Ponca War Dancers* (Point Riders Press, 1980) and *Cowboys and Indians Christmas Shopping* (Point Riders Press, 1992). His most recent books include *Family Matters, Tribal Affairs* (University of Arizona Press, 1998) and *Winning the Dust Bowl* (University of Arizona Press, 2001). He has been honored by the Native Wordcraft Circle as well as by *Studies in American Indian Literatures*, which devoted the Spring 2003 issue entirely to his work and includes critical essays and a selected bibliography of his work. There is also "An E-mail Sampler" of the extended commentaries, critiques, and experiential descriptions of travel Revard has sent to a wide range of friends and colleagues throughout the years.

Right alongside the Osage County Courthouse in Pawhuska, Oklahoma, is a vacant lot that has been asphalted for the poor souls to park who have come in to face the music–for Driving Under the Influence, for bootlegging, assault, breaking and entering, marriage and alimony disasters, and (for that matter) for the foreclosures or sales and leases, I suppose, which those with property, vehicles, or spouses to offend with, or to law over, must come in to a county courthouse and face up to. I'm told that in this waterproof blackness once stood a house rented by my grandfather not so long before I was born, where my uncles carried on a small but brisk business in bootleg whiskey which they bought wholesale down by Tulsa, from three Creek Indian brothers who (unlike most producers of white lightning) actually aged their product in charred whiteoak casks buried for several months or even a year. So my uncles always had a good market for the stuff they ferried up to Pawhuska in a Model A coupe with oversize springs, not just to bear the extra weight but so the car would not sag low enough to let the cops know it had a load of whiskey in it.

Before long, though, the police officers developed an informant network–or, as my surviving uncle puts it, they paid some snitches to get in good with the Osages who otherwise would never tell who sold them the whiskey. Eventually the snitches snitched on my uncles, and my grandfather–who never lied in his life, and would have nothing to do with lawbreaking, but couldn't keep his boys from getting up to such things–had to do thirty days in the County Jail for it. The cops had come round to the house on evidence offered by the snitches, and although various uncles had rushed into the bathroom and busted the bottles and poured and flushed frantically, enough hard evidence was sopped up in rags to present in court. Uncle Woody, though–then about fifteen–had stashed some gallon jugs down behind foundation blocks, so the family could eat for the week needed to get a new batch of quality stuff. Never after that would the uncles rent a house in my grandfather's name: if a bust came, they'd be hit; he wouldn't.

What's always agreed when this story's told is that there were no jobs around, so with no legal ways to eat, it was by quenching illegal thirsts that the DNA and RNA on this side of my genes could egg me on. There were, of course, people making an honest living in Pawhuska then. Just across that vacant courthouse lot, a back yard faced the house my folks called theirs; in that yard stood the cultured, responsible mansion of the Mathews family, whose Osage son John Joseph Mathews had already been soldier (flying instructor in the First War), scholar (two years at Merton College, Oxford), courtier (Paris, Morocco, Sunset Boulevard). He would soon return to Pawhuska and write *Wahkontah: The Osage and the White Man's Road* and *Sundown,* classic accounts of what whiskey, cars, white sex and drugs in the black flood of oil money were doing to the Osages. The Mathews house still stands on Big Hill's brow next door to the old Osage Agency, a few steps from the new Osage Clinic where in 1981 I went with my Osage stepfather to beg anodynes for my mother, dying of cancer. Doctors don't lose their jobs, come recession or depression, just as bootleggers never lack for clientele—each making more work for the other, I suppose. In 1978 when I brought some Indian Literature students down from St. Louis to Pawhuska, where my Osage folks gave a traditional dinner for them, John Joseph Mathews guided them and me around the Osage Museum, where his picture now hangs, and we had some good words about our different days in Merton College, Oxford. (Gatsby didn't really get its library, where in fact the ghost of Duns Scotus still has the old book-chains to rattle.)

I think now of Grandpa looking out through the jail bars at the big house where maybe Joe Mathews was already writing, and I think of my pregnant mother and uncles, looking in both those directions. There was another man in the jail there about that time—the one who master-minded the murder of a good many Osages for their oil money, a story made into a novel later by Joe Mathews' stepson. Now here they all are, looking out from these words at strange readers. The past has windows, the future only doors, and God knows who may be looking at us through the peepholes where in this ragged English I knock for some of us.

I guess I've happened because in 1930 among the customers of my uncles there were some mixed-bloods with lots to spend and lots of appe-tites to spend it on, and these apparently had an eye for beautiful nubile daughters of bootleggers, as witness my twin sister and me. Our father, whom I never recall seeing in person, died in the 1960s down in Texas, it is said, which is also where an uncle, a pretty well-known country-and-western singer whom I am supposed to resemble closely, now makes his career. Twice unlucky, our mother did better the third time: she married our stepfather Addison Jump, and we have four half-Osage brothers and sisters now. Had I been old enough to notice such things or remember them, it must have been a wonderful change for us, moving from small marginal houses rented under the eyes and often the clubs of the law to the roomy modern house on Big Hill where we had a maid and a spaniel and a telephone and presently a new Pontiac Eight and a Model B pickup, the latter for use in farm work when we would move from Pawhuska out twenty miles east to Buck Creek valley, five miles west of Bartlesville, the eighty-acre meadow with some tillable land where I grew up, prime bluestem hay and a twelve-year-old house wired for electricity with its own Kohler-plant generator, a two-story garage also wired, its own cistern and well and inside bathroom working off water pumped from the well by a cranky two-cylinder engine in the motor house, a haybarn and stock barn and windsock on a pole for the plane that the previous owners had landed out behind the haybarn they used for a hangar. I sit typing this in the upstairs of the old garage, a fan on to bring the ovenlike June air in somehow cool as I look east over knee-deep wild flowers and bluestem hay to the eastern prairie hills behind which Phillips Petroleum's research plant smokes, seethes and sucks in hundreds of cars each morning, then spews them out each evening to spread out along U.S. 60 into Bartlesville or out this way in Osage County—did I say that Osage County is in fact the Osage Reservation, so I was born "on the res" in the Agency town, not far from the Osage Agency? Better stress that for east-of-the-Hudson friends of the Indian who would like to know that a child of the wild who doesn't look much Indian was actually born on an Indian reservation and lived among the Indians when he was growing up. Did I say that Phillips Petroleum, whose world headquarters are in Bartlesville, Oklahoma, got its start in 1917 and still derives considerable income from Osage oil, and that Uncle Frank Phillips, founder, was an ol' Iowa farm boy who would give a big Sixty-Sixth Birthday Party for all the school-children of the rural schools in Washington and Osage Counties? Have I mentioned that on the memorable occasion we children who attended Buck Creek (District 66) School in Osage County went in to this party at the old Bartlesville Civic

Center and Uncle Frank came out on stage, between acts such as a basso singing "The Man with the BAY-AY-AY-AYS . . . VI-OHL" and Gretchen Wienecke (later on Broadway in *Silk Stockings* as Gretchen Wyler) doing a sexy long-legged postpubescent dance? Uncle Frank told how he did it, worked hard, got up early, freely enterprised, started as a barber or maybe it was farm boy, always treated the Indians fairly, and we could do the same. Then he gave each of us a sack of hard candy and fruit and a silver dollar. But he did more than that for us children: he owned Woolaroc, down in the heart of the Osage Hills where there had always been a spring, and he had bought several square miles of rolling blackjack-covered hills around that spring, dammed it for a lake, built him a lodge, and brought back trophies from Africa – elephants, springboks and bongo antelopes, and lions – and a skeleton of "an Indian who died on the Trail of Tears," and lots of wonderful things from the Spiro Indian Mound where he bought digging rights. Better yet, he had live water buffaloes and American bison and wapiti and peacocks and swans and parrots and so on wandering around under the blackjack trees and scrub oaks, and I recall one school picnic at the end of the year, early May or so, when we were driving in the teacher's car, redheaded Mrs. Nameless who was caught (I heard say years later from an older kid whose folks were willing to gossip as mine were not) by one member of the school board, *in flagrante* on her desk at night in the schoolhouse with another board member, and so had to be replaced next year by another teacher, this time not a divorcee like her but a happily married woman who to the scandal of the board and neighborhood got pregnant and finished the year, my fourth grade, teaching us to add while giving us a practical example – when we were driving along the entrance road at Woolaroc in Mrs. Nameless's car, I was watching a group of wapiti of which one still had his antlers and just then his left antler fell off his head. It was hell getting them to believe me but I pointed out that he still had only one antler, the right, and if anybody wanted to go over there the other antler would be lying on the ground. In those days we said *laying:* it's a wonder somebody didn't say it might be *laying* on the ground but I was *lying* in the car.

So Frank Phillips helped to educate us in the Trail of Tears and the ways of elk antlers, but I never got the hang of founding a big oil company. So let us go back to Pawhuska to see what hung me up. A sense perhaps of impermanence, of being one of those who could be told to jump and cower for good reasons. Our houses did not last. When Uncle

Woody and I drove down past the Osage Agency to the old Pawhuska cemetery to see the house where he remembered my being born, it was another vacant lot. "I be damned," he said, "it was right in here." It was one of those town margins, trees, the yards not lawns, the grass that grows instead of being cultivated. These people work for others or they make a bare living or they never quite get the groceries paid for and they are trying to keep up with the other bills. So it was no surprise when we drove round the other end of Pawhuska, out where U.S. 60 leaves on its way to Uncle Frank's town, and saw a vacant lot where the old hospital had been, the one where we were able to do our small first wauling. No surprise, but strange, to see it had melted into air, into thin air, that second floor where we had run down the corridor and turned in to see my younger sister Ireta (Lay-ta-wee-sa, her Osage name was), and my younger brother Jim, and then Josephine, and finally Junior. These red bricks of the hospital had been so solid; our grandfather had hauled them up on contract, had helped build that hospital. The mules he had still used until about then were Old Beck and Jude, same ones who had pulled the covered wagon from the Current River in Missouri into the oil-booming Agency town of Pawhuska, after our grandmother had died.

All that work, the new brick town of Pawhuska my white grand-father had helped build, the rented frame houses where we scuffed along. Vacant lots. Doctors, lawyers, merchant chiefs knew what; we at their bidding stood or sped. It was for the Agency and the Superintendent later to say what must be done with the oil money, and of course at first that was all needed to buy the eighty acres, to put in the barbed-wire fence—driving the posts in with the big sixteen-pound maul, stretch-ing the wire with the rope-and-pulley so tight it twanged like a banjo and the post-staples screeked with the strain when we nailed them in. To dig the pond, my stepfather Addison big and powerful, my grand-father Aleck short and masterful, the uncles swarming and laughing and swearing, the metal slip scraping and sleekly digging into the earth, grating into rocks that jerked and twisted the handles in my grandfather's hands as he held the slip on course and hyaahed the mules, and us barefooting in the slate-smooth part behind as the earth began being moist then muddy. Money went on a team of horses who died within a month, and on the pickup with which we dragged their corpses out behind the barn for the coyotes and the buzzards. We did not have to pay the buzzards to demonstrate flying, their slow wheeling in Spencerian ovals across from the western hills and bluffs until they circled above our meadow, quarter-mile up, watching usurious from their naked red heads as they prepared to come down, then tilting, slanting down, running out of updraft, sweeping and swinging almost out of control down to bring up braking, to drop short of the great bloating corpses, fold their wings like not quite reliable umbrellas, perching, lowering heads, picking, seizing, tearing, gobbling. But the *cattle* we had to buy, the *pigs,* the seed corn and seed barley! and with no threshing machine, the neighbors to feed at the harvest dinners! But now we had a bluewater pond for cattle, and fish came into it, and willows began growing and elms and hackberries along its dam, persimmons and buttonbush and such up in its swampy top areas where the redwing blackbirds perched and oiled their hinges and nested and complained and flaunted and sometimes were shot from the tall willow, now that it had grown all the way up, by my older brother who could hit a crow on an electric wire at a quarter-mile with his singleshot .22, with Long Rifle cartridges at least. Yet this was a crazy bunch trying to farm in the middle of the Depression, and the uncles being killed by police or fellow bootleggers, all the stories of Uncle Carter getting shot when he came out of the bank he had just robbed by police who had set him up with a snitch—entrapment it would be called today but then they considered it a feather in the cop-cap; and about his being shot while hijacking a bootleg shipment coming in from Joplin by the bootlegger with that hideaway gun which Carter and his buddies had not found when they patted him down as they took over the car and Carter was driving him off onto a side road to leave him there to walk back while Carter and buddies went off with the whiskey. And the much more guarded stories afterwards about what happened to the bootlegger with the hideaway gun after he was let off in court on a justifiable homicide, how someone nameless had followed that guy for two years and nearly got him in a little dusty town in Texas, but the guy got the wind up and skipped out just ahead, and finally that summer or late spring some years after Carter's funeral, word came that the killer was resting in peace.

And Cousin Roy who had sat across from the Pawhuska Courthouse with his squirrel rifle, him only thirteen years old, waiting for the cop to come out who had killed his dad, our Uncle Aubrey, the cop who beat Aubrey to death in the cell and then said he fell out of his bed and hit his head on the floor, and the cop came out of the courthouse and Roy had him in his sights and just couldn't pull the trigger but went to California the next week instead, hopped a freight with a buddy and landed in Truckee where he worked in a sawmill, then got into the migrant worker circuit with some other Okies that he knew from Pawhuska, worked the truck farms from lettuce down in the Imperial Valley up through the artichokes and tomatoes, the fruit trees in the Central Valley, the cherries and apples up in Washington, put the damned grapes and tomatoes and lettuce on the tables of good old Uncle Frank and Uncle Winthrop and married a really good woman, smart, who saved up, and they had five kids, and bought them a used Airstream trailer after Roy got out of the Marines and they all worked with the kids chipping in and hell they got them a little house on the edge of Porterville and there they were up in the edge of the Sierras and Roy could hunt him bears or deer or whatever and had half the damn year off to do as he pleased, go bass fishing, what Grampa would have loved to do in Indian Territory no doubt if there'd been some honest way to do it, and Roy saw to it that his mother came out and had a little house down the street with plenty of time and grandchildren, and there was the orange tree and maybe the apricot tree in Roy's back yard—so far as I'm concerned he redeemed his time. So I'm glad he didn't shoot that cop, and glad the freight trains were free for hoboes in those days, and glad there was a California before Steinbeck and Ronnie dumped the wrong myths into its margins. Yeah, I saw references to Okies out there when I got out to be semanticist-linguist on that computer and dictionary project funded by the Defense Department at a think tank, but I visited Roy and Celestine and their kids, when we lived in Pacific Palisades.

Well, so that isn't very Indian, is it? I should mention that Grandma Jump always had the cool quiet house with beautiful rugs and sofa and Indian blankets on the easy chairs and across the sofa-back, you know those Pendleton blankets all red and green and blue with their deep soft wool. When my mother and stepfather got married, Osage oil money was still coming in, and his grandmother, Grandma St. John, was still alive and had some head-rights to the oil money, as did his mother, Grandma Josephine Jump. So there was always fresh fruit on that big mahogany table in their dining room, and outside a big new Oldsmobile and a new pickup with camper canvas on it, and there were Aunt Arita and Uncle Kenneth who was a football player and boxer and went to Notre Dame just before World War II, and I vaguely recall when Uncle Louis (for whom my older half brother was named) was killed in a car crash who had been going to be a dentist in New Orleans and drove too fast. And Aunt Arita was smart, could type and do everything and she read books, so my idea of Indians was not purely "Gettum up Scout" or "I will fight no more forever," let alone Twain's Injun Joe or the rest. The summer after the war I stayed over at Grandma Jump's to help Uncle Kenneth, still having bad dreams from Iwo Jima, get the farm south of Pawhuska going again, and Aunt Arita had Marcel Proust's stuff around in a bookcase, and to get a break from shoveling oats one day I took a copy of *Swann's Way* into the outhouse and good old Proust would have sniffled if he had seen how the red wasp with black wings, trapped in a black widow's web down in the toilet hole's semidarkness, interested me much more than *Remembrance of Things Past*. I have a little better sense now of what Proust was up to and may try again to read him one day. Not in an outhouse though—he still can't compete in that league.

But I also had little sense, as a kid, how rough a time and how wild and varied a time Grandma Jump had had before I was born. Born in the 1890s, she was put into a convent school at ten, forced to speak English. (All her life she spoke with an Osage accent, though not until I was in college did I suddenly realize that that was what made her English run so counter to the usual cadences of pitch and stress; it was just the funny way she spoke, the "Indian" way, until in college I heard this guy who was a native speaker of Greek and his melodic runs were so different—it suddenly hit me, Hey, you dummy, Grandma talks with a "foreign accent"!) Then at age fourteen Grandma was married off by her folks to Jacob Jump (I am told this is a translation of an Osage name that refers to the buffalo jumping forward). So she had only four years of being taught English. She was widowed twelve years later and had quite a life for the next twelve and more, until her oldest son Addison married my mother. She was a strong woman, quiet but always knowing what was on both sides as well as in front of her, and she had many friends in the tribe and was very much respected and listened to. Photographs from her younger days show a tranquil, forceful woman, handsome and unperturbed by the camera. She had a terrific laugh, loud and slow, which like her English speech rang the Osage changes, and it broke out oftenest for puns and wordplay. My stepfather, her oldest son Addison, was born in 1910, soon after the Osages had been forced to accept individual allotment of their reservation lands, and when the old ceremonies were being thrown away. So Addison was put into a military school, beaten if he spoke Osage, and had the language taken from him except for his understanding quite a lot of it. The younger children were educated, like him, in schools where Osage was being killed. So Grandma Jump's mother, Grandma St. John, whom I knew for almost eight years before she died when I was ten (she must have been eighty), barely spoke English, and her daughter (Grandma Jump) was fluent in English but spoke with a strong accent, and her grandchildren (my stepfather, uncle, aunt) had Osage peeled from their tongues and were left with English, only a little tangy with something which those who have grown up on the res would recognize, even over the telephone, as an Indian accent on their Oklahoma speech.

Grandma St. John, shorter and slighter than her daughter, was quiet too in the way of an Indian woman, but when I knew her she seemed less queenly than her daughter, maybe less imperial is the phrase. I remember the time she came out to our place in the country, maybe a time when one of the younger children was born, and she made some meat pies for us, a whole Indian feast with fry bread and beef stew I remember, and I loved the meat pies, which we had not had at home before. By then the money at our place was almost all gone, the hard times were on us. We had a Pontiac one year, then two succeeding years we had new Buicks, we had a cook, a whole house full of new furniture and heavy window drapes that seemed regal to me, things trucked up from Tulsa, an expensive furniture store there, silverware and all, and always room for one or two or three uncles for whom there were still no jobs with wages, the house crammed and overflowing with children, so it seems. But suddenly the money was gone, the Depression took hold on us too, the long rainless baking summers dried up the pond, we sold off the cattle, the last Buick went sour soon after its radio had brought us the Louis-Braddock fight; we killed not only the pigs but the sow, and Addison was having to work in the hayfields and hoeing corn and so were all us boys, even Uncle Woody and Uncle Dwain were out on the road selling magazines, the only job they could find and lucky to get it. They drove from Brownsville, Texas, to Butte, Montana, selling *McCall's, Newsweek, Redbook;* postcards would come in, or letters from Butte on thin, quangly sheets of copper, or a crate of grapefruit from Brownsville. But when was it they and Uncles Arthur and Bert went out to Utah and worked for the Mormons and had to do without coffee for breakfast with those strict people there, as Uncle Dwain said like to died every morning? Twelve gallons of honey it was, I think, that they sent us from Utah that time, in gallon cans.

One thing was that with seven kids there were always plenty for games, cowboy and Indian if nothing better, tree-climbing, swimming or fishing or hunting rabbits, squirrels, out on the meadow or up on the hills around our valley after the meat and adventure. And when I was just old enough to appreciate the extra company there were our Ponca cousins, because Uncle Woody had met a Ponca girl at the Osage dances one year in September—they used to dance in June and also in September—and by December they were married, and presently there were Darlena and Buck and Carter Augustus and Cordell and Craig and Kathy. And because there were no jobs and we had the Osage money in the early days there would be weeks, months even, when Aunt Jewel and the Ponca cousins would be staying over with us and Uncle Woody out on the road, if he wasn't laying low avoiding a bootlegging rap. One reason why, when on a February day in 1973 I read in the St. Louis newspaper that Indians had taken over the hamlet of Wounded Knee and Carter Camp was serving as their spokesman, I was both worried and proud, and why I went up there in March to see what the hell was going on inside there, was that these were my Ponca cousins that I grew up with running around the yard there or out in the haybarn or off on Buck Creek. And another reason was that before my mother had married Addison, Aunt Jewel and her folks had helped keep me and my twin sister down on the Ponca res at White Eagle for quite a while—the first photograph of my twin sister and me, aged about one year, is sitting in front of an Indian blanket, taken down there at White Eagle when Aunt Jewel kept us there.

I don't have to say things, then—do I—about extended families, and hard times shared, and a peculiar sense that being Indian meant being very rich and very poor, quietly dignified and raucously funny; I haven't even said anything about Uncle Gus, the brother of Aunt Jewel and a traditional Ponca who had been sent on his vision quest and was trained to be Ponca leader, who became a wonderful wardancer and was among those who first brought the "fancy" wardance onto what I guess I can call the "powwow circuit." He gave you that sense of a man who was a great dancer before he even walked out there toward the drum and started to dance, who could make you know that this was a warrior, who let you see what it was that so impressed the Europeans, when they came into this continent, in the people who appeared to speak with them. It was a role; he stepped through this door from 1491 to dance for us, came out with eagle wing and vision. But the dance was Gus—not all of him, but the way light is not all of the sun: what you saw him by was this intense brilliant presence. Besides, he was just one hell of a natural athlete; as Uncle Woody tells it, Gus never lost a fifty-yard dash when they were betting on him. And Aunt Jewel, that little brisk-stepping woman I remember who could stand with her back to a wall and bending back toward it walk down it with her hands and put the hands flat on the floor between her feet and the wall: even now, if you came along to a dance or to a bingo night down at White Eagle I might not have to tell you which was Aunt Jewel; I have heard the Poncas say, laughing, you would know that was Gus McDonald's sister, just from the way she holds herself. No, not just a queen. Every inch an Indian woman. And laugh, when did we all quit laughing unless we were arguing or fighting? Or—well, yes—starving, like when all we had one Christmas to eat was some cowfeed and milk.

Let's see, then. Earliest memories of small frame houses around the ragged edges of Pawhuska, of mules and uncles and homebrew and whiskey, then of the Ponca res for a while, a time when Aunt Jewel and her great-aunt and her mother took care of us. Her aunt remembered when the Poncas were forced down from Nebraska into Oklahoma, and I have written in "How the Songs Came Down" (in *Ponca War Dancers*) of the song we used to ask Aunt Jewel to sing us later, the Ponca song we thought of as one to go to sleep unafraid with, and how it turned out that its Ponca words said, "What are you afraid of? No one can go around Death." The aunt had made it when, in Oklahoma, her brothers were so discouraged and the whiskey was getting the Poncas down so far, and it was a strongheart song, a warrior song to encourage them. Of her brother, Uncle Gus, I have written in "Ponca War Dancers," and of my uncles Carter, Arthur, Bert, and Dwain in other poems also printed in the 1980 volume *Ponca War Dancers*. I try now to think of each poem as a giveaway talk, one honoring that relative, the way at the end of a dance there will be a time when the Indians ask the head of the occasion—the M.C., I will call him—to call up some of their folks, and the women will be given a shawl, the men a blanket, or some such gifts, and the speaker will tell why the person is being called to receive this. With good thoughts and a good heart, we tell of what this person has done that has made us want to honor him or her, and of the good feelings that exist between our folks and this person.

When I wrote "How the Songs Came Down" I was thinking of all the places I had been, and of how each person is so like a black hole out of which no light could ever emerge to another, and I began it thinking of how, there in the St. Louis suburban area where I now live, I could lie at night and look northward out the bedroom window into the leaves lit by a full moon and streetlamp with the new leaves just softening all that light, and I could see a couple, fortyish, overweight, in Bermuda shorts and T-shirts walking down the midnight center of the street below us, knowing we were there and knowing what we would have been doing but with no idea who we were, who our folks were, what we were like as persons, and ourselves no less ignorant of them, though they must be neighbors living in the next block or two. Then there was a mockingbird singing out in the catalpa just past our back yard, in the alley, and I got to wondering about a bird that would sing loudly at night when the owls would be just hunting by ear for such prey, and this began to get together with the black hole thing, the way something in us sings or shines out for the strangers, friend and foe, though in theory it is not possible. So I was thinking too that it is not only people who are so in the dark to each other, but people and rocks, clouds, trees, birds, and creatures, and of how the memories in us both stay and go the way water stays and goes in a beaverpond, the fish in it like our strange unseen theories and perceptions and memories, time flowing on through the dam of molecules in our brain and our "self" drifting there for a while. And how dangerous it is to let out that energy, how at risk we are if we do sing to the owls, like the mockingbirds.

But thinking that way I had a picture of us as kids in a summer night under a full moon, those times before air conditioners when we would go take our pallets out on the front porch in the moonlight there in the Buck Creek meadow, and then how the radio shows had once a series about werewolves and the eerie howl over the radio scared the scatology out of us kids there under the full moon and thinking of the coyote howls up in the hills around our valley-floor meadow. So we were out there, and Aunt Jewel and Ponca cousins were there, and Aunt Jewel sang us the Ponca song as we were going to sleep, over and over. And I had (only a little time before I wrote the poem) heard from Aunt Jewel what the words of that song meant: "What are you afraid of? No one can go around Death." And it struck me that this is how the songs come down, how we sing and let the owls listen, how Indian songs stay alive and help our people survive. So I was able to finish the poem and give her back some honor for the courage she gave us and still gives. But just so the Anglos don't think this is a song they should not listen to, or need not, I took a little swipe at old Willie Yeats in its last line, since

I can't ever be disgusted enough with his damned mechanical birds in Byzantium, and I cast Aunt Jewel in bronze there on our front porch but a living bronze of American Indian, Ponca that is. That way I was able to honor the mockingbird, our American singer that takes all the other songs and shouts them at the moon and to hell with the great horned owls, and honor Aunt Jewel, when I said:

> She tells her children lately now, some of
>   those real old things,
>   now that the time has come
>   to pass them on, and they are ready
>   to make new places for what she
>   would sing into
>   the moonlit darkness like
>   a bronze and lively bird.

If there are so many birds in the poems that come to me, it is because on the meadow and with the elm, catalpa, poplar trees around a house where birds would have only these trees except for the willows of the ponds half a mile away, our trees were where the orchard orioles, robins, turtledoves, scissortails, bluebirds, kingbirds, dickcissels came to perch and sometimes nest and sing or shout. And the mockingbirds and shrikes, the (once) indigo bunting in the garden, the yellow-headed blackbirds, flickers, redheaded woodpeckers and yellow-bellied sapsuckers, the meadowlarks flying and singing out over the meadow, landing twenty feet away from their sideways-tunnel nest down under the tall green hay and wildflowers so they could take a cautious periscope peek around before ducking under the grass and scuttling along their trails to the nest . . . and the bobwhites with their fifteen-egg nests, and sparrow hawks and the redtail and Swainson and red-shouldered hawks, the turkey vultures, the marsh hawks cruising and tilting low over meadow. How do kids in cities survive with only movies and discos and dope, broken glass in alleys and neat front lawns? For us there were baby rabbits that our cats would bring in stunned but alive, and skunks that educated our dogs but cats must have learned to let alone without getting sprayed, since I never saw a cat come in sneaking and stinking the way every one of the dogs, one time or another, did.

Sure, there were the dances, Osage and Ponca mainly. Not, for us kids, the way it was for uncles and the older Indian folks. Uncle Woody and Uncle Gus used to go roostering off in the Model A to one powwow where Gus would win the prize for the fancy wardance, then on to the next to repeat it; we kids never went along. It never occurred to me to learn the languages, though when Grandma St. John and Grandma Jump were there they always spoke Osage to each other, and Uncle Woody learned to speak Ponca with Aunt Jewel while he was hiding out from the Feds down at White Eagle, the time the U.S. marshal, old Smithy Leahy, sent word along to Woody that he knew Woody was there and knew he would be coming over to Pawhuska to his brother Carter's funeral—*but to come at night.* Uncle Woody did that, and sat up all night with the body, and went back to White Eagle without being arrested. Leahy knew Woody would understand the message: Smithy would not have arrested a man at his brother's funeral, but he had some chickenshit deputies that would have done it and he could not control them during the day when they were on duty. All those stories, all that language, all those days, passed over our heads. Uncle Woody in the Aleutians during the big war, later working for Rocketdyne in California and the Atomic Energy Commission at Hanford Plutonium, in Las Vegas (Lost Wages, he calls it, and would love to live there), in Porterville, fighting forest fires up above Los Angeles, or in the Sierras, their kids going to Haskell Indian School, my sister Ireta for a little while at Chilocco Indian School.

So like the mockingbird I have more than one song but they are all our songs. It has seemed to me that no one else will sing them unless I do, that when Ovid or Virgil or Horace promised someone he would set them among the stars as long as the Latin language should last it was not a bad idea, and it did not have to be some semi-pro like Corinna whom one fitted for a constellation, nor even some semi-thug like Octavius Augustus Caesar; it could be my grandfather, James Alexander Camp. When Octavius died he was holding together pieces of an empire; when my grandfather went he was bringing in wood for our fireplace. My uncle Augustus McDonald was a better dancer than Augustus Caesar, or Nero for that matter, and my cousin Carter Augustus Camp a better singer of Forty-Nine Songs, not to mention he was once elected national head of the American Indian Movement and is now on the Ponca Tribal Council and going in to Washington, D.C., to confer with the present emperor. Who knows, he might have his finger on the button one day and wield more power than that other Augustus. Somewhere, a kid on the Res . . .

Schooling. A one-room country school a mile from home, eight grades, my twin sister and I walking to it one spring to see (I now see) whether we were up to starting it that fall although just turned five in March. The long folding bench of maple wood at the front of the room where the teacher held recitations – imagine eight grades, all subjects, kids from five years old to seventeen, up to thirty of them, for a hundred and fifty dollars a month – was smooth and comfortable, and we were up to the test, and we graduated at thirteen as valedictorian and salutatorian after serving as janitors during our eighth grade for the nine dollars a month which allowed us to contribute a little more at home than just a pair of starving mouths. Good teachers, tough and tender Miss Conner with whom we listened at noon to Bob Wills and his Texas Playboys on KVOO from Cain's Ballroom in Tulsa; jovial avuncular Mr. Loyd who hitchhiked from Bartlesville every morning that war year of our eighth grade, played softball with and prayed over us, harmonized beautifully on "Walking in a Winter Wonderland" with a young woman from town who came out to the Christmas party but would not marry him. Ahem, distinguished career, spelling down the school when I was in the third grade, graduating as valedictorian of all Osage County – no, just covaledictorian, since Dicky Dickson of Indian Camp School in Pawhuska and I tied for high average scores for five years on the State Tests. The shock of going in to the 3,200-student seventh-through-tenth-grade high school in Bartlesville where I knew no one but had the blessing of a twin sister to tell the girls that I was better than I looked, and report to me which ones would not turn me down flat. A kind of social limbo at first, not one of the poor defiant West Siders, nor rich insufferable South Siders: an Outsider. At age thirteen and very small for that age, up against it with the boys but able to do enough kamikaze stuff in the lunchtime football games on the grass and concrete and enough country-style wrestling to keep from getting too badly bullied the first year. So unbelievably many girls were so incredibly beautiful, I might as well have landed in Hollywood on a movie lot in that Sweater Girl time. No money for dates, no car, no line, had to get right back to the country and work after school, mostly then at training greyhounds – I hope there is never a place in any future life for cleaning out a hundred or so kennels of stinking hay, or raking the bones and crap, getting up at four-thirty or five in the morning and walking or running the dogs three to five miles before school, and after school cleaning kennels, grooming dogs, killing and skinning and butchering cattle or horses for them to eat, helping cut and stack firewood, plowing and harrowing the coursing fields for the trials.

I loved the races, I liked very much the dogs, and it was great to go one fall to the National Coursing Trials in Kansas, a week off school, all-night drive to Wichita and then Abilene, the week of predawn breakfasts and feeding the dogs and walking and grooming them under the reddening skies and trying to learn secrets of dog-diet from rival grooms, psyching out the competition, spending a few nights at the skating rink and being treated as rich visiting celebrities by the local high school girls—what a change for Johnny Kendall and me from the Bartlesville girls who by this time had us pegged as no mon, no fun. Could've hooked me for life on betting if I had won a few more and had that kind of luck with girls on the results, but luckily I failed to cover the touts at the trials who offered a hundred to one against our white and brindle bitch Miss Border that we thought would surely lose to the fawn Frieda who had always outrun her in Oklahoma, and then Miss Border came out of the slips, sore foot and all, and beat Frieda up to the rabbit on the first turn by a yard, and outcoursed her like a damn little whippet, so when Miss Border killed the rabbit stylishly and cleanly with a single snap and I ran over to clean the fuzz from her throat, snap the leash on her, and lead her out of the coursing park past the judges who were dropping those red marbles down the winner's hole for Miss Border (instead of the white ones for Frieda), I was on the one hand dancing on air for our little brindle and white bitch but on the other thinking how to dodge what would be said to me by Mister Kendall about not at least putting up a couple dollars at those hundred to one odds offered just as I was going into the park with her to get her into the slips. Ah well, what he said was nothing to what my College Algebra teacher said when I got back into Bartlesville College High School without the homework I had promised to do in order to be allowed to go to Abilene. Still, it was worth getting the C that semester in math. And for some reason gambling never got hold of me after that.

Very little Indian in high school except a beautiful Cherokee girl that picked somebody else, dammit. Senior year, they put me up to compete for a college scholarship in a couple of things and I won one, a kind of radio show, College Bowl, that now would be classed as a trivia quiz, emceed by a brilliant speech and drama man from the University of Tulsa, Ben Henneke, later its president. This got me to the University of Tulsa. Now why the hell should I go through standard college stuff? Good teachers, wonderful friends, Professors Eikenberry and Hayden educated me so far as I was disciplined enough to get what was offered. I am embarrassed by remembering failures to learn, but they and others there were the best teachers I could have found anywhere. They put me up for the Rhodes Scholarship and it was given to me. Then the honor which is for me the highest: Grandma Jump and the Osage elders held a naming ceremony in September 1952 and gave me my name, in Pawhuska at the Legion Hall; Chief Paul Pitts, Mr. and Mrs. Wakon Iron, Hazel Lohah, and many others signed the copy of Mathews' *Talking to the Moon* that was given me that night after the hand games and all. A great kindness.

So, sent to Oxford, I am reclaiming what's worthwhile in Europe for our people, am calling the Muses to Oklahoma, where the cowpond we made is as live as those springs in Greece that in the spring of 1975 I toured with wife and kids in a little rented Volkswagen that we drove almost up Mount Olympus. But I expect the Muses to behave like the strong Indian women they are over here, and to sing Arcadian songs, in the Osage Hills, that Okies can follow. I'd like to bury Caesar, not keep on praising him. The thousand-year Rome, thousand-year Reich, five-hundred-year Ameropean empire are more than my meadowlarks can fly up to the stars. And less than they want to fly with, since they need nesting places in the Fifth World of nonaligned bluestem. I have tried to turn the old stories and the new sciences into present myth, in the poem "Dancing with Dinosaurs" (in *Ponca War Dancers*). It is "science" that birds were once dinosaurs, science that some of them migrate over the Atlantic from Maine to Venezuela, flying nonstop at twenty-odd thousand feet for three days and nights; and I have imagined that the dinosaurs learned this when the continents separated and the Atlantic came between them and their winter homes. Then I have seen that we put on feathers to survive, as the dinosaurs did, and that we sing as the birds do; and have raised this into a myth that like the birds, when we dance in our feathers to bring the new children into our circle, when we sing the old songs, we are doing just what the old Osage Naming Ceremonies, linked to our creation stories, describe:

> now as we face the drum
> and dance . . .
>   . . . to honor on a sunbright day
> and in the moonbright night
> the little girl being brought in
> becoming one of us
> as once was done for me,
> for each of us who dance,

I have called them here
to set them into song
who made their rainbow bodies long before
we came to earth,
who learning song and flight became
beings for whom the infinite sky
and trackless ocean are a path to spring:
now they will sing, and we
are dancing with them, here.

Into a star, the old singer sang as he moved toward the House of Mystery where the child he would give its name was waiting among the assembled representatives of the clans, arranged to repeat the starry order: *Into a star you have cast yourself.* I am naming, as I go, as I approach the House of Mystery, those who have cast themselves into our star and are walking with us here. I am Carter Revard (Nompehwathe), at Buck Creek, Oklahoma, June 21, 1984.

JIM BARNES

On Native Ground

Jim Barnes, of Welsh and Choctaw ancestry, was born in Summerfield, LeFlore County, Oklahoma. He earned an M.A. and Ph.D. in comparative literature at the University of Arkansas. Since 1970 he has taught American and French languages and literatures, world literature in translation, and comparative literature at Truman State University in Kirksville, Missouri. In 1978 he was awarded a National Endowment for the Arts Fellowship in Poetry. He has published eight books of poetry, two books of poetry in translation, a book of criticism analyzing the structure of works by Thomas Mann and Malcolm Lowry, and an autobiography. In 1980 his translation from German of Dagmar Nick's *Summons and Sign* (Chariton Review Press) won the Translation Prize from The Translation Center (New York). His 1992 book of poetry, *The Sawdust War* (University of Illinois Press), won the Oklahoma Book Award in Poetry, and his autobiography, *On Native Ground: Memoirs and Impressions* (University of Oklahoma Press, 1997), won the 1998 American Book Award. His most recent books of poetry include *Paris* (University of Illinois Press, 1997) and *On a Wing of the Sun* (University of Illinois Press, 2001). In addition to his faculty position, he is presently writer-in-residence and professor of Comparative Literature at Truman State University, where he also edits *The Chariton Review*, an international journal of poetry, fiction, essays, and translations.

§1

I was five years old the last time I heard the mountain lion scream.

That was in Oklahoma, 1938, when times were hard and life was good—and sacred. But a year later the WPA had done its work: roads were cut, burial mounds were dug, small concrete dams were blocking nearly every stream. The Government was caring for its people. Many were the make-work jobs. A man could eat again, while all about him the land suffered. The annual spring migration of that lone panther was no more. The riverbanks that had been his roads and way stations bore the scars of the times, the scars of loss.

In my mind the rivers must always run free. But in truth today I do not recognize them. They are alien bodies on a flattening land where everything has been made safe, civilized into near extinction. Sounds of speedboats drown out the call of the remaining jays and crows. The din of highway traffic carries for miles now that the timber has fallen to chainsaw or chemical rot. Green silence in the heavy heat of summer afternoons is no more.

The Fourche Maline River and Holson Creek flow through much of what I have written. I suspect they were always there, even back in the mid-1950s when I wrote my first bad short story and my first bad verse. My sense of place is inexorably linked to these two streams and to the prairies and woods between them.

I was born within spitting distance of the Fourche Maline, on a meadow in a house that no longer stands. A lone clump of gnarled sassafras and oak rises out of the meadow a short mile northeast of Summerfield, in the hill country of eastern Oklahoma, where the land was once heavy with wood and game. Nobody knows why the clump of trees was not cut down when the land was first cleared for the plow. Once there was a house a few feet east of the trees. The broken tile of a well long since filled still rises a few inches above the earth. But you have to look long, for the tall grass hides it like the night. I cannot remember a time when the house stood there. My mother says that, as a child, she lived there for a short while at the turn of the century when her parents first moved up from Texas. But she does not recall the house, nor why it ceased to be.

Maybe the maker of the house knew why the trees were left in the middle of the field. At any rate, the trees are still there and are not threatened. Local legend has it that they once guarded a rich burial mound, but now no mound rises among the trees. Instead, a musky sink in the middle of the clump shows the scars of many a shovel and many a firelit night. The story of one night in particular sticks in my mind, though I was much too young at the time to know of the night at all. But like bedtime ghost stories, some things told again and again when you are young and lying with your brothers and sisters on a pallet before the hearth of the fireplace later illuminate the dim, unremembered years. It is the story of how my brother outran a horse.

Before I could stand alone, we lived on the lane that borders the east edge of the field where the trees still stand. My brother was nearing manhood and owned a horse and was a night rider. He learned that three men, neighbors and good-for-nothings, planned to dig in the trees. He asked to join them. He longed to prove himself a man. They had visions of gold and told him there was money buried there.

So when the October moon was dark, they gathered in the clump of trees and hung a lantern over the chosen spot. There was frost on the limbs of the sassafras and oaks. My brother broke first ground, and a hushed moan moved through the still trees. He dropped the shovel; later, strange pieces of bone-red matter began to show up in the dirt at the edge of the pit. While all were gathered about, another moan, much louder than the first, moved through the night—and my brother leaped out of the dark pit. But the good-for-nothings held him fast and howled with laughter as one of their cronies strode into the circle of the lantern's light, drunk on erupting mirth and bootleg whiskey. Everyone had a good laugh at my brother's expense. And he laughed too.

But the laughter was short-lived. A deep, low moan—ghostly but unmistakably human—rolled up from the bowels of the black earth. There was for a moment, my brother recalls, a stillness like doom upon all of them. Then everybody was running, running: the good-for-nothings were running, the original moaner was running, my brother was running, and all the beasts of the field. A great shadow passed beside my brother. It was a horse. The moan persisted, even over the sound of thumping boots and racing hoofs. Now my brother passed the horse, and burst through the barbed wire fence at the edge of the field with one wild bound. He flung himself down the lane and plunged through the doorway of our house and hugged himself close to the dying coals in the fireplace. An hour passed before he began to cry.

Several days later my father filled in the pit and brought home the lantern, dry of kerosene, the wick burned to a crisp.

The clump of trees in the middle of the field was the hub of the universe of my childhood and my adolescence. We always lived within sight of the field. And after the field became a great meadow, I found several days of bone-breaking work each summer helping a cousin bale the tall and fragrant lespedeza that had been urged to grow there. But never did I seek the shade of those trees for my noonday rest. For me, they were too ghostly, foreboding, sacred. In my mind's eye I could see beyond all doubt that here was the final resting place of the broken bones of some great Choctaw chief. He had made it just this far west. He had come within sight of the blue Kiamichi range to the south, which was to become the last home for his dispossessed people, and had fallen dead on the spot from a homesickness of the soul. Among the sassafras and the oaks he had been buried with all the pomp and honor that was left to his migrating children. For me, the spot was inviolate.

And thus it has remained. Only recently have I had the courage, and the reverence, to penetrate the gnarled clump of trees in the middle of the meadow. I went there in midafternoon and sat as motionless as I could while the sun dropped well below a long, low line of trees far to the west. Sitting there, I tried to grasp something I could not name, something I knew was gone forever. I could not invoke it. I did not know its name. Once, just as the sun went down, I heard a hawk cry out high above the clump of leafless trees. Perhaps there was a moan. But I did not hear it.

Named by the French who early explored eastern Oklahoma, the Fourche Maline is by literal definition and observation a dirty stream, though one which once teemed with all the life that water could possibly bear. It was home to some of the world's largest catfish. I have seen mudcat and shovelbill taken from the river, on bankhooks or trotlines, huge fish that ran to more than a hundred pounds each, their hides so scarred and tough you had to skin them with wire pliers or Vise-Grips. Bullfrogs loud enough to drown a rebel yell, turtles big as washtubs, and cottonmouths all called it home, dared you to enter their domain. I can remember bear tracks on the shoals, mussel shells bitten in half.

The Fourche Maline was always a sluggish river, at least for the last twenty-five miles of its course. Though its head is in the western end of the Sans Bois mountain range, where ridges are still thick with government-protected scrub pine and savannah sandstone, and the water begins pure and clear, it is soon fed by farms and ranches with runoff from cornfields and feedlots and by worked-out coal mines as it snakes its way eastward to join Holson Creek. I can recall a time when the Fourche Maline cleared in early summer even as far as its mouth, and the water of the deep pools tasted of springs. Now the river runs ever more slowly, if at all. Its life grows stagnant out of season.

Conversely, Holson Creek—named for Holson Valley, from which it heads northward—was in the past a clear, fast-running stream. It flowed through the pines of Winding Stair and Blue mountains, through pastureland thick with native grasses, among stones that seem still today old as the sky. When I remember Holson Creek as it was in my youth, I can smell the odor of water willows, sharp in the summer, and hear the sounds of barking squirrels, of rapids and small falls, the banks rich with a treasure of arrowheads.

But now both rivers are slow, dammed. Where they meet, mouth to mouth, a lake begins. And for miles back up both streams it is difficult for the eye to discern movement of water, except in flood time, and then there is no guarantee which way they may run.

The land and streams are changing. Even what is protected pollutes: in the wildlife refuge, near the confluence of the Fourche Maline and the Holson, there are so many deer now that tick fever has thinned even the equalizing coyotes and has put salt fear into the veins of poachers, who once knew—who once were, right along with the coyotes—the true balancing force in nature.

Though fishing is sometimes fair, gone are the days of the scream of the mountain lion, the days of the big catfish. No one has seen a bear track in forty years. I doubt you could get snakebitten if you wanted to. But I am a child of the past. I live it in my waking dreams. The white clay banks along the Fourche Maline still hold their lure and the lore I assigned to them. I dug caves there. I danced the old songs. I attacked wagon trains or, on the other side, killed Indians. And once in a rare sundown, I realized that here in the bottomland stood the only native holly tree I knew of anywhere in the great wooded valleys between the Sans Bois mountains to the north and the blue Kiamichi to the south. The holly tree is gone, victim of the backwater of the Corps of Engineers. When backwater rises, is held like a cesspool for weeks on end, all flora and fauna rooted to place die. Even a simple child knows this.

What's more, and the hell of it all: I see but little hope, rather mainly dissolution of river, of land, and thus of spirit. You can see it plain on the faces of those who have witnessed, have lived, these civilizing years. Their faces are not lined without cause; there is something in the blood that needs rivers free, forests and prairies green with promise. Maybe lack of fuel and the death of automobiles will help, but I doubt it: I know people who will hike ten miles or more carrying a six-pack just to be able to throw the cans into a stream to see how long they will stay afloat while they are pumped full of lead.

We have been called a nation of tourists. But I suspect, deep down, some of us somehow know where home is—and what it has become.

§2

Home for me will always remain the Great Southwest. That the Southwest is a rich cultural region, few will deny. But what its boundaries are is a moot question. For William Bartram in his *Travels* in the early 1700s, the old Southwest was Alabama, Mississippi, Louisiana. But this did not last. In later years Washington Irving showed us Arkansas and eastern Oklahoma as Southwest territory. Cherokee Sam Houston took us to Texas. The Santa Fe Trail opened up New Mexico, and the region expanded on to California. Useless to argue boundaries.

But there are things in my lifetime I cannot help associating with the term *Southwest*. My grade school geography and history classes taught me that Oklahoma, Texas, and New Mexico were the Southwest. My high school library had one book that was passed off as Southwest literature—J. Frank Dobie's *Coronado's Children,* a book that made me dream of buried treasure from the Brazos River to the Superstition Mountains. He made it all come alive—that feeling for west Texas and Oklahoma—and he did it through his characters, the spinners of tall tales, Coronado's children.

The cultural Southwest means always for me Indians, their land and their customs and their languages. The Native American languages are going fast. It is no small wonder that they have held out this long. There are mighty few Yuchi speakers left today. Ten or twelve years ago I believe there were some two hundred acknowledged Oklahoma Yuchis living, and of those perhaps four or five native speakers. How many languages we have lost! The Yuchis, who came from Georgia with the Creeks in forced migration, are virtually no more. That great tribe believed that they came from the East, across a great water—a belief that seems borne out by the so-called Metcalf stone that was unearthed in Georgia back in the 1960s bearing characters from the Phoenician alphabet.

Some years ago I spent several hours with one of the few remaining Yuchi speakers, listening to her and trying to transcribe a few phrases of the language. I remember her saying that the typical greeting in Yuchi is "Wa-hin-gi?" (Where are you going?) or "Sen-ga-le-la?" (How are you?) She spoke of many things Yuchi: I tried to transcribe. Several days later we met, and she greeted me with "Sen-ga-le-la?" Wanting to appear miraculously fluent, I replied, with the only phrase I could remember then, "Yubo-ah-tee-tee-onde-de-tah," which means "I want an orange." She laughed long and hard, then said, "You must try harder." Words I try to hang on to.

Tomorrow we will be able to count the fluent Choctaws on one hand if something is not done today. I was raised in Choctaw country, LeFlore County, and count myself one-eighth *Chahta*. I was raised on the language and the foods, practically all that was left us then of the culture. I have eaten *chongkus chom pooey* (pork backbone boiled in hominy) and *tom fuller* (meat and cornmeal cooked in a cornshuck) and hickory nut soup—to my infinite delight. But now these have passed away like so many other things Choctaw. In a few years Choctaw will become a rare language. I hate to see that happen, but it is bound to come to that unless something more is done. I can recall the day when "Halito, chin achukma?" (Hello, how's your fat?) was a familiar greeting in eastern Oklahoma, around Talihina and Summerfield. You will find few replies to the question today.

I am proud of the Choctaw blood I carry, and I am equally proud of the Welsh blood in my veins. But I object to the term *regional writer* or *ethnic writer* or even *Native American writer,* though it may apply to a number of us in a general sense. I don't think I could be called a Kiamichi poet or an Oklahoma writer by any far stretch of the imagination. In my work, place names are important, but they are usually important not because of any geographical sense but because of the names themselves. "Antlers," for example, in "Stopping on Kiamichi Mountain" (*The American Book of the Dead*), carries with it the name of a very old town in Oklahoma but also a pretty good-sized rack of horns. So if I use "Antlers," it's because I can get mileage out of the image as well as the place name. A poet not too long ago came out with a very short poem—and I thought a very bad poem in a very good magazine—and one or two lines went something like this: "Spoon, spoon, I love the sound of spoon." I guess that's the way I feel about many of the place names in Oklahoma and elsewhere: the *sounds* are good.

I object to terms like *regional* or *Native American* for art and artist. As a magazine editor and a lover of good literature, I don't care who writes the poem, where it is written, or what it is written about. Whenever the universal grows out of the specific and vision is achieved, you can tell yourself here is art and it should be preserved. Such a work is, for example, N. Scott Momaday's *House Made of Dawn*. I doubt anyone would call Momaday a Southwest writer (true, by birth he is largely Native American); his novel deals with the people and the land of New Mexico, but also Arizona, Oklahoma, southern California. It is a book of vanishing Americans in all their many faces, many skins; it is a book that documents the failure of a way of life, ways of life, the failure of the individual, of society, of religion, of myth. It is a book that touches the human heart and head and universalizes the human struggle to survive, to prevail, in this hopped-up, turned-on world. The message is as clear in Momaday's work as it is in Ralph Ellison's *Invisible Man* when Jack the Bear finally realizes that to survive we must change, must reject, must affirm, must love, must hate; we must know that ambivalence is the condition of being human and that we are subjects of loss.

Momaday is hardly *just* a Native American writer. I know of no fuller expression of loss in contemporary American literature than the Sermon and the Peyote Ritual of *House Made of Dawn*. The celebrants know what is to be done—the world as it is must be admitted, affirmed, but also remade, recreated. The four blasts of the eagle bone whistle to the four great corners of the world. In the beginning there was a sound, a single sound at the very center of the universe. In the agony of stasis, sound comes, the first word and—if we are lucky—the poem as world, the world as poem.

There are several contemporary writers that I associate with the Southwest—that is, Oklahoma, Texas, New Mexico—though I do not see them as *regional*. Then I ask myself: Is Albert Goldbarth a Southwest writer, a Southwest Jewish writer? He has been living, writing, and teaching in Austin, Texas, and has recently done good (weird) work with the character of Sam Bass. Is Speer Morgan, from Ft. Smith, Arkansas, a Southwest writer hiding out at the University of Missouri? His fairly recent *Belle Starr: A Novel* would seem to say yes. But here he comes with a novel called *Brother Enemy*, a work set in a Caribbean banana republic. Is Speer Morgan a Caribbean writer? Or is Winston Weathers a Southwest writer in scholar's disguise at the University of Tulsa? He is of Osage heritage, but his works go far beyond both Osage country and Tulsa.

There have been many, many anthologies of Southwest literature and Native American literature to tell us just who are the American Indian writers, just who this and who that, along with pedigree. And there will no doubt be more. But we must not be misled. The writer is first a writer, second a Native American, a Black, a Chicano.

There may be works about a place, about a people, by a writer native to the area; but none of this gives anyone the right to catalog or label the works *regional, Native American, Black,* or whatever. Is Ralph Ellison, born in Oklahoma City, a regional writer? Is his work to be listed as Black literature only, when it is so universal that it is horrifying? Is his *Invisible Man* a product of his Southwest heritage (Hey, boy!), his southern heritage (I yam what I yam), his New York heritage (Sibyl, you been raped by Santa Claus)? A writer, whoever he may be, if he believes in art as art, will bring everything to bear upon his art, ethnic or otherwise. The work of Ralph Ellison, N. Scott Momaday, J. Frank Dobie—all are larger than the cultural and geographical boundaries we might try to fence them with.

§3

IN DEFENSE OF SOBRIETY AND LYING

A few years back I submitted a manuscript of poetry to a well-known university press. In four or five months the manuscript came back with words of praise, generally; but it seems the book was rejected because, as the editor put it, the work was "unrelentingly sober." Well, I think maybe the editor who said that did not like poetry of images, poetry filled with the sense of loss yet with an affirmation of that loss. Unrelentingly sober—I hope not because I don't occasionally have a sense of humor. If I've entirely lost my sense of humor, then I'm not of much worth. It's a dangerous thing to do or have done. Sober, unrelentingly sober, too, because when I get an image going or a metaphor working, I will try to carry it throughout the poem and weed away anything that is extraneous, anything that's not tightly connected to the major image of the poem. That is why, for example, in "Elegy for the Girl Who Drowned at Goats Bluff" (from *The American Book of the Dead*), water, stone, and bone are carried throughout the five stanzas:

The sun strikes water like soft stone,
oblique and torn by surface waves.
Below, in the still place of stone,
the slow fish nuzzle through the caves

you seldom know are there at all
and rest among the drowned girl's bones.
Above, the bluff is too brittle
for a date in stone. The long day downs,

and she alone records the passing.
You think you know her now, the scream
that cracked the bluff, the siren song
that wails its way into the dream

you sometimes have. Dark water.
Darker still the night. You wait
for the water to take the sky, for
the floating moon to turn stone white

as the skin of dead fish. You know
she sees you stranger to this place,
her empty eyes wide against the night,
her empty hands, her empty face.

Of course, you can kill an image by overworking it. I try not to do this; I try only to stay true to the image throughout the poem. I am always trying unrelentingly to succeed at that particular task. And the effect is usually a sober one, in opposition to the drunken one or the dizzy one, which would be failure, in my view.

I have no theory of poetry. I feel no need for one. But I do have complaints. Looming large today is the Poet-as-Speaker. Surely here at the end of the twentieth century, by this time surely, we must understand

that the poet does not speak. The poet creates a voice, and that voice
speaks.

LA PLATA, MISSOURI: CLEAR NOVEMBER NIGHT

Last night in La Plata an avalanche of stars
buried the town in constant light the way the red
coalburners on the Santa Fe used to send fires

climbing night and falling back again, burning sheds,
hay, carriages, whatever was set along the track.
An avalanche of stars, last night the Leonids

fired every farm with ancient light, curdled milk
in Amish churns, and sent dogs howling through field
and tangled wood. Never was there such a night like

this. Lovers sprang from one another's arms, reeled
away from lurching cars and thoughts into a state
of starry wonder no human act could have revealed.

As if by common will, house lights went out. The late
work left, families settled out into the snow
unaware of cold, unaware of all except that state

which held us all for those long moments. We saw
and saw again the falling stars course Bear and Swan,
take field and farm, take all, and give it back as though

a gift given was given once again. Our lawn
on earth was full of promise in the snowing light.
Earthbound, we knew our engine on a rare November run.

(copyright © 1985 Purdue Research Foundation, West Lafayette, IN)

Confessional poetry? No way! It is high time the poet quit lying about
his poetry. It is high time critics stopped being cretins. There is no such
thing as autobiography or biography. One cannot write one's life, or anyone else's. It is impossible. The greatest biography is fiction; the greatest
autobiography is lie. One has to take a few facts here and there, make
transitions between, and hope somehow to capture the essence of the
thing or person one is writing about. Essentially, poetry works the same
way, because for each poem there must be created a voice to carry that
poem—a speaker, not the poet, to say what is to be said. The best poetry
is dominated by speaker and image, image and speaker. The voice is the

fiction (the lie) in respect to the poet's life. The poet may be using a few facts that belong to his experience, but he has to expound these facts in a certain way to create a universal. He must *think* he is speaking, and he must make it real. Momaday does it in *House Made of Dawn* (pure poetry throughout); Ellison does it with Jack the Bear; Bobbi Hill Whiteman does it in her work, and James Welch and Joseph Bruchac and Ernest Gaines and Garcia Lorca. For the writer the experience is not real in sense of fact. He uses whatever he can to enhance the initial fact or image that he is working with. The fiction, the lie, is a mixture of anything, many things, that the poet cares to stir up that will make the poem work as art.

From the total experience of the poem comes an experience of the speaker, and it is in this combination of fact and lie that Truth stands. If it means something to you, if it affects you, it is a certain truth. If it makes you see, if it makes you realize, if it makes you grow, then it is somehow true. Great truths have come out of lies. All great analogy is lie, from the analogies of Plato on down. There is a certain truth that comes out of Plato's relating the vision of Ur or the story of the Cave, and we learn something about ourselves from such fiction. For me, then, only fiction (only lie) is the greatest of all truths. In all honesty, I can say I have never learned anything about the world and its importance by reading a newspaper, that bastion of daily fact. But believe me, I learn, *I learn,* today when I read and reread Momaday, Ellison, and our other good ethnic or otherwise contemporaries.

GERALD VIZENOR

Crows Written on the Poplars:

Autocritical Autobiographies

Gerald Vizenor was born in Minneapolis, Minnesota, in 1934. He is an enrolled member of the Minnesota Chippewa Tribe, White Earth Reservation. Vizenor earned his B.A. from the University of Minnesota in 1960 and conducted his graduate studies at the University of Minnesota and Harvard University. At present he is professor of Native American Studies at the University of California, Berkeley. He has received many awards including the Lifetime Achievement Award from the Native Writers' Circle of the Americas in 2001, the New York Fiction Collective Prize, and an American Book Award from the Before Columbus Foundation in 1988 for his novel *Griever: An American Monkey King in China* (Fiction Collective, 1987). He received the PEN Oakland, Josephine Miles Award, Excellence in Literature, for *Native American Literature: A Brief Introduction and Anthology* (HarperCollins College Publishers, 1996) and for *Interior Landscapes: Autobiographical Myths and Metaphors* (University of Minnesota Press, 1990). In 1989 he received an Artists Fellowship in Literature, an award for professional achievement, from the California Arts Council. His screenplay *Harold of Orange* won the Film-in-the-Cities national competition at Robert Redford's Sundance Film Institute in the summer of 1983 and won the Best Film at the San Francisco Film Festival for American Indian Films. He has published many books of poetry and fiction, including *Hiroshima Bugi: Atomu 57* (University of Nebraska Press, 2003), *Bearheart: The Heirship Chronicles* (University of Minnesota Press, 1990), and *Earthdivers: Tribal Narratives on Mixed Descent* (University of Minnesota Press, 1981). His nonfiction includes *Fugitive Poses: Native American Indian Scenes of Absence and Presence* (University of Nebraska Press, 1998), *Shadow Distance: A Gerald Vizenor Reader* (Wesleyan University Press, 1994), and *Wordarrows: Indians and Whites in the New Fur Trade* (University of Minnesota Press, 1981).

One can say anything to language. This is why it is a listener, closer to us than any silence or any god. —John Berger, *And Our Faces, My Heart, Brief as Photos*

Each autobiographical utterance embalms the author in his own prose, marking his passage into a form that both surrenders him to death and yet preserves his name, acts, and words. —Avrom Fleishman, *Figures of Autobiography*

This is a mixedblood autobiographical causerie and a narrative on the slow death of a common red squirrel. The first and third person personas are me.

Gerald Vizenor believes that autobiographies are imaginative histories; a remembrance past the barriers; wild pastimes over the pronouns. Outside the benchmarks the ones to be in written memoirs are neither sentimental nor ideological; mixedbloods loosen the seams in the shrouds of identities. Institutional time, he contends, belies our personal memories, imagination, and consciousness.

Language is a listener, imagination is a mythic listener, he pleaded and then waited for the light to turn green at the intersection. Imagination is a presence, our being in a sound, a word; noise, ownership, and delusions remain, the material realm reduced to scenes on color television in the back seat of a white limousine.

"Myth makes truth," wrote Avrom Fleishman, "in historical as well as in literary autobiography." Myth makes noise, war, blue chicken, and mixedbloods too, mocked the mixedblood writer. The mixedblood is a new metaphor, he proposed, a transitive contradancer between communal tribal cultures and those material and urban pretensions that counter conservative traditions. The mixedblood wavers in autobiographies; he moves between mythic reservations where tricksters roamed and the cities where his father was murdered.

The Minneapolis *Journal* reported that "police sought a giant negro to compare his fingerprints with those on the rifled purse of Clement Vizenor, a twenty-six-year-old half-breed Indian . . . found slain yesterday with his head nearly cut off by an eight-inch throat slash. . . . He was the second member of his family to die under mysterious circumstances within a month.

"Three half-breed Indians were being held by police for questioning as part of the investigation. . . . Seven negroes were questioned and then given the option of getting out of town. . . .Captain Paradeau said he was convinced Clement had been murdered but that robbery was not the motive. The slain youth was reported to have been mild tempered and not in the habit of picking fights. Police learned that he had no debts, and, as far as they could ascertain, no enemies."

Clement William Vizenor was born on the White Earth Reservation. He moved to Minneapolis and became a painter and paperhanger in the new suburbs; he was survived by his mother Alice Beaulieu, his wife LaVerne, three brothers, two sisters, and his son Gerald Robert Vizenor, one year and eight months old.

Bound with mixedblood memories, urban and reservation disharmonies, imagination cruises with the verbs and adverbs now, overturns calendar nouns in wild histories where there are no toeholds in material time, no ribbons on the polished line. The compassionate trickster battens on transitions and listens to squirrels, windlestrat patois, word blossoms on the barbed wire, androgynous rumors in college chapels; the seasons are too short down to the mother sea. The end comes in a pronoun, he roared on an elevator to the basement, birth to death, decided overnight in a given name.

"When we settle into the theater of autobiography," wrote Paul John Eakin in *Fictions in Autobiography*, "what we are ready to believe—and what most autobiographers encourage us to expect—is that the play we witness is a historical one, a largely faithful and unmediated reconstruction of events that took place long ago, whereas in reality the play is that of the autobiographical act itself, in which the materials of the past are shaped by memory and imagination to serve the needs of present consciousness." Here we are once more at the seams with pronouns and imagination in an autumn thunderstorm.

"A good hunter is never competitive," Vizenor repeated, a scene from his autobiographical stories published in *Growing Up in Minnesota: Ten Writers Remember Their Childhoods*. "The instincts of a survival hunter are measured best when he is alone in the woods. In groups, people depend on each other for identity and security, but alone the hunter must depend on his own instincts of survival and must move with the energy of the woodland."

Survival is imagination, a verbal noun, a transitive word in mixedblood autobiographies; genealogies, the measured lines in time, place, and dioramas, are never the same in personal memories. Remembrance is a natural current that breaks with the spring tides; the curious imagine a sensual undine on the wash.

Ten years ago he wrote about what he chose to remember from an experience twenty years before that, when he shot and killed a red squirrel. He was alone then, the autumn of his second year of college, his first year at the University of Minnesota; he was single, an army veteran with two volumes of photographs to prove that he had driven a tank, directed theater productions, survived a typhoon, and walked with the bears in the Imperial National Forest on Hokkaido. When he faced the camera he wore a pensive smile, and at nineteen he had captured two dreams to be a writer.

The sun was warm, the wind was cold, and the oak leaves were hard on the mound behind an abandoned house north of the cities; the ponds where the whole moon had crashed overnight were calm. In the loose seams of his memories he pictured Aiko Okada at Matsushima in Japan; he remembered his lover there, the loneliness that winter, the old women with their cloth bundles on the train back to Sendai. The squirrels whipped their tails and waited four trees back from the mixedblood.

He folded his cold ears and remembered a scene from a movie: Barbara Stanwyck climbed the stairs, opened a door, and shot a man in his bed; and a soldier in the audience at the army theater shouted, "Cease fire, police your brass and move back to the fifty-yard line." The audience roared, he roared with them; now the audience roars in his head and he smiles in the woods.

He praised Kahlil Gibran then, on the train with chickens and maimed warriors, and later in the leaves; he mentioned Lillian Smith in the barracks and repeated a line from her memoir *Killers of the Dream*, "The heart dares not stay away too long from that which hurt it most." He had been accepted at Sophia University in Tokyo, but at the last minute he decided to return home. Who would he be now in his autobiographies, he wondered, if he had stayed in Japan?

He has never been able to tame the interior landscapes of his memories: the back stoop of a tavern where he fed the squirrels, while his grandfather drank in the dark, breaks into the exotic literature of Lafcadio Hearn. Tribal women in sueded shoes mince over the threshold in the translated novels of Yasunari Kawabata and Osamu Dazai. Alice Beaulieu, in her sixties, married a blind man because, she snickered, he said she looked beautiful; and now, in the white birch, their adventures in the suburbs to peddle brooms and brushes overturn the wisdom of modern families—the blind man and his old stunner soothed lonesome women in pastel houses, and no one bought a broom.

Matsuo Basho came to mind on the mound with the squirrels that afternoon. Basho wrote, in his *haibun* travel prose, that the islands at Matsushima "look exactly like parents caressing their children or walking with them arm in arm. . . . the beauty of the entire scene can only be compared to the most divinely endowed of feminine countenances," and at the same time Vizenor remembered a woman who told him that his haiku were too short; she dismissed those poems that were "less than seventeen proper syllables." She would never understand mixedblood autobiographies.

In the distance he heard laughter and smelled cigarette smoke: a hunter in a duck blind in a marsh behind the mound. Silent crows were on the trees. He pinched the side of his nose, abraded the oil with his thumbnail, and rubbed it into the dark grain of the rifle stock. He remembered laughter on a porch, through an open window, at the river, and snickers deep in the weeds behind the cabins at Silver Lake, a Salvation Army camp for welfare mothers. He had taught their children how to paddle canoes that summer, how to cook on an open fire, and how to name seven birds in flight.

He ordered a laminated miniature of his honorable discharge, bought a used car, a new suit, three shirts, a winter coat, and drove east to visit friends from the army. Two months later he was a college student, by chance, and inspired by the novel *Look Homeward Angel;* his two dreams, and much later his grammars, blossomed when his stories were praised by Eda Lou Walton, his first teacher of writing at New York University.

Professor Walton turned her rings, fingered the chains and beads at her thin neck when he lingered in her office; touched, he must remember that she was touched, even amused by his mixedblood meditations. His manuscripts were scented with her lavender water when she returned them with three unpunctuated phrases: the first a comment on imagination, the second on narrative, and at last a note on usage. "Wild imagination," she wrote on his third manuscript, "the boxelder sap stuck to my fingers . . . person and number, horrid grammar." This, the praise and criticism, was a marvelous association because she once shared an office with Thomas Wolfe.

I walked into the woods alone and found a place in the sun against a tree. The animals and birds were waiting in silence for me to pass. . . . When I opened my eyes, after a short rest, the birds were singing and the squirrels were eating without fear and jumping from tree to tree. I was jumping with them but against them as the hunter.

Here, in the last sentence, he pretends to be an arboreal animal, a romantic weakness; he was neither a hunter nor a tribal witness to the hunt. He was there as a mixedblood writer in a transitive confessional, then and now, in his imaginative autobiographies.

He has been the hunted, to be sure, cornered in wild dreams, and he has pretended to be a hunter in his stories, but he has never lived from the hunt; he has feasted on the bitter thighs of squirrel but he has never had to track an animal to the end, as he would to the last pronoun in his stories, to feed his families and friends.

He understands the instincts of the survival hunter, enough to mimic them, but the compassion he expresses for the lives of animals arises from imagination and literature; his endurance has never been measured in heart muscles, livers, hides, horns, shared on the trail. His survival is mythic, an imaginative transition, an intellectual predation, deconstructed now in masks and metaphors at the water holes in autobiographies.

"Language is the main instrument of man's refusal to accept the world as it is," wrote George Steiner in *After Babel*. "Ours is the ability, the need, to gainsay or 'un-say' the world, to image and speak it otherwise. . . . To misinform, to utter less than the truth was to gain a vital edge of space or subsistence. Natural selection would favour the contriver. Folk tales and mythology retain a blurred memory of the evolutionary advantage of mask and misdirection."

I raised my rifle, took aim, and fired at a large red squirrel running across an oak bough. He fell to the ground near the trunk of the tree, bounced once, and started to climb the tree again. The bullet passed through his shoulder, shattering the bone. His right front leg hung limp from torn skin. He fell to the ground and tried to climb the tree again. He instinctively reached up with his shattered paw, but it was not there to hold him. Blood was spreading across his body. He tried to climb the tree again and again to escape from me.

The slow death of the squirrel burned in his memories; he sold his rifles and never hunted animals. Instead, he told stories about squirrels and compassionate tricksters. Once, he leaped over a fence to block a man who raised his rifle to shoot two squirrels. Later, a few months before he wrote the autobiographical scene repeated here, he witnessed an accident: an automobile had crushed the lower spine and pelvis of a red squirrel. He watched the animal scratch the cold asphalt with her front paws; she hauled her limp body to the wet maple leaves at the low curb. Closer, he cried and the squirrel shivered; then he warmed her with his hands and hummed with her down to the mother sea.

He was a survivor. He knew when and where to hide from the hunters who came in groups to kill—their harsh energies were burned in the memories of his animal tribe. I was alone. My presence and my intention to kill squirrels were disguised by sleep and camouflaged by my gentle movements in the woods. I did not then know the secret language of squirrels. I did not know their suffering in the brutal world of hunters.

The overbearing hunter learns not to let an animal suffer. As if the hunter were living up to some moral code of tribal warfare, wounded animals must be put out of their miseries.

The squirrels in his autobiographies are mythic redemptions; he remembers their death and absolves an instance of his own separation in the world. The transitive realism is a mask, the blood and broken bones rehearsed in metaphors to dishearten the pretend hunter. He refused to accept the world as a hunter; rather than contrive stories or misinform, he fashioned a blood-soaked mask that he dared the hunter to wear in his autobiographies.

Three decades later he read *And Our Faces, My Heart, Brief as Photos* by John Berger, who wrote that the "opposite of to love is not to hate but to separate. If love and hate have something in common it is because, in both cases, their energy is that of bringing and holding together—the lover with the loved, the one who hates with the hated. Both passions are tested by separation." He learned that hunters and squirrels were never opposites; the opposite of both is separation. Both the hunter and the hunted are tested by their separation from the same landscapes. Gainsay the sentimental and decadent hunter to forbear the squirrels in trees and autobiographies.

"I write for myself and strangers," said Gertrude Stein, a secular oblation that would become the isolation of imaginative writers. The mixedblood autobiographer is a word hunter in transitive memories, not an academic chauffeur in the right lane to opposition; those mixedbloods at the treelines, he warned, are wild word hunters with new metaphors on separation.

When the squirrel started to climb the tree again, I fired one shot at his head. The bullet tore the flesh and fur away from the top of his skull. He fell to the ground still looking at me. In his eyes he wanted to live more than anything I have ever known. I fired a second time at his head. The bullet tore his lower jaw away, exposing his teeth. He looked at me and moved toward the tree again. Blood bubbled from his nostrils when he breathed. I fired again. The bullet shattered his forehead and burst through his left eye. He fell from the tree and watched me with one eye. His breath was slower. In his last eye he wanted to live again, to run free, to hide from me. I knelt beside him, my face next to his bloody head, my eye close to his eye, and begged him to forgive me before he died. I looked around the woods. I felt strange. I was alone. The blood bubbles from his nose grew smaller and disappeared. I moved closer to his eye. Please forgive me, I pleaded in tears. Please live again, I begged him again and again.

"The man who takes delight in thus drawing his own images believes himself worthy of a special interest," wrote Georges Gusdorf in his article "Conditions and Limits of Autobiography," translated by James Olney and published in his book *Autobiography: Essays Theoretical and Critical.* "Each of us tends to think of himself as the center of a living space: I count, my existence is significant to the world, and my death will leave the world incomplete. . . .

"This conscious awareness of the singularity of each individual life is the late product of a specific civilization. Through most of human history, the individual does not oppose himself to all others; he does not feel himself to exist outside of others, and still less against others, but very much *with* others in an interdependent existence that asserts its rhythms everywhere in the community.

"It is obvious that autobiography is not possible in a cultural landscape where consciousness of self does not . . . exist," wrote Gusdorf. "Autobiography becomes possible only under certain metaphysical preconditions. To begin with, at the cost of a cultural revolution, humanity must have emerged from the mythic framework of traditional teachers and must have entered into the perilous domain of history. The man who takes the trouble to tell of himself knows that the present differs from the past and that it will not be repeated in the future; he has become more aware of differences than similarities."

He blinked at me. His eye was still alive. Did his blinking eye mean that he had forgiven me? Please forgive me, I moaned again and again, until my self-pity fell silent in the woods. Not a bird was singing. The leaves were silent. He blinked again. I moved closer to him, stretching my body out on the ground next to him, and ran my hand across his back. The blood was still warm. I wept and watched the last of his good life pass through me in his one remaining eye. I sang a slow death song in a low voice without words until it was dark.

"Artistic creation is a struggle with an angel, in which the creator is the more certain of being vanquished since the opponent is still himself," continued Gusdorf. "He wrestles with his shadow, certain only of never laying hold of it."

Chester Anderson smoked too much when he edited the ten autobiographies that were published in *Growing Up in Minnesota.* Borrowed books and sprouted markers, notes in his winter coat, and the thin manuscript of my thirteen autobiographical stories returned in a manila envelope smelled of sweet pipe tobacco. The professor lowers one shoulder, as he does when he rides in the wind with a genial smile, and leans closer to listen; no one has been a more sensitive listener.

The crows were written on the poplars that winter when the autobiographies were published by the University of Minnesota Press. The shadows between metaphors vanished in scheduled seminars; personal memories shivered in the buckram and perished on neap tide phrases; memories were measured and compared in a tournament of pronouns.

A teacher at Macalester College in Saint Paul, an *agent provocateur* in reflexive literature, said that my stories were not true. "These are not believable experiences," she announced in the chapel where several authors had gathered to read. Her haughtiness and peevish leer, broadened behind enormous spectacles, reminded me of a high school teacher who refused to honor one of my stories because, she ruled, an adolescent would not have such experiences.

"Mature speech begins in shared secrecy, in centripetal storage or inventory, in the mutual cognizance of a very few. In the beginning the word was largely a pass-word, granting admission to a nucleus of like speakers. 'Linguistic exogamy' comes later, under compulsion of hostile or collaborative contact with other small groups. We speak first to ourselves, then to those nearest us in kinship and locale. We turn only gradually to the outsider, and we do so with every safeguard of obliqueness, of reservation, of conventional flatness or outright misguidance," wrote George Steiner in *After Babel.* "At its intimate centre, in the zone of familial or totemic immediacy, our language is most economic of explanation, most dense with intentionality and compacted implication. Streaming outward it thins, losing energy and pressure as it reaches an alien speaker."

The two dreams to be a writer remain the same as when they were captured in a photograph on a train near Matsushima in northern Japan. The islands there are endowed with "feminine countenances" and mixed-bloods must hold back some secrets from the alien speakers in the academies.

JACK D. FORBES

Shouting Back to the Geese

Born in 1934 Jack D. Forbes (Powhatan-Renate-
Lenape and other indigenous descent) was a professor of anthropology and chair of Native American
Studies at the University of California, Davis for
many years. Included among the most recent of
his more than twenty books is *Columbus and Other
Cannibals: The Wetiko Disease of Exploitation, Imperialism, and Terrorism* (Autonomedia, 1992) and
Black Africans and Native Americans (University
of Illinois Press, 1993). He continues to publish
journalism in a variety of places. A fiction collection,
Only Approved Indians: Stories (University of Oklahoma Press), appeared in 1995, and his novel *Red
Blood* (Theytus Books) was published in 1997.

.,:‚"

My Delaware and Powhatan ancestors lived along the bays and tidal rivers of the Atlantic Ocean's western edge. I was also born within sound of the sea but in southern California, near a bay where sea lions dried themselves in the sun. In the first few months of my life, it seems to me, I could hear the sea lions barking, I could smell the salt water, I could watch the snowy-white seagulls from my mother's arms. The muffled sound of the surf penetrated my consciousness then and even now pulls me back to oceans, to seas, to the quiet dunes.

> I was conceived in the spring
> April probably
> soon after the
> Great Earthquake of 1933
> which caused my mother
> to become pregnant
> or so she says. . . .
>
> I was born in January
>   within sight and smell
>   of the Pacific
>   in a place where
>   it used to be
>   always spring
>   now one tells the seasons
>   by smog reports
>   and television schedules
>   and I never go back there.
>
> (from "A Spring Poem")

To survive the Depression my father bought a half-acre in a rural Mexicano–Okie–poor White area. There I spent most of my first eight or nine years.

In depression flats of
South El Monte
Between the Rio Hondo and the
    Rio San Gabriel
On a half-acre of flood ground
My father
With his own hands alone
    built our home. . . .

My pants were always torn
    And hitched up on my legs
Poor country boy always with a
    duck in one hand
    or a goat
Chewing at my belt
    or licking me.

(from "Earth-child Remembers")

Those were hard times, but growing up poor has given me a sense of loyalty to working people, to the oppressed, and to the struggle for human dignity which I don't think I'll ever lose.

Depression days—
Daddy walking the streets of L.A.
    wearing out his shoes
Staying in a flop-house hotel
    trying so hard to find work—
Did you cry Daddy?
    Worrying about us so. . . .

But I never knew that we were poor
Wading in the river
    catching minnows
    and tadpoles. . . .
Fighting, rough and
    tumble
Falling in love in Grade 4 with
    a sweet Mexican girl
    when I became well known
    as a singer. . . .

Earth-child I am
    always free and wild

Little rebel with
    uncombed hair
Out on the ploughed earth
    smelling manure
    from the dairy—
    it still takes me back there. . .

(from "Earth-Child Remembers")

Plants, trees, animals, places, and the mother earth herself have always
been of extreme importance to me. When I was about nine my family
moved into a northern section of Los Angeles, and there I would have
psychologically perished had it not been for a range of hills that came
up to our back yard. The hills were full of animals—deer, snakes, coyotes,
birds—and I spent much of my spare time crawling along deer trails
through brush and exploring draws and canyons. In one nearby canyon
was a giant oak tree, and under its branches, where they brushed against
the top of a sharp rise in the canyon wall, I had one of my favorite hiding places. Like an animal of the earth, I loved to rest in such secret places,
where I could see but not be seen, and where I could dream.

When young I had a dream—vision
    I joined the bee and wasp nations
    they adopted me
    and I helped them
    in their lives
    and to guard against invaders
    and they were my friends
    I've always liked bees on my skin
    seeking salt

but now I understand that
    that dream was a map of my own life
    helping many nations
    to find justice.

(from "A Spring Poem")

That mother oak tree, a group of pines, a prickly-pear thicket, secret
trails, and the canyon itself soothed me from the pain of contact with
white middle-class urban children and teachers with whom I could not
relate. My first real act of civil disobedience occurred when construction

equipment was moved in to build a dam in my canyon. I fought them at night, a guerrilla war of damaging what I could and spilling out diesel fuel and oil onto the sand. I was just a young boy then and I lost. The giant oak and the canyon exist now only in my mind.

I saw a lot that I loved destroyed—not only there but in El Monte del Sur, which became an industrial zone, and all over southern California, where freeways, smog, and development chipped away at a land that was still beautiful when I was a child.

I was lucky to have grown up when there were still clear skies because I have witnessed how much we have lost from so-called "progress" and "development." A lot of people, now, know that only from pictures.

In my high school days I used to sit at night on top of the Eagle Rock, a giant rock overlooking the Eagle Rock Valley sacred to the Indian people; I grew up—later—in the desert and in dry canyons with Indian rock-writing on the walls above; I grew up along trails in the timber-covered mountains; and I also grew up hitchhiking all over southern California and riding streetcars to every part of Los Angeles. In high school I often cut classes to explore the city, and I got a lot of my education in the downtown streets.

> I used to peer into
> dark bars
> On Main Street
>   with B-girls
> Sitting on stools
>   legs crossed and bare
> Dank moldy odors
>   dirty floors tobacco stained
> Looking for
>   wise women. . . .
>
> I used to go to
>   downtown streets
> Where men with no legs
>   people talking to themselves
> With frozen stares
>   fixed on sidewalks
> Dirty with old spit
>   and unexplainable stains
> Looking for
>   wise men.

("Looking for the Wise,"
in *Poo-tah-Toi:*
Davis Literary Anthology,
Davis Arts Commission, 1981)

Actually I started that learning process early on, since my father was a truck driver and I used to go with him a lot.

My father
    walked these streets
Staying in cheap hotels
    looking for work
    fifty years ago
And he and I both
    driving trucks
All around these
    alleys
Delivering milk and
    cottage cheese
    butter
    ice cream
To restaurants forgotten now
Starting out at three a.m., a
    little boy at his side
    sitting high in the cab
    of a big truck
One day I got my own
    so I know,
    I know these streets.

("Los Angeles Despues de Treinta
Años," in *City Country Miners . . . ,*
City Miner Books, 1982)

I not only roamed the city, day and night, but managed to find my way to the Southwest Museum and its library, to the Los Angeles Public Library, and to the L.A. Indian Center when it was out on Beverly Boulevard. In these places I was able to learn more about Indian history, to meet reservation people, and to get in the habit of reading lots of books. Sometimes I would be getting very poor grades but I would be reading voraciously. In a lot of ways I was self-educated—in nature, in the city, and with books from the libraries.

I can't overstress the importance to me of the Southwest Museum and especially of the people there. Ella Robinson, the librarian, and M. R. Harrington (an authority on the Delaware-Lenàpe people and part Indian himself) were really helpful. Ms. Robinson was always finding books for me, and M.R. used to show me notes that he had taken in Oklahoma with Delawares and in Virginia with Powhatan people. I was obsessed with an interest in everything Indian, and M.R. published the first research article I ever wrote on my own Powhatan people—in 1956, in a journal called *The Masterkey*. Earlier, however, my aunts and my father were my main teachers. My dad and I used to play games to see how much I had learned about Indian history, the names of all the different tribes, and so on. From him and other working-class men I also learned about labor union battles and the struggle for justice.

In high school a bunch of us boys who shared a sense of rebellion and alienation grouped together.

But we weren't bad
Only outcasts
Mexicans, half-breeds, poor whites
Working-class
We didn't know.

Just rebels
Cigarette-smokers
Wine-drinkers

The girls—some of them—
thought I was too rough
Middle-class white girls
They didn't know a god-damn thing.

But women have always been very important to me:

I used to like to show off for girls
A little boy doing great things
I still do
Like a boy I am
Accomplishing great deeds so the women will sing about me
Under their breaths
Not telling their lovers.

(from "Twenty-five Today")

I used to go to the L.A. Indian Center in the days when *Talking Leaf* was just a mimeographed newsletter and Stevie Standing Bear was director. But my contacts with the Indian community became minimal later when I was going to college. The two colleges I attended were both overwhelmingly white, and there were very few U.S. Indians or even Mexican students. But by the time I became a senior and from then on, through all of my graduate work, practically all my research related to Native American history and culture.

As far as my writing is concerned, I guess it started pretty early. One of my great-grandmothers had tried her hand at poetry, and my grandmother and father also had a bent toward writing. My dad, of course, as a workingman, had no energy at the end of the day for much of anything; but earlier he had tried to study law on the side, and he and I both studied with a big used British encyclopedia set that we had purchased for ten cents a volume. So he encouraged me even though physical labor prevented his being able to do any writing.

In high school I wrote articles for the student paper and became sports editor and associate editor. That helped my prose a lot, so much so that a friend and I tried to establish our own magazine when we were about sixteen or seventeen. After entering college I started writing lots of essays just for the fun of it and, later on, a few poems and a short story. As a graduate student, however, I had to switch over to the left side of my brain and focus completely on analytical and scholarly exposition. That remained my dominant form of writing until 1979, or for about twenty years.

In 1959 I started teaching at a junior college and began to work with ethnic minority students. Soon after that I helped to establish the Native American Movement and the American Indian College Committee, and became involved with Native affairs in an active way. That activity has continued without a real break ever since. I also managed to visit the Virginia area and Oklahoma, becoming closely involved with Powhatan, Delaware, and eastern Indians' organizing activities. For many years I edited and published *Attan-Akamik,* the Powhatan newspaper, and I also helped to organize the Coalition of Eastern Native Americans.

In one of my poems I describe something of my feelings when visiting the Virginia area:

Sleek modern Dulles Airport crowds
Should I shout to them?

That man's a CIA agent
A government may be overthrown
Senators, bureaucrats, flunkies
Rushing to planes, taxis, cars
Should I shout to them?

"I'm an Indian – I've come here, to
Virginia to see Indians, to see
What's going on"
I might shout. . . .

Native People hunted buffalo at Dulles
where the jets take off.

And it wasn't very long ago
Either. . . .

Anyway it's all been replaced by
Schools where Indian children
Walk and sit like ghosts
Unrecognized by White lords
Who say just another high-yellow
Nigger. . . .

I could tell you how hard it is
To hide right in the midst of
White people. It is an Art
Learned early because Life depends
On dissimulation and harmlessness.
To turn into a stone in the midst
Of Snakes one pays a price. . . .

Yes I could shout at Dulles
But it wouldn't be wise.
The White Lords don't really like
To have Native Indians in
Virginia.

It reminds them of something.

(from "When I Didn't Shout
in Dulles Airport")

Of course, working with Powhatan-Renàpe people and with other eastern Indians brought home to me the full impact of colonialism and also the difficulty of being Indian if one is also part African. Being a mixedblood myself and also a mixture of many tribes, I had long been aware of the significance of being a "half-breed." Back on the east coast, however, I became increasingly aware that those of us who looked European and Indian had a hell of an advantage over people who looked Indian and African. I thought that that differential treatment was so much white racist bullshit and still do.

I really resent white people trying to dissect us and tell us what it is that makes a person a Native American.

How much Indian blood do you have?
What tribe are you?
    Oh, I never heard
    of that one.

I must remember to
    put on
My beads and turquoise
    when I go out today
Among strangers
    Palely examining
My nose
    and eyes
    and cheekbones
    and skin
For signs of aboriginality.

("Beyond the Veil,"
in *Ceremony of Brotherhood,*
Academia Press, 1981)

I'm very proud of my tribes—all of them—surviving in the face of terrible obstacles.

Yes I could tell you about these people.
Native Sons of Virginia fooling
Genocide, managing somehow to hold on to
Indian-ness. "We're really Indians.
We are Powhatans. Pocahontas sprang
from us although the White ladies of the
DAR have her now, in Richmond, at
Tea parties.

(from "When I Didn't Shout in Dulles Airport")

I started teaching full time at the college level in 1959, and since then I've lived in many different places in the U.S.A. and Europe. I find, however, that it is very hard to survive in your average white North American area. Thus I try to live in a cosmopolitan, racially mixed university town (if I can) and take shelter with other nonconformists.

Islands of exiles
    finding refuge
In Alexandrian splendor
    Soft siberias
Where dissenting spirits
Are drunk by each other
    shielded from Red-neck stares although
Reminded by the dregs in their glasses that
    Christian mobs
Destroyed the wisdom of Alexandria
    burned the libraries
    And can do so again. . . .

College towns
    if just the right size
    and far north enough
Are sometimes like islands
    Safety-valves
Where restless souls who cannot
    make it
    go to
    write poems
Gurgitating obscenities
    at their cousins in Des Moines
And in helpless rage
    Plotting
    revolutions
And hatching plans for rehabilitating
    prostitutes in
    San Francisco.

("Island-Hopping")

During most of the seventies I lived out in the country on seven acres, moving into an old house that resembled the one my father had built forty years earlier. It was a good experience, to be back on the land again and living close to D-Q University, but it wasn't all easy.

Seven acres
Out in the clay
Just west of here
    became a place of
Refuge
    for me
And all my friends, along a dirt road
    with neighbors making angry
    faces
At the Indians
    moving in.

Hauling water
    in buckets
From a creek or in plastic jars
    from town
Making sure my new friends
had drink, while our
    roots dug down deep
    into the ground.
Together. . . .

Some fools
Think
Plants exist
For them—
A lie so arrogant to see
I've been the servant so I know
When they say "come and work for
    me. . . ."

Without the air
    the earth
    the plants
We cannot be—
Working hard
Seven acres
Taught much to me.

("Seven Acres")

Since the early sixties I have been very active in developing Native American Studies and Indian institutions including, D-Q University and Tecumseh Center at the University of California, Davis. Going along with this has been a lot of fieldwork and research relating to the conditions of Native Americans and other struggling peoples, research that has involved also a personal commitment to seek justice within this alienating, materialistic society of North America.

Hard narrowed Indian eyes
    glinting steel-like
Peering into white faces
    looking for
The wisdom they're said to have
    but where?
Eagle-nose between cheek bones high
    smelling out
Odors so refined of perfume
    whiskey and rotten
Corpses strewn on street car
    right-of-ways
Abandoned by General Motors
    in the sallow alleys
Careening back of every
    elegance.

Narrowed slits of half-breed eyes
    disrobe the gowns
The suits and jewelry fine
    casting them along with
Junked autos and ghetto slums
    into barrios piled
High with lies and tricks
    Stacking up the filth
And debris in huge mounds on
    boulevards lined with
Trees and exclusive shops
    sending slop into
Salons where ladies rich scream
    and run to escape
The flood of their own
    social excretion.

(from "Looking for the Wise")

In 1978 I started composing a few songs. Then in the summer of 1979 I wrote the first draft of a still-unpublished novel. That flipped me over to the right side of my brain. It was an unbelievably enjoyable summer, running every morning, writing, and also composing songs.

During the academic year of 1979–80 I started writing poetry again for the first time in many years. I also tried my hand at short stories and developed a great love for that form. I was on the right side of the brain for the entire year and it was a fantastic experience, like becoming young again, becoming free and "real." I was also able to help a lot of Indian students write their first poems and stories and we organized a Third World Literature Group. Two German scholars, Hartmut Lütz and Bernd Peyer, were visiting with us at Tecumseh Center, and they helped to inspire me with their own enthusiasm. It was just a very good "mix" of people that year, one of those special times.

And 1979 marked another turning point in my life. I decided that I had been for too long cooped up inside the United States and that I needed to see what other countries were like. Since then I have lived for a year in England and a year in Holland, and made several trips to Mexico and Europe. I find that I really need the stimulation of new environments and especially the relaxation from tension to be found in other societies. More and more I am becoming interested in the worldwide struggle for human rights and in the common problems of all peoples.

I have continued to be involved in analytical research on topics that I believe are important to the struggle for justice, but I also manage to find blocks of time when I can write fiction and poetry. The latter is perhaps the most satisfying, existentially, but it is also the most demanding in a sense because it requires (for me) a leap into the unknown world of my deepest feelings and memories.

Above all, I continue to seek wisdom and understanding wherever I can find it, and I continue to survive psychologically because of Native American religion and philosophy and what they teach about the sacredness of all living creatures.

Wandering through years of life
    following
Older and older streets
    listening
Carefully within as well as without
    hiking along
Mountain paths and
    forest trails
With more patience and
    humility
Among the poor and the
    suffering

As my wisdom grows from
    seeds collected
Here and there, without looking
    I am finding
In old hotels
    and on reservations
In ghettos
    and barrios
On little farms
    and in the hills
Among children
    and mothers
With love in their eyes
    for a little one
In so many different places:
    Wise men
    Wise women.

(from "Looking for the Wise")

Bound, yes bound I am
    connected
    I am part of the Spring
    the animals
    the Earth
    on that path
    which is called Life
    that magic adventure
    I am, at fifty,
    still a child
    dreaming of bees
    and
    shouting back to the geese.

(from "A Spring Poem")

DUANE NIATUM

When the Words Began to Dance

It Was a Joy to Play

Duane Niatum, an enrolled member of the Klallam Tribe (Jamestown band), was born in 1938 in Seattle, Washington, and has spent most of his life there. He received his Ph.D. from the University of Michigan in 1997 and has taught at several universities across the country. He has published several essays on contemporary American Indian literature and art, but he is better known for his poems and short stories. He has edited two anthologies, *Carriers of the Dream Wheel* (Harper and Row, 1975) and *Harper's Anthology of Twentieth Century Native American Poetry* (Harper and Row, 1988), and his books include *Ascending Red Cedar Moon* (Harper and Row, 1974), *Digging Out the Roots* (Harper and Row, 1977), *Songs for the Harvester of Dreams* (University of Washington Press, 1981), *Drawings of the Song Animals: New and Selected Poems* (Holy Cow! Press, 1991), and *The Crooked Beak of Love* (West End Press, 2000). His work has appeared in more than fifty anthologies, and his poems, stories, and essays have been translated into thirteen languages.

I protect my Klallam and Twana roots and the Coast Salish path because my good name is a measure of its people, languages, and arts.

Duane Niatum, during the Moon of Chinook Winds, 1985

JOURNEY TO HURRICANE RIDGE

The climb up the trail to the ridge
will be slow and steady,
the view acute and the passion outspread wings.
The sky point, setting the direction,
off the memory for breaking ground
crosses our path like an osprey's eye,
far above the cloud banks
floating within blue-currents.
The dance hangs between day and night
where red cedar and star settle with the ants
and mosquitoes on the horizon.

The climb will be slow and steady,
impregnating us in a flow of sunlight
flowing back down the mountains.
The nerves, elders of the blood,
trace their roots to the edge,
to rock, lichen, and crow.
We have come to rest with the molecular,
the lava layers exposed to eternity.
When the veins pulsing in our toes
give themselves to the sky
we hear the earth's core shift.

With sky pounding through our hearts,
the snow under our feet will shape
for our children the rivers

of these mountains and their songs
settled in our gene pools.
Guests of dead pines and spruce,
the windbreakers, the wind bleaches
us white as the sun.

Even the deer family we watched
near the forest and valley below
will leave footprints to chance
on the snow for others climbing beyond
themselves for the lost connection.
With the sky howling in our blood
we touch earth to unknot the spine.

(*Greenfield Review*, revised July 2003)

I was born in Seattle, Washington, in 1938. I am what is called a breed in American Indian country. My ancestry is a very mixed pool of Klallam and Twana and French and Italian streams. My American Indian origins stem from my mother's side of the family. I grew up around her family, until I was asked to leave the home at almost seventeen. My father was a ghost. The man I thought was my father divorced my mother when I was about five or six. Many, many years later my mother told me my real father was an Italian-American sailor.

One day in my life at Port Hadlock, I was on the beach of my ancestors, or maybe it was on Hurricane Ridge Trail, or riding in a canoe on the Dungeness, Hoko, or Elwha rivers in the heart of Klallam country, when I made a promise to my grandfather never to lose touch with his Coast Salish traditions, never to abandon our red cedar roots, never to forget any creature that shares this world, never allow or participate in a rape of the earth or sea. Now, at forty-seven growth rings from this clearing, our pact continues to feed my imagination and strengthen my will to keep to this bond. In short, my spirit mated for life with the Northwest Coast, Puget Sound, and Seattle (centered there between two mountain ranges that extend as far as the eye can dream). Even were I to move to another part of the world for a year or two, the spirit of the region is the strongest guardian of my path and art. So I invariably gravitate back to Seattle, city of hemlock, madrona, sea rose, and mushroom. Today I know why: it is a spiritual connection that draws me frequently to my grandfather's house and to a land that is no more.

Grandfather's home was on the Olympic Peninsula, where his parents and his grandparents lived before I was born. Their homes were close to my great-great-grandfather's village, Old Patsy, on the beach at Port Hadlock Bay. Because my family has been salmon fishermen and whalers for generations, I am an animal of the currents and the tide. For this reason I feel it is my duty to protect the beauty and healing power of the unique heritage that emerges from nature and not from books. I am convinced that I am most alive and most fully a part of a community when I am living as one with the people, the animals, the fish, and the birds of the Northwest Pacific Coast. After all, it was on this part of earth that a song sparrow once perched on my left shoulder when I was a child of seven or eight. One day I had climbed up a cedar tree to sit on a branch and watch the rain and the light fall to earth. The cedar was about one hundred yards from my grandfather's house, which he had built as a youth. And it was in Seattle's arboretum, on a sunny day in June, while lying on a blanket reading Roethke's poems aloud to a woman-friend, that a tiger swallowtail butterfly circled our blanket three times and then landed at the center of my left hand, to look directly into my eyes and inner nature before flying away. As you might have guessed, nature is my musical staff and measuring stick, the open-ended journal I carry with me at all times. If my life was void of nature, my words would fly like crows without wings or swim like salmon without gills. The world would continue to be experienced, but only as a fun house labyrinth, which, to me, is an accurate way to describe the fragmentation of industrial urban society. Like the creatures from the forests and mountains surrounding Seattle and other nearby cities, Trickster teases us at every entrance to the fun house maze and boasts often that he or she or it created this abstract mind-vacuum, mostly out of boredom at watching us periodically leap from its traps.

It is nature that shows me the way to deal with our fragmented urban society, with the city, and with Trickster. Nature offers me a sense of order, balance, and proportion: the clarity of organic light! As Jorge Guillen once so beautifully said, "clarity, uttermost strength, my faith is fulfilled in you." Experience has taught me that an art grounded in the natural world gives wholeness of vision. Denied it, everything we see and experience is seen and experienced as if by a stranger imprisoned in the void.

I began writing poetry and short fiction when I was twenty. In my youth I had read a little poetry and fiction outside of school, but the verbal arts were not my first influences. I studied the alto saxophone very seriously during my teenage years, and music was my first love and obsession. As a young musician I was very ambitious. I dreamed of becoming a great jazz player, perhaps as good as Charlie Parker. Bird was a hero of mine as a youth in the city. Music was uplifting to me and I was gladly its captive. As is true with all the arts, my taste has included both the traditional and the avant-garde: Bach to the Beatles. Later, when I put all my energies into writing, my musical ambitions became more modest. I am proud to say I have kept to this more realistic and sensible approach. I could never purify the tone of my instrument. I put the instrument down after I nearly threw it against the wall in a rage of frustration. That evening I took to the street and got quite drunk in a bar in Yokosuka, Japan. I was in the navy and it was 1958. In the bar that night I began writing my first poem. I have never stopped writing since that night, and I never played a musical instrument again.

Not long after this event I decided to be a storyteller for life. Becoming a storyteller has been, of course, a gradual process, but time has only reinforced my belief that writing is the thing I need to do. At first I read the Beat writers—the poets, the novelists, and the playwrights—but by 1961, at Theodore Roethke's and Nelson Bentley's urging, I came to know the poets who turned my head around: Hardy, Eliot, Thomas, Stevens, Williams, Auden, Bogan, Paz, Yeats, Neruda, and Vallejo, to name just some. These poets made poetry a love affair and much, much more. Looking back at how long ago I first courted the Muse, I can see today that poetry and fiction were the only parts of my existence that showed any sign of continuity or reality. I was struck with awe. Art appeared to be the one vehicle that could carry me through the chaos of living in an age where speed and abstraction and destruction were the new gods and science was at the top of the new totem of fashion and technology.

I am convinced I would never have survived my teens and twenties had it not been for the nurturing power of art and the friendship and love of a grandfather I remember from my youth. As the black sheep of the family I needed some guidance, and my grandfather became my guardian-spirit. The arts and his friendship offered me a little hope for the future when my inner and outer worlds looked like a twisted mess. They still look that way to me today, but today I feel all right. I have learned that arrogant pride is the real threat to psychic and spiritual growth. Luckily, some things can be learned and some things can be changed.

Actually, it was the Impressionist and Post-Impressionist painters, their work and their lives, that inspired me to try my hand at writing poetry. I could never see or read enough about these artists: I read their diaries and letters, their journals, and their biographies and their autobiographies. I even discovered the artists who inspired a few novels. After several lives and numerous selves later, my idea of what life and the world might be is continually expanded by these painters. Yes, from them I learned a great deal about poetry and music and drama and dance, and have found that their collective vision has been helpful in forming my own aesthetic.

I remember Elizabeth Bishop once telling us in class that you are either an "ear" poet or an "eye" poet. Well, what with our feeble efforts at handling sensory fragmentation, I am reluctant to take sides, but I confess to being very much an eye poet. I know the visual image is not the total picture, but it is central to the creative action in painting as well as in poetry. Also form and rhythm. Furthermore, the influence from these painters added pleasure to my responses to painting, sculpture, and architecture. Thus the visual and rhythmic patterns I experienced will continue to play a part in my own point of view, will go on giving depth and range to my aesthetic. The reward, what it produces itself, will always amaze me. Besides, as Wallace Stevens said, poets must occasionally turn to painters to find a new direction for a poem.

The joy I felt in discovering art spawned a chief interest of mine, which I have to this day: collecting paintings by friends and paintings by artists whose work I saw in galleries. Eventually, I want to write a series of poems on the work of such painters and sculptors as Guy Anderson, Henri Matisse, Paul Klee, Odilon Redon, Auguste Rodin, and Constantin Brancusi.

The transforming magic of dream also plays an important role in the direction and development of my art. My tribal traditions and my personal and public histories have taught me to look closely at the dreams that stir us when we are awake. As Antonio Porchia said, in his special way, "When I am asleep I dream what I dream when I am awake. It's a continuous dream." This is similar to the wisdom of the Australian Aborigines, who have told their children since the first dawn, "He who loses his dreaming is lost." It is a noble perception from a most ancient and humble people. For me, until I am dead, the eternal flight of dream will present a symbolic web of emotions and feelings, songs, ideas, images, and paradoxes that will help me deal with speed, high and low technology, the mass media, and the noise and clichés of advertising, politics, education, and war, both private and public. I believe that by living in harmony with the values of my

American Indian and European ancestors, the chaos of everyday life will become more tolerable. For this reason, specific people and their unique characteristics are placed in the foreground of my verbal canvases. This relates directly to an important idea I learned from my Klallam and Twana Indian grandfather and great-uncle and their parents when I was a child. By humbly approaching anything in the world, inside or outside of ourselves, we can experience a consistent sense of order and harmony because of the spiritual nature of ourselves and the universe.

I received a bachelor's degree in English (in writing) from the University of Washington and a master's from Johns Hopkins University (in a similar program). Living in Japan for two years, within its traditional culture, and especially near its art and poetry, had a major influence on my first approach to the arts. I saw some parallels between Klallam and Twana ancient traditional beliefs and art and those of Japan and China. I mean their ancient traditions, of course. Modern Japan imitates all the worst aspects of our consumer culture. Nevertheless, I can see enough similarities in the arts to create a hybrid way of looking at things and at oneself. For me this is all that is required for growth. If it stops feeding my imagination, I will let it go. Moreover, it taught me something important: the art of restraint, holding back, and understating both the object and the feeling for the object. No better influence could exist. I will forever be grateful.

Since I enjoy visiting other countries and meeting people from other cultures, I want to spend a good deal of what is left of my life traveling in Europe, Central America, South America, and Asia again, if I am lucky. Which leads me to comment briefly on my eclectic lifestyle: I value living with diversity, and the idea of a "world tribe," now popular among the "enlightened," does nothing but drive me to the pun table. Men and women, children and the elderly, who mirror contrasting values, arts, faces, and ways of being and doing are what make me happy and sad, love and hate, appear and vanish. Of course, I want to believe in a United Nations that struggles to maintain world peace and fellowship among nations, but I do not envy their difficult and thankless task. Yet I am against any individual or state that advocates the creation of a uniform species of humanity.

I am eclectic in my opinions about aesthetics, too. Furthermore, I do not write for an "elite." Any person who sees the arts as an integral part of his or her consciousness can understand my work. My literary and social roots are in the earth and sky philosophy as well as in the art of my North American Indian ancestors. I am in awe of the "unrealism" of the world at the odd moments of ego-death (not such an uncommon event as we all would like to think?). Yet mine is not quite the same aesthetic as the Dadaists or the Surrealists, in that I feel, like Louis Simpson has pointed out, that "the poet must find the logic of the dream." Robert Lowell made a relevant comment on the subject too: "Unrealism can degenerate into meaningless clinical hallucinations or rhetorical machinery, but the true unreal is about something, and eats from the abundance of reality." In other words, we do allow the images from below the surface—the imagery from dream or fantasy, or even the ones that appear in broad daylight—to arise within our consciousness. We must select from these interconnected labyrinths the images and symbols that truly "burn through the paper." So I see little to be gained by paying too much attention to the "make it new" zealots. If I step through life with an open mind, vulnerable to chance and the endless stream of paradoxes, I am sure my work will continue to grow, too. Does not the tension come from the play between what you have read and what you will eventually write, and what you experienced in the past, day by day, night by night, and what you later imagine you experienced? If things fall apart, dry up, or fail to jar themselves loose from the obvious, then I will know it is time for me to quit writing. Megalomania is not my straightjacket. But a problem I do have is the reluctance to ignore for one second a person, animal, bird, book, or art object. Each of these separate yet connected realities has as many masks and dreams and dances as the stars and planets and winds in a worm's eye, and are every bit as alluring as the inner wars and divisions of the Self!

Honesty in presentation of image or idea is an absolute value with me. Yet when writing about people, what counts is accuracy of feeling and emotion. It goes without saying: if you are describing a scene from nature, then the details should be accurate. Eudora Welty, one of America's finest storytellers, once said that her characters' emotions were the only element in her fiction that had some direct relationship to her own life. Now, depending on the poem or story, this has become my own point of view. You see, each poem or story demands its own images and landscapes. We slowly discover that all births do not produce identical offspring, nor the same voice or cry. We should glory in this and be thankful that they do not! Our characters change as much as we change while growing older.

Moreover, art and society may not always reflect the same world. Two sources helped me grow as an author. Roethke and his generation taught me much about poetry and the arts; my grandfather and great-uncle taught me a great deal about human society and Nature. These early influences gave me the strength to believe in a sense of wholeness in the universe, which sustained my belief that I chose the right road for myself. Which points to something else I have learned over the years: the need to fight for one's values. Papa Roethke knew this only too well: "I fear those shadows most that start from my own feet." Thus, sooner or later we come to recognize that the worst destroyers often come from within the dark recesses of our own minds. Roethke and his literary fathers and mothers taught me the ways of art and my grandfather and great-uncle taught me the ways of nature. I grew to love Roethke's poetry because it celebrates a worldview very similar to the tribal values of my Coast Salish ancestors. The importance of Roethke's role in the development of my own voice should now be clear: spirit kinship.

The main focus of my writing, whether poem or short story, has been to chronicle the inner life of the artist—to turn the constant battles waged within the psyche and its rare moments of bliss into mental images and metaphors and feelings. This struggle covers and gives substance and shape to my canvas, and sets the stage for revealing one central theme: the quest for the meaning of survival and loss.

I have learned that I survive best in Washington State. Perhaps it is because through my mind's eye I can still see a day when I was a boy of nine or ten, swimming more under water than above it, kicking my way along, drawn onward by the sea's foliage and creatures. With mask and flippers secured I would play in the water for hours, sunup to sundown, almost never needing rest during those days I explored what the beach and the Deep Beyond offered to my imagination. I am, without being too tricky about it, sometimes a kin of the seal of dark caves, moonlight, and white foamy tides. Over the years I have learned how much I am an exile child of the sun. Because the moon is in my blood, I feel the clearest light is the color of yellow cedar ash and moon dust. As an exile of the sun I search the night like a bat in search of the dream cave's end, the reality and release into the waves of stars, the renewal of dawn.

New York City, once called the literary capital of America, has been my home for a few years. Although I lived in the Big Apple as early as 1964–65, it was not until 1973, when I accepted an editor's job at Harper & Row, that I lived there again. I admit that New York City has been an inspiration to me. It is, for example, home to some of the best museums in America, as well as to the center for the performing arts. Yet I do not believe—as some diehard New Yorkers do—that to remain in one of the provinces of America is to doom oneself to mediocrity. I have found that resisting the conventional response to experience is as challenging for the New Yorker as it is for a Portlander or a resident of Seattle. In fact, over the years I have met a few artists and writers in New York who were more conventional, socially and aesthetically, than many people I know from the West Coast. Yet there is a kind of magic to New York City. It captivates you in an uncanny way, like the sirens in *The Odyssey* or the creatures seen in *Through the Looking-Glass*. The atmosphere is decadent, theatrical, loud, garish, and manic—like a giant Raven and Coyote circus. Yet I do not find it necessary to make a permanent home there in order to become a better writer. Thus, living most of my life in Seattle and on the West Coast has proved to be the right choice for me. It is the same choice each artist must make. Some artists thrive in New York City, others quickly wilt and expire. Call it Fate if you will, but somehow I learned early what catastrophes awaited me were I to choose New York as a permanent home. So my trips there are frequent but not long in duration. Being a "realist junkie" (in the opinion of a former sweetheart), I need to feel more connected to the physical universe than is possible to achieve in a social and physical abstraction such as New York City.

Still, it would be nice to live in Europe for a few years, to allow my European self an opportunity to surface and take charge of the direction of my canoe. But I am not the least bit ashamed of considering myself a Northwesterner at heart. I was born here of two worlds: the American Indian's and the white man's. For better or worse I must live in both worlds. I have no choice. Like artists around the world, my strengths and weaknesses are entwined in the earth from which I was born and where I have spent most of my life. The Pacific Northwest Coast and surrounding seascapes offer a sense of freedom and physical reality one is not able to experience in the cities of the world that I have visited. But what is wonderful about life in the United States is the variety of landscapes and people and the freedom in the air. Yet too many people fail to accept or admit that within freedom are the seeds of its own prison. The so-called free-spirits do not like to think about this possibility. To me, the art of true freedom is how well you learn to move around inside a net with a thousand-and-one knots.

For anyone wondering what I think is the poet's calling, I can, at least, say this: Pablo Neruda, who came as close as anyone can to defining the impossible, believed that if the world's poets have a specific calling, it is to sing until the hour of their deaths. He said we must give back to the people their own impulse to break into song and unite the community in the oldest bond of nature's: the impulse to sing. Perhaps Auden named for us this general calling: to help purify the language of the tribe or cross verbal-swords with the cliché mongers. In an age that trivializes everything in our lives, this is no easy task! To reach out and connect with another human being in song has always been a chief concern of man and woman. It surfaces, no doubt, from the desire to momentarily—even for less than a fleeting second—purify the body and its spirit from the void and it own finality, the last isolation ward. This probably has to do with two basic questions the first poets asked: Who am I? and, Why am I here?

I have made every effort to maintain a relationship between my poetry and fiction and the oral traditions of my Coast Salish people, for I greatly respect their traditions, socially and aesthetically. They are a shield against the social and spiritual plague of the twentieth-first-century consumer culture. Perhaps a few of the Coast Salish values have found a home in my work. Yet, it is difficult to determine just how strong the connection between my art and their paths is. I have had to use their tribal values in my own way but in a new context. Only time will tell whether I have succeeded or not. (On some days it seems very close, on other days, very, very far away.)

I want to mention one other important influence in my life as a writer. The gods were kind and over the years sent four special women my way. My relationship with them, though occasionally clouded with intense chaos and pain, nevertheless offered genuine material and inspiration. Furthermore, the first woman I loved as an adult I married. We had a handsome and healthy and highly spirited son who is now a man and living a life of his own. I really love women and value their companionship, their imaginations, their humor. For this reason I think my oldest and truest friends have been women. They can be tender and supportive with the most difficult and trying of people (that is, people like me). I have a few male friends that for the past three decades have been there when it counted, through the nightmarish ups and downs, but the majority of my friends, past and present, have been women. Thus, my experiences and dreams with them have found their way into many of my poems and stories.

It would be a pleasure and relief to settle down and teach at some college or university for two or three years, to see if it is the right job for me. I have a secondary education teaching certificate from Washington State University, alas, now expired; a year's experience teaching at the Johns Hopkins University; another year's teaching at the Evergreen

State College; a quarter teaching at Seattle Community College; and a quarter at the University of Washington. I taught a semester at a Seattle high school, and for more than a year at a Seattle elementary school. For a year I taught poetry and short fiction writing to senior citizens in Seattle centers. These experiences, however, have not been long enough or consistent enough to show me whether career teaching is right for me. I still need to be tested to see if I can do an adequate job for the rest of my life. I would *never* teach if I thought my students were not obtaining something different than what the run-of-the-mill educator gives them (often it is a mere tape-recorded series). I find full-time teaching physically and emotionally exhausting. Yet I have not found a satisfactory alternative to teaching for a livelihood. So I am still in limbo about what to do. If I find an alternate profession that will help me make a living and avoid being so much of a burnout, I will take it.

Finally, I want to mention a change in my last name. After my great-aunt Patsy gave me her father's Indian name, "Niatum," in the spring of 1971, I have published under that name. In 1973 I went through the Washington state court system and legally made it my last name. I think of this name-taking as a sacred trust, and I have reason to believe that if I live long enough, Young Patsy's name will turn out to be what ultimately changed my character and life.

PAULA GUNN ALLEN

The Autobiography

of a Confluence

Paula Gunn Allen, Laguna, Sioux, and Lebanese, is a poet, novelist, and critic. She was born in Cubero, New Mexico, and grew up on the Laguna Pueblo. She obtained her B.A. in 1966 and M.F.A. in 1968 from the University of Oregon and earned her Ph.D. at the University of New Mexico in 1976. She has taught widely and in 1999 retired from her position as professor of English, Creative Writing, and American Indian Studies at the University of California, Los Angeles. She has received many awards, including a National Endowment for the Arts Creative Writing Fellowship in 1978 and the Lifetime Achievement Award from the Native Writers' Circle of the Americas in 2001. She received the American Book Award from the Before Columbus Foundation in 1990 for *Spider Woman's Granddaughters: Traditional Tales and Contemporary Writing by Native American Women* (Beacon Press, 1989). And she received the Susan Koppelman Award from the Popular and American Culture Associations and the Native American Prize for Literature. Among her books of poetry are *Life is a Fatal Disease: Collected Poems, 1962–1995* (West End Press, 1997) and *Skins and Bones: Poems, 1979–1987* (West End Press, 1988). Her books of prose include *Off the Reservation: Reflections on Boundary-Busting Border-Crossing Loose Canons* (Beacon Press, 1998) and *The Sacred Hoop: Recovering the Feminine in American Indian Traditions* (Beacon Press, 1992).

．，：；"

TUCSON: FIRST NIGHT

for Larry Evers

the stars.
softness on the brutal land.
the song.
rest here. The reflective
pause (reflection)
what things we do, being
(hands like butterflies in July evening sun) I recall
water calling down the grass
moment hovers.
Do I say clouds? See how they piled
over the mesa,
the rocks that made one boundary of my home
found there alongside the blue-framed door
that meant entering
(the land is central to this)
focused or unfocused
the eyes form shapes to be dissolved
where time is finally illusion
carved out of rock, motion, a word to put upon the stones,
The road was the other boundary.
The highway went around us before I was born:
motion elliptical as the thought I took,
moving away until found, it holds: "the Road," we said,
implying that time had no changing.
     (Like Plato in our innocence)
clouds that were there
are here. Now. My mind and the sky,
one thing on the edge of surmise (sunrise).

(from *Coyote's Daylight Trip*)

143

When I was very little, two of my favorite songs were "Pistol-Packing Mama" and, a couple of years later, "Don't Fence Me In." Both appropriate, given that I grew up in cowboy and Indian country, descendant of cowboys and Indians, among other ancestors. "Pistol-packin mama, lay that pistol down." I liked the idea of a mama who carried a gun. I was about four when I learned the whole song by heart. "Don't Fence Me In," of Bing Crosby fame, must have been popular a few years later, maybe during the Second World War, maybe when I was six or seven.

But I liked it because it was about a world I understood, one that had horses and cattle and unlimited vistas, and where fences were signs of an unwanted civilization. I liked it because I knew that riding along forever, not bound, not held in, was my life, and that the comfort of fences, forever denied me, should not be a source of unease. I remember my sense of that song, its defiance, its aura of loss. For to me it had such an aura; underlying its rebelliousness was resignation and reconciliation to that loss. As if, given the situation, it was best to choose what was inevitable anyway. "Let me ride through the wide open country that I love; don't fence me in." I knew the cottonwoods, the ridges, the mountain, the stars and the moon in the song. I knew the urge to go, somewhere, anywhere, into the forever boundless openings of the West. I knew that good fences make strange neighbors and good possessors, and that burgher order might be fine in its place, but its place wasn't the sort I wanted or recognized.

My life was more chaos than order in any ordinary American, Native American, Mexican-American, Lebanese-American, German-American, any heathen, Catholic, Protestant, Jewish, atheistic sense. Fences would have been hard to place without leaving something out, and my senses were already lost, maybe to the moon.

Of course, I always knew I was Indian. I was never told to forget it, to deny it. Indians were common in the family, at least on my mother's side. In fact, unlike many people I meet who are claiming they're "Indian" or reluctantly revealing it, far from being denied, my relationship to the pueblo down the line was reinforced in a number of ways. I was told over and over, "Never forget that you're Indian." My mother said it. Nor did she say, "Remember you are part Indian."

I grew up on the Cubero Land Grant, in New Mexico. I grew up with wilderness just up the road, with civilization much farther away. I grew up in the hollow of the land, a hollow that was filled with grass and flowers, à la the white eyes, planted and nurtured by my halfbreed grandmother, a hollow that was heavy with trees.

My life is history, politics, geography. It is religion and metaphysics. It is music and language. For me the language is an odd brand of English, mostly local, mostly half-breed spoken by the people around me, filled with elegance and vulgarity side by side, small jokes that are language jokes and family jokes and area jokes, certain expressions that are peculiar to that meeting of peoples who speak a familiar (to me) laconic language filled with question and comment embedded in a turn of phrase, a skewing of diction, a punning, cunning language that implies connections in diversity of syntax and perception, the oddness of how each of us seems and sees. It is the Southwest, the confluence of cultures, the headwaters of Mexico. It is multiethnic cowboy, with a strong rope of liturgy and classics tied to the pommel, a bedroll of dreams tied up behind, and a straight-shooting pistol packed along. It's no happenstance that the Gunn in my name has been good fortune, or that the Indians I knew growing up were cowboys. As most of the cowboys I knew were Indians–the others were Chicanos, Nativos, and a few Anglos, though their idea of cowboy was mostly a big hat and western clothes (long before they found fashion in New York). Rednecks–Redskins: an odd thing, a dichotomy to Americans who go to movies and believe what they see, a continuum to others who take their history straight from life.

The triculture state, as New Mexico is often called, is more than three-cultured, as it works itself out in my life. It is Pueblo, Navajo and Apache, Chicano, Spanish, Spanish-American, Mexican-American; it is Anglo, and that includes everything that is not Indian or Hispanic–in my case, Lebanese and Lebanese-American, German-Jewish, Italian-Catholic, German-Lutheran, Scotch-Irish-American Presbyterian, halfbreed (that is, people raised white-and-Indian), and Irish-Catholic; there are more, though these are the main ones that influenced me in childhood, and their influence was literary and aesthetic as well as social and personal. The land, the family, the road–three themes that haunt my mind and form my muse, these and the music: popular, country and western, Native American, Arabic, Mexican, classical like operas and symphonies, especially Mozart, the Mass. The sounds I grew up with, the sounds of the voices, the instruments, the rhythms, the sounds of the land and the creatures. These are my sources, and these are my home.

STORIES ARE ROADS, STORIES ARE FENCES

North of the house I grew up in was the mountain. East of it were the tall rock mesas we called "the hills." In a southerly direction, parallel to the line the hills made, ran a paved road, old Old Highway 66. It meandered slowly past our house and my grandmother's house next door, which was separated from ours by two lawns, bordered on one side by a dirt area where we played, the huge galvanized metal barrels where we burned trash of various sorts, the coal shed, and the clothesline; on the other by a couple of flower beds. Just past my grandmother's front door the road curved sharply and crossed the Old Arroyo, climbed the hill, and ran northwest for a mile or so until it turned a left-hand corner at the cattle guard and, a few yards farther on, joined up with Highway 66, next to my mother's uncle's wife's world-renowned cafe.

To the south of grandma's, the road traveled alongside the Arroyo, a deep cavernous slit in the earth. Hand in hand they moved then, past the store that was next to my grandparents' house, down the way past Mrs. Rice's house, past Macano Valley that held the old Cubero grave-yard in its fingers, on down almost truly south to where it connected to Highway 66 (since bypassed by I-40) and thence to Laguna (lake, home, and land-grant/reservation of the Keres Pueblo tribe named Laguna Pueblo).

At that juncture the road and the arroyo parted. The arroyo some-where down the line joined the San Jose River that borders Old Laguna village on its eastern edge. It eventually meets the Rio Puerco, which, in its turn, joins the Rio Grande in its southward journey to Mexico and the Gulf. The road, transformed into the highway, crosses each in turn on its way east to the Sandias.

Some miles past Laguna proper, but still on the Laguna reservation, you pass a road going off to the north. It crosses Laguna land and links the Canoncito Navajo Reservation/Land-Grant to the highway. Farther along is Correo ("mail"), which I always remember, when I pass by that way at the distance that I-40 now runs from there, as the home of some Texans named Harrington whom I went to school with in Albuquerque: the daughter I was best friends with; the son I had a crush on when I was ten, for which I got in a passel of trouble when the nuns at the convent school caught me passing love notes to him over the back fence at their convent in Albuquerque. That was the same Harrington family, the father's older brother, who was the second husband of my Laguna halfbreed aunt Jessie, my grandmother's older sister. He died of a heart attack that struck him as he was riding horseback across a cattle pond before I was born.

From Correo the highway goes through Rio Puerco (Pork River), where Jido, abuelo, grandfather—my father's father—beat his car to death once or twice because it got stuck in the quicksandy bottom when he tried to cross from the Canoncito/Seboyeta side; where my mother's brother went over the side when he fell asleep at the wheel and nearly died; where you're two-thirds of the way to Albuquerque, an important point when you're small and get carsick.

Before my time, old Old 66 went from Correo around in a southerly direction to Los Lunas (the moons, but really the Luna family who homesteaded there or something) and then to Albuquerque. It must have been a long trip, but pretty. You'd have come into the city (then really a very small town) along the Bosque, curving and winding along the cottonwood-crowded banks of the Rio Grande. But the way we came in was fine too: you'd get to the top of the dreaded Nine Mile Hill and gaze across the wide valley at the strong towering hugeness of the Sandias and down at the river—the Bosque—and the trees and lawns and houses and business buildings of "town," as it was referred to by everyone I knew, so welcome to eyes drained of energy by the semidesert starkness, the huge layered distances, the forever sky that had shaped the long road there.

Or it would be night, and from the height of the west mesa you'd look down at the necklace of light nestled comfortingly on the velvet darkness of the valley. It matched wondrously the deep night sky, brilliant with its stole of stars.

The west mesa was then the Atrisco Land-Grant, since sold by the heirs for development. Snow Heights, now, and snowy with neo-Spanish and pretend California ranch-style homes that the rising middle class of the city affect.

From Albuquerque, the road leads right smack into the towering ridges of the Sandias ("watermelons") that rise 5,000 feet off the valley floor; and next to them, softer, the Manzanos ("apples") bound the eastern rim of Albuquerque. The highway barely makes it through the canyon, Tijeras Canyon ("scissors"—affectionately known to some of us as tiger-ass). Beyond the mountain lies Texas (and how it lies!), Oklahoma, and the Plains, and somewhere beyond them (maybe in Ohio, because my mother's family, whose paterfamilias came from there, always called it Back East), is THE EAST. (Surely you've heard the joke, "Poor New Mexico, so far from heaven, so close to Texas," a joking sigh attributed to Governor Armijo, or was it Governor Larrazolo?)

THE HIGHWAY IS FOREVER

If you go right on the old highway out of Cubero, from the cattle guard southwest of the village, you will pass King Cafe and Bar, where the wife shot the husband a few years ago and got out on $10,000 bail; next comes Budville, once owned by the infamous Bud, who was shot in a robbery. The main robber-murderer later married Bud's widow. They were living happily ever after, the last I heard, and it served old Bud right. Or so most people around there believed, at least in the privacy of their own thoughts. You pass Dixie Tavern, owned, last I heard, by a mixed-race couple I grew up with, the man Polish—no, Scandinavian. He taught me to schottische when I was a young teenager at a party at my aunt and uncle's on my mother's side. His wife is a Spanish/Chicano woman, one of the prettiest of our generation of Cubero women, and I used to flirt with her covertly. She never noticed (small wonder). They bought Dixie Tavern after Lawrence lost his hand in a mining accident.

Then you go by a small bar that was owned by a Cubero Mexican/Spanish-American family, then the Villa (pronounced "vee-ah" except by Granddaddy, who said "sa wee-ah"), which consisted of a cafe, motel, and general store built by my grandfather on my mother's side, run by her uncle and his wife for the greater part of their working lives.

It's of course closed now. Has been most of the time since they retired a passel of years ago, though my brother and his wife ran it under the new name of Country Villa for a time in the seventies. They served crepes, carnitas, and mother's fresh-baked bread, had art shows of local artists' work, and showcased entertainment from the area on weekends. Contrary to some more soured predictions, it was successful, which cost so much they had to close it down.

From the Villa, you pass Bibo's, a store and whatnot along the highway (now called Los Cerrillos, the hills—famous to me when I was small because Vivian Vance, the actress, had a house there), then San Fidel, where I went to the mission school for a couple of years and where I used to hang out at a cafe when I was in high school and listen to the jukebox playing "Born to Lose" and "I Walk the Line."

I went there on a couple of dates with a Mormon kid (dead long ago in an industrial fire) who made me feel like a fallen woman because I drank Coca-Cola (a stimulant) and smoked cigarettes. He was a sweet boy, in spite of his shock at my wicked ways.

Just west of San Fidel are McCartys and Acomita. There's a gas station and cafe near the highway, announced garishly by bright yellow signs.

My great-great-uncle Beecher lived there. I think he was clan uncle when he died. Or was it his brother? He's the one who used to scold Grandma Gunn, my mother says. She remembers when she was little and living with Grandma, who she thought was her mother, and Uncle Beecher would come to their house in New Laguna (that's in the other direction from McCartys) and scold, and Grandma would cry. My mother doesn't know what he said. She was very small, and he talked in Indian so she didn't understand.

From McCartys, the malpais (bad country). It's a beautiful stretch of lava flow that has a clear stream and fish and grass and my German grandfather's ranch that was named El Rancho Gallito (the Little Rooster Ranch)—aptly enough. It is bordered by the Acoma Reservation, and Acomita and McCartys are Acoma villages. Their lives and ours are intertwined, whether any of us likes it or not, woven together like those of the fish, water, and plantlife, the livestock and railroad, the mesas that climb slowly toward the mountain's vastness.

If you follow the stream you will cross the railroad. You will come to Horse Springs. You will come to the foothills of the mountain. If you follow the highway, west, you will come to Grants, Anglo town. Uranium Capital of the World. Before Ambrosia Lake and Paddy Martinez, when I was young, it was the Carrot Capital of the World. Before that, before I was born and when I was very small, it was the Pumice Capital of the World. When I lived there in the late fifties and very early sixties, I called it the Paranoid Capital of the World.

More or less connected to Grants (which began as a house where people driving cattle or sheep from one pasturing place to another would stop and get fed or drink coffee, and which was owned by a family whose last name was Grant) is Milan, named for my uncle's wife's (the couple who ran the Villa) brother. Their family came from Spain via Mexico, where he and his sister—my uncle's wife—were born, I think— or was it she was born in Mexico and he, the youngest, was born in Gallup, U.S.A. (sort of)? Their other siblings were born in Spain, and one of their relatives married my mother's cousin, the daughter of the aunt who had married the Harrington—though the daughter was by my great-aunt's first husband, a Jew, emigrated from Germany early in the twentieth century.

My mother's cousin and her husband took over the store at Laguna (the one that had been my great-grandfather's, the one that was managed by my father and Uncle Johnnie, the Indian one) and ran it until their deaths—his from an accidental gunshot, hers from emphysema caused by too much smoking and not enough crying, perhaps, or was it by force of proximity to Jackpile Nine? Quien sabe? as they would say at Cubero. Who knows?

Going west from Grants and Milan you pass Anaconda, the housing development and mill where people who work for Anaconda Company in their uranium mines live; where my oldest sister lived for a time when her husband, the Italian-American chemist, worked at the mill; where my next older sister lived for a very long time while her husband, a metallurgist, worked his way up from the Jackpile Mine at Laguna to the mill and then to California and then to Gallup—which is miles down the road from Anaconda.

Just west of Anaconda is or was, last time I looked, Bluewater Inn, a dancing place and restaurant where we used to go. It's where I went the first time I got drunk. I was dating the then editor of the Grants *Beacon* (believe me, Grants is a strange place to place a beacon!) and dreaming about being a writer. For a few months I wrote a column for the paper I called "Cubero Quotes." Bluewater Inn. Where the editor taught me to jitterbug to his whispered renditions of "Alexander's Ragtime Band." He called me his "Lebanesian Slave Girl" because I wore silver bracelets on my arm given me by my grandmother (the halfbreed Laguna one). We didn't get married, though the thought crossed his mind. Me, I was going for a career. I thought I would marry, if ever, in my late twenties.

East of Grants and the Bluewater Inn is the top of the world. The Continental Divide. That's at Top of the World, near Thoreau (pronounced "threw" or "through") and Prewitt. Off to the south lies Zuni, tucked into the endless march of mesas that glimmer in the blue distance from the top of the world.

Then comes Gallup, Indian Capital of the World and Home of the Gallup Ceremonials, or so the garish Chamber of Commerce signs proclaim it. It's a colonial town, a frontier town, blasted and despairing. A white-owned town carved out of the Navajo Nation on its east side, fittingly enough.

West beyond Gallup is the endless stretch of highway that runs through Arizona and, blessedly, crosses the Colorado River and the Sierras, whence it descends into paradise. That's where dwell all good things like movie stars and farmers' markets and fresh fruit stands and Disneyland and housing developments by the square mile—orange groves, oil derricks, and the rich white people who aren't Anglos or Texans but just people, just Americans (not like our white people who aren't people anymore than the Indians or the Chicanos are people but rather Anglos, Tejanos, Indians, La Raza, Nativos, whatever). YOU know, PEOPLE, like are in the magazines and on the radio. You know, like in the surveys and the polls. As in "People do this and that" or "People think such and such." People, like live in the America that all the American stuff is developed for and said about and sold to and by. As in "People won't buy frozen food. It's too expensive, or too hard to transport, or dangerous." Or "People won't vote for this or that." As in almost everything said by Americans and supposed by them to be about the human race.

I always knew that those sentences didn't mean us, we who lived in confluence. It meant somebody else, those who lived in California. Or The East.

My life is the pause. The space between. The not this, not that, not the other. The place that the others go around. Or around about. It's more a Möbius strip than a line.

THE ROAD IS STORIES, IS DREAMS

The last time I dreamed about the Road, as we called the tiny dirt road that ran past our house to connect in one direction with the highway and in the other with the mountain on one side, the hidden Laguna village of Encinal on the other, was late summer of 1984. In the dream my mother, my sisters, and I were in our old house in Cubero. The old one built of stone, plastered with adobe mud. The one that had huge beams, not the cool kind that the rich buy for their trendy Southwest houses but hand-hewn ones made at great effort by whoever had, long before I was born, made the original structure. The beams weren't round; they were square. The walls weren't adobe brick; they were stone.

The interior was calcimined once a year when I was small (how I love the clean smell and taste of it still) and heated by coal stoves; later we had white folks' paint and butane.

My folks put in a bathroom and indoor plumbing just as I was born. My mother heated my bottle (and my sisters' before me) on a wood-stove fire, one she had to light for middle-of-the-night feedings. The house had wooden floors—pine, not hardwood, and they were shellacked, linoleumed, or painted with what was supposed to be wood-colored paint but was a sort of sick orange.

In that dream, my sisters and I were gathered, and my cousin—the one who died over twenty years ago of Hodgkin's disease, the one who was the eldest son of my uncle the halfbreed and his wife who ran the Villa—came in; and we visited for a while and talked about moving back, how we would share the space, what mother wanted for us, what had been her plans. My cousin said he had to go and went out the back door, down the slate stone path. He crossed the narrow packed-dirt path edged by sandstone rocks set upright in the ground that divided our yard and lawn from Grandma's, past her lawn, past the poplar tree and down the cement walk that fronts her house, and out to the road. He was returning to where he lived, somewhere in the Arroyo, somewhere beyond the store and the lumberyard, beyond the old barn-warehouse that belonged to my father's store, Cubero Trading Company.

My sisters and I went to my grandmother's front yard and there took the arms of an unknown woman who had died. She was why we were there. We took her arms and walked her through our house to our front yard. We laid her in a white stone coffin, and put on the heavy stone lid. Cenotaph, maybe, not coffin. Not exactly tomb. She walked there, in the dream, though she was not really conscious. She walked with our guidance and our help. When I woke up, I knew somebody was about to die, because my cousin lived in the Arroyo—not in the physical one, but in another one that is in about the same place but that occupies another space. He goes from the physical Big Arroyo to the metaphysical one, the one where the dead live, the place the Lagunas and Acomas call Shipap. He comes sometimes to tell me when somebody is about to die.

A little over two months later my brother called to tell me that my grandmother, the halfbreed Laguna one, had had a serious stroke. She remained comatose for two months, entombed in the coffin of her body. Not conscious, not dead. Just caught in between. When she died in January of 1985 she was buried next to Granddaddy, in the Jewish part of the cemetery.

If they came to colonize, those non-Indians in my family, they didn't succeed. The dead still walk Cubero, as they walk this entire land. Capitalism, imperialism, racial hatred and racial strife notwithstanding. Perhaps Mr. Bibo, Mr. Gottlieb, Mr. Francis né Hassen did not come here to steal Indian land. Perhaps they came to keep the dead alive.

Another time I dreamed about The Road (these are not dreams, though they often occur while I am asleep), Uncle Johnnie showed up.

He took me from The Road across the Little Arroyo (as we called it). It is the one that comes down from the mountain and brings irrigation water from the mountain dam into our front yard; just beyond our house and grandma's it crosses under the old highway and empties into the Big Arroyo.

We went into my parents' house, the one I grew up in. This was years after the house no longer belonged to us, you see, but there we were, in the Cubero house, at a party. There were a lot of people there, all family. A lot of noise. You get a houseful of Lebneni/Chicanos, a houseful of halfbreeds, a houseful of folk from every imaginable background and food style and noise style, and you get a lot of noise, a lot of party.

I was standing at one end of the living room and looked up to see my granddaddy and my grandmother entering. And as I looked at him (this was years after he had died) his skin color began to change, to glow with a golden pink radiance that I have since learned goes with the sort of love that is life itself, and he looked at me, in that light, and shrugged. The people in the room were almost shadows, so radiant, so vibrant had he become. They were people in a dream; he was not dreamed but seen. And what passed between us was lengthy, but it boiled down to this. He understood that he had been seriously misunderstood for his life, in his life. What the nature of the misunderstanding had been. Had seriously misunderstood what others saw when they looked at him, when he spoke to them. He came from Germany, remember. (How was he to know the variant signal-systems of those around him, from such different systems, such different thought streams?)

He looked at me, and shrugged, vulnerable, small. Just a simple man who only tried to get by. To do as he was taught. To live a decent life. He told me that in his posture, his gaze, his shrug. Perhaps in his thought. For we didn't speak, only exchanged a long long look. But I understood. Not only Granddaddy, but all of us. We are simply all trying to get by. But some of us are sure, until we die, maybe, about who we are and what is right and who is deciding these things; some of us, like Granddaddy, believe we know for sure the difference between what is good and what is not.

And some of us are forever denied that sureness. We live on the road that the dead walk down. We ride it out of town and back. By its meanders we discover what is there, what is not. By its power we are drawn into a confluence of minds, of beings, of perceptions, of styles.

It is a singularly powerful place, the road that runs across the middle of the lands, the roads that run, everywhere, bordering the Big Arroyo that leads to the other place, that connects us to it and them to us. It's that road that is the center of my life; it goes to the mountain, the one called Mt. Taylor, Old Baldy, Ts'pin-a (Woman Veiled in Clouds), Kawesh-tima (Woman Who Comes from the West). The names of the mountain refer to the people who see her. She knows her real name and that she belongs only to her own self, and her dreams and memories, like her plans, are hers, not ours, to judge. And the road that goes to her also goes to town; it goes to the East and to the West; it goes to California, America, and it stays forever home.

ON THE ROAD

The events of my own life (as distinct from my community and family life, if such distinctions are possible) are fairly simple. Some of their connections are elegant, like a good mathematical proof; others are not yet jointed, joined. Throughout, the social and personal events are mirrored or reinforced by those that are more properly literary, that have a definite effect on my work.

Essentially, my life, like my work, is a journey-in-between, a road. The forty years since I left Cubero for convent school have been filled with events—adventures on the road—all of which find their way into my work, one way or another. In my mind, as in my dreams, every road I have traveled, every street I have lived on, has been connected in some primal way to The Road, as we called it, like Plato in our innocence. That Road has many dimensions; it exists on many planes; and on every plane it leads to the wilderness, the mountain, as on every plane it leads to the city, to the village, and to the place beneath where Iyatiku waits, where the four rivers meet, where I am going, where I am from.

JIMMIE DURHAM

Those Dead Guys

for a Hundred Years

Born in Nevada County, Arkansas, in 1940, Jimmie Durham (Wolf Clan Cherokee) is a graduate of the École des Beaux-Arts in Geneva, who has lived in New York City and Cuernavaca, Mexico, and currently lives in England. In the 1970s and '80s he was active in the American Indian Movement and was a founding director of the International Indian Treaty Council at the United Nations. A collection of his poems, *Columbus Day* (West End Press), was published in 1983 and *A Certain Lack of Coherence: Writings on Art and Cultural Politics* (Kala Press, 1993) also includes some of his poetry. He has most recently been active as a visual artist with several exhibitions in Europe. Catalogs of his important Munich and Berlin exhibits, *Jimmie Durham: Between the Furniture and the Building (Between a Rock and a Hard Place)* were published in 1998 in Munich (Kunstverein München), Berlin (Berliner Künstlerprograam DAAD), and Cologne (König).

.;.;"

speaking to the reader (teaching)
(critical)

I want you to hear these words. Now I am speaking to you about our lives.

That is the way we begin speeches in Cherokee, and then we say what we would like to see happen, with a simple statement that begins with "I want," as in "I want us to go to Washington and tell them just what's going on down here." The way white people exhort in their speeches—such as "we should . . ." or "we must . . ."—sounds to us not only arrogant but devious. Is this guy trying to hide from us his own thoughts? Then why speak? (They often do speak only for the purpose of hiding their thoughts.)

I want us to have an Eloheh Ga ghusdunh di at Dhotsua's old Ghadjiya in Goingsnake District, because it is now 1984, exactly one hundred years since the Allotment Act when our first new century of trouble began, and also when Dhotsua started the Nighthawk and told us that the U.S. government had no power to allot Cherokee land. "We follow the Bright Path of the One Who Allots each plant and animal and Cherokee and whites to their proper places."

Dhotsua died fighting. Before him, before 1884, hundreds of brave Otashtys and Beloved Women died fighting. They walked a straight path and they won our lives for us and I have got to tell you that when I ride this New York subway I practically hate them. How the hell did they do it? Could they always find the money for the Con Edison bill or did they eat in the dark?

Sequoyah invented writing, marched on Washington, became the Uku of Arkansas and Texas, and then split for Mexico to make a treaty with Santana. "He was never known to make a foolish move."

But I did, and my brother did, and Larry Red Shirt sure did.

Now here is what happened that makes me call for the combined fires of the Council of Everything, and why I also ask my uncles to prepare

157

for me an Ado dhlunh hi so di so that I can change myself: in 1984 I became forty-four years old, which is the average life span for an Indian man.

Is it a good thing to write about your own troubles and worries? Paul Smith, a Comanche guy with a weird history, said, "In this century the story of any Indian is a typical Indian story, no matter how different." Which means to me that in this allotted century of lives in dispersed parcels we are still the people, with a common thread.

I remember Greg Zephier with his bad heart, joking about turning forty-four and how we all laughed. But last year my brother died a month before his forty-fifth birthday. He was working as a farm laborer in Louisiana and just conked out. It was very hard for me, because we had been on the outs with each other for a few years. Just that month I had finally figured out some things about him and figured out that I really liked him. It was in my mind to come home in November and he and I would go fishing and I would explain to him how I liked him.

He was not happy that year he died; everything was going wrong. But he liked being outside all the time, and he told me how he liked seeing a wild pig in the fields once in a while. The guy who owned the farm or one of his sons would sometimes shoot the pigs and would roast them up. My brother was not invited and they never offered him a pig to take home. I am glad of that, because I can imagine my brother trying to lift a dead pig into the trunk of his car all by himself, or trying to clean it all by himself way over there in Louisiana.

My first memory of him is also my first memory of my father. We were in a creek back home, swimming and running around. None of us had any clothes on, and my mother was also there but I think she had on her dress. My father made a little millwheel in the creek with sticks and magnolia leaves. It really worked.

When we were little we were very thin and not growing well. I had had rickets and my brother had something or other. But we were happy, with our sisters and dozens of cousins, and our parents, aunts and uncles, great-aunts and great-uncles, and two grandparents, and yellow jackets coming up out of the ground to sting us, and diamond-back turtles. My brother and I were like twins and went everywhere with our arms around each other's shoulders. We slept in the same bed until I left home. As teenagers we often had the same girlfriends. When we were twelve or so we had to go to the doctor because we were not developing right. Some hormone trouble. We had to dissolve bitter yellow pills under our tongues, and he would spit his out, so he stayed little and thin until he was about eighteen. People would call him Midget. In the family we called him Geronimo because he was so wild and because he admired Geronimo so much. He used to tell people that he was part Apache. I would say, "Me, too!" and he would say, "No, you're not, you're part coon." Once he told some people that I was a dog, but that was only because we were hunting ducks without a license and he was protecting me.

He was my best teacher when we were little because I was selfish and did not like anybody. He was generous and liked everybody, so he would interpret their mysterious actions to me and also ran interference between me and my mother. Once I tried to kill him with a hoe and almost succeeded, which scared us both. My brother was especially kind to me the rest of the day because he knew how I must have been feeling, to almost kill my brother. So we developed some secret bird whistles to signal each other in school if we got in trouble.

In the third grade I pulled a knife on another kid and the teacher took my knife away. The next day, after a family meeting over supper, my brother went as an official delegate from our family of woodcarvers and told the teacher that I had to have my knife back. She gave me and the knife into his custody.

Just a couple of months before he died he told my mother that he had always been afraid of everything, and that was why his life was so bad.

My father is called Son in his family because he is the oldest. He had three brothers and three sisters. One sister died young and the brother next to him died next, at forty-four. My father really took it hard, and I thought I understood. Only I wanted to say, "Your sons and daughters and grandchildren are with you." When he would look at me it was like partway he was seeing a stranger, even an intruder, and partway seeing his brother instead of me. I did not understand until my brother died. For us, history is always personal. (I remember the Trail of Tears and Sequoyah's efforts as though I had been there.) History is directly involved with our families and our generations; tied with sacred white cotton string to the sweet and intense memories of our brother or sister is the desperate and intense hope of each generation to change this history.

I knew all along that in my parents' generation, as in their parents' generation and in mine so far, the history begun in 1884 has been bad for Cherokee people. It was bad before. What period in human history could be worse than 1784–1884 for the Cherokees? In the 1680s we were first invaded by European armies and settlers, so 1684 to 1784 was pretty bad, all right. Two epidemics of smallpox in that time, each wiping out fully half of the population.

But I could not know with my heart what the hope and desperation means to each of us for our own individual lives when the history wastes and lays down in stupid sugar cane fields our own brothers.

You think that they have finally killed you, because part of your life is the plans for redemption, and you cannot do it without all those people, especially brothers, who will give you the courage of their own returning to the battle.

A great Otashty Wahya has fallen dead in the sugar cane fields. An average Cherokee guy died at the average Indian male life span.

And I am forty-four in 1984, the close of a century, so either way I think about dying. Something is wrong with my stomach and my guts— they don't work. There is something painfully wrong with my throat, behind my Adam's apple. I don't want to go to the doctor because either he will tell me things I do not want to hear or he will say, "It is nothing that cannot be fixed up for a few hundred dollars," which I don't have.

In 1972 I joined the American Indian Movement and for the next eight years gave my life to it. Then it kind of all fell apart and left me feeling bad. Then last year my brother died, and this year I turned forty-four with some "physical problems," as the doctor says.

So that is why I want my uncles to give me the ceremony of Ado dhlunh hi so di. I need a change. I need to be changed like the old men change Tsola. But those uncles, my grandmother's brothers, are all dead, and my grandfather's brothers.

My uncle Jesse was in those old days about nine feet tall. He was extremely thin and wore overalls with a blue serge coat and a John B. Stetson hat, along with whatever shoes he had—sometimes hightop black tennis shoes. He did not always wear shoes. Uncle Jesse's eyes were fierce black but he was very kind. He gave my brother and me whiskey and told us about women. His shotgun was part of his eyes. He made sweat-lodges and taught us to go hungry and to use tobacco. For ceremonies he said you could use Camels but no other cigarettes. Camels could be changed into Tsola, medicine tobacco, and when we went fishing we had to spit tobacco juice into the water and on the bait as an offering. He and Tom and Doc were crazy old guys. They were not alcoholic, I guess, but pretty drunk.

Doc had something to do with my grandfather's death, long before I was born, and people did not speak to him. They said he had been drunk. But my father took me to see him where he lived back in the woods.

This year 1984 is the last of a century that has been different from those before it, which means that next year something even weirder will probably start up. Does anyone know where we have been since the Allotment Act? Now this is how the last hundred years was different: the Allotment Act was the first time they made a legislation affecting all Indians— the first time they completely ignored the treaties and acted as though we were some subminority to be legislated. In their hateful system, then, it was only natural that the first piece of legislation should say that we had to own land privately instead of communally, that we, in other words, had to begin being someone other than ourselves. The mere concept of parcels of owned land is an insult to Cherokees. Spiritually, it is like what if we were in power and we told the whites, "This guy Jesus was a stupid, filthy no-good and you have to get rid of all those churches and Bibles, and you Jews have to obey our laws and un-obey your own laws." Talking about it is impossible; in our own language the possessive pronouns can only be used for things that you can physically give to another person, such as, "my woodcarving," "my basket."

Communally, and that means physically, that piece of legislation broke us up. Once they got the idea, though, they really kept piling it on. This has been the century of legislation: 1924, 1934, 1954, etc. So we all got confused. Do we have the right to be ourselves without U.S. permission, in spite of U.S. death-and-poison spells?

Hna quu huh? It did something else, too, na? 1884 invented Indians. Before, we were strictly Cherokees or Sioux or Apaches. When they legislated that we were all "Indians" and homeless, they lumped us all together, and this century has seen us trying to pull all those fingers into a fist.

They are not as smart as they think they are. Aren't they like the bear who got beat by a mouse? We know very well that if you put death-words on someone's corn, that kernel could wind up in your own soup. They put death-words on us but we are the corn they cannot swallow.

This is the century where we began to be Indians, as well as Cherokees or whatever. I have never believed that for a minute, no matter how much I say it, or listen to other guys' speeches. My brother never once believed that we would all pull together into a fist. Larry Red Shirt didn't believe it.

Of course, we know our sorrows and we know our fears better than we know our families. The betrayals and little dishonesties are bushels of kernels of poison corn, but do we know where we are going?

Now I want to say things you may have heard me preach about before, but the words are not empty. I know your brother died last year, or your daughter. It has never been truer than now that your daughter is my daughter, my brother is your brother.

I am not trying to get you to join my movement. I want an Eloheh Ga ghusdunh di where everyone shows up. Because Charlene La Pointe just showed me that those battered Sioux women in that shelter she runs on the Rosebud Reservation are my sisters turning to face an old century, then turning to face a new one, and Donna Thunder Hawk and Charon Asetoyer and Phyllis Young just showed me something.

So now I see the lives and hearts of those uncles, and my mother and father, through my brother and his grandson. I am the uncle, I must be the uncle now.

I want us to meet at Dhotsua's Ghadjia, whatever the hell happened to it; they turned it into a stompground or burned it down, but we can find it. Hna Quu, dini yotli! Alia liga! Wait, now. I didn't get finished yet. I just remembered something else.

HOW COME HE WROTE IT LIKE THAT?

So here's what happened: I showed the piece to a woman who is a good critic and she had a lot of criticisms and I agree with all of them. So then I wrote to Brian Swann and Arnold Krupat and told them I wanted to make some revisions, but I guess I didn't really want to because this is a last-minute addition. It is almost 1986, two years after the first writing.

In the first place, didn't he notice that the title is too close to *One Hundred Years of Solitude,* and anyway, wasn't the Allotment Act passed in 1887 or something? Yes, it was, and I can offer no explanation for why we always think it was 1884. Maybe that just *seems* right to us.

Then she said she didn't like the ending at all. "You're *still* being selfish; tell us *what* Donna Thunder Hawk, Charon Asetoyer, and Phyllis Young showed you." "Just leave out the part about preaching; it does sound preachy and we know you can write better than that."

That one guy said that the piece seemed to be written in several voices, no clear style, and that it seemed to be telescoped, as though I had written it in a hurry without taking time to develop the different ideas.

For one thing, my father died this year. But at least he died on a fishing trip with two of my nephews. So when I went back to revise it, all the stories had changed.

But here is the real thing: I absolutely do not want to communicate anything to you. Another woman I showed it to said that I always seem to hold something back, that we never get to see inside, even in my poetry.

So you're probably saying if he doesn't want to communicate, why does he write? Here is the real truth: I absolutely hate this country. Not just the government, but the culture, the group of people called Americans. The country. I hate the country. I HATE AMERICA.

Now, if you ever come to my house I'll invite you in and act pleasant, and we might even become close friends. My hatred is really not as absolute as I need it to be. Why wouldn't I hate this country? Because you are a nice person? Because it makes you feel bad for me to hate this country? You want me to be properly indignant about "injustices" and still be on the side of you and your friends who are also "trying to bring about some changes in this country?"

Don't ask a white man to walk a mile in your moccasins because he'll steal them and the mile, too. Only, just try standing in my shoes for a minute. The *fact* of the U.S. is destructive to Indian country. Every piece of progress, social or material, is more destruction to Indian country. I'm not even going to bother to develop that idea, but why don't you just think about it—until the sun rises (that means all night long)?

Here is what I don't understand: how come so many Indians don't seem to (or at least don't admit it) hate this country? Simple—we hate ourselves and each other instead, and now there we all are, out there trying to impress the white folks with our one thing or another.

I do not want to entertain you in any sense of the word. I would hate it if you all came to understand me. And I'd really hate it if I wrote something like those "sensitive and honest" novels some black writers are doing, so that any white person with a few bucks could spend a quiet evening being entertained by our sorrows, and gaining in power by "a better understanding" of our predicament, our dreams.

Where am I supposed to go, and what am I supposed to do? Some folks say, "Why don't you go back home and live with your own people and those woods you claim to love so much?" In the first place, those woods are destroyed. In the second place, I am a human in the world in this century, just like you. It doesn't matter to me that there are contradictions that are irresolvable, because they *are* irresolvable. To be an Indian writer today means being on no path, contradicting yourself at every turn, so at least I want to face that condition and not "act nice," pretending it isn't true.

Anyway, I'm not sure I like Indians all that much, either. Our intelligentsia, the writers and artists, are such a bunch of stuck-up, apolitical, money-grubbing, and flaky ripoff artists, and our political leaders are usually crooks and pretentious bastards or either somebody's puppets. Our regular folks are usually drunk or bad-mouthing their neighbors. Do you know that out on the res we have just as much child abuse and wife-beating as the rest of the country? Alienated, man; this is definitely not the old days. The people that work in offices, they're the worst: petty, banal, officious, completely distrusting and cynical, and they always have that self-righteous superior attitude and they're always incompetent. Our elders are all off being gurus to some white weirdos and talking about how some big earthquake or flood is going to solve all our problems.

I didn't give up hope; *I* been hanging in. But those other guys. Walking around, AIM-lessly. There is a whole crowd of professional Indians, now; folks who wouldn't lift a finger if they weren't paid to but come off all concerned about our condition. They know they'd be out of a job if we ever got our act together and changed the condition.

Let's see, what else. That's all I have to say right now, except like I said, hna quu, dini yotli! And I guess I'll throw in a couple of poems here. Oh yeah, I meant to say that the reason I used several voices, or styles, is that I wanted to experiment with mixing different Cherokee speech patterns as a way of showing confusion and the fight for some clarity within that confusion. I'm sorry if it didn't work out right. Anyway, here are the poems. One thing, though – I wrote the first part of this piece as though I were writing to Indian people, with one half of my brain; with the other half of my brain I was writing to the white folks, because who reads all these things? The white folks.

If we read – now here is a subtle point – if we read, we read like the white folks. We become like the white folks for the duration of the reading; that is, we read passively, to be entertained instead of to be motivated to organize to take back our land and all of our rights, no bullshit and no stopgap measures. But anyway, how many Indians are reading this? A few of my fellow writers. But maybe, a couple of college students who need to see how crazy it got. So here are the poems.

GUY FINDS TWO DEERSKINS IN MANHATTAN!

Dateline Manhattan Island, April 22, 1984
A man claiming to be an American Indian
Discovered two deerskins today, on a trash heap
At 108th and Columbus Avenue.

The guy said he had no knowledge concerning
The origin of the skins or who placed them on
The trash heap.

"The hair is thick and shaggy, like northern deer
Have, so I don't think they were brought here
From Oklahoma, Texas, or Arkansas," he said.

"Immediately upon discovery I consulted
a wise woman from Brazil, who said that I
Should try to tan them," he claimed.

The Brazilian woman, who may also be at least
Part Indian, stated that she gave no such advice.
According to her the guy is always finding
Dead animals or remnants and bringing them to
Her apartment, which is furnished with a hammock
And purple walls.
"He believes that the coyote spirit leads him to
Things like that," she said in an interview.

The guy later denied her version of the story.
"I have no idea what's going on in Manhattan," he claimed.
"But obviously many animals lived here at one time.
And there were some Puerto Rican dudes hanging out
Close by so I wasn't sure if I should take
The skins or not. It was Easter Sunday and
Those guys would think I was nuts."

In the week previous to this incident a near-by
Church burned to the ground, and on Good Friday
(April 20) Russell Means of the American Indian Movement
Spoke at a meeting on Columbus Avenue near 107th.
Means has no known connection to the
Guy who found the deerskins.

I AM ONE OF THOSE INDIANS

I am one of those Indians that fly around.
When we fall off cliffs we yell AIIEEE!
And keep zooming, never hit dust or bounce
From boulders. (Hi na?)

I am one of those Indians you may see flying
Around the Empire State Building in late Spring evenings.
But we are not steel workers or high walkers,

And our flying does not come from being bucked
From the backs of rodeo broncos.

The Bureau of Indian Affairs assigned me this special job
As part of the Termination Act of 1954.
(Their Acts come in the fours; 1884 was the
Allottment Act, 1924 the Citizenship Act, 1934 the
Re-organization Act, and in 1984 I turned 44, to
Which I reply, Nunh gi! Nunh gi! Nunh gi!
Nunh gi!)

Ancestral graves and my specific gravity were all
Terminated in '54 and I act accordingly. I act
like a flapping Redskin. We are not stars or birds
or ghosts; more like flying peeping toms. I am
One of those Indians that fly around witnessing
prophetic novas in burnt-out toasters.
(Ka, ni, hi na?)

DIANE GLANCY

Two Dresses

Diane Glancy (Cherokee) was born in 1941 in Kansas City, Missouri. She received her M.F.A. from the University of Iowa and teaches Native American Literature and creative writing at Macalester College in St. Paul, Minnesota. Her latest poetry collections include *The Relief of America* (Tia Chucha Press, 2000) and *The Shadow's Horse* (University of Arizona Press, 2003). In 2003 she was awarded both a National Endowment for the Arts Fellowship and the Juniper Prize from the University of Massachusetts Press for *Primer of the Obsolete* (2004). Her recent novels include *Stone Heart: A Novel of Sacajawea* (Overlook Press, 2003), *The Mask Maker* (University of Oklahoma Press, 2002), and *Designs of the Night Sky* (University of Nebraska Press, 2002). *American Gypsy* (University of Oklahoma Press), a collection of six plays, was published in 2002.

．，．，"

My Cherokee grandmother could not write. I have her X on the land deed when the farm was sold in northern Arkansas, just before Norfork River was dammed and their land went under water.

Neither did she speak more than a few words when we visited. But not speaking, she spoke to me, and it is her quiet influence I feel again and again. I think in some way I am drawn to words because of her.

I was raised by an English-German mother. My father, one-quarter Cherokee, was there also, but it was my mother who presented her white part of my heritage as whole.

I knew I was different, then as much as now. But I didn't know until later that it was because I am part heir to the Indian culture, and even that small part has leavened the whole lump.

When I was growing up, everything was done in order. It was the influence of my mother. My socks were folded and in their place in the chest of drawers, and my bed was made. Outwardly I was orderly, but inside I was Indian. I have a fierce shyness. I recognize the Great Spirit in all things. I speak to animals and rocks. And though the Cherokees are more sedentary than other tribes, I must travel now and then. In my spirit dreams, chevrons of geese and wild herds of striped antelope crawl up the back wall of my head.

Still, I know little of my Indian heritage.

My great-grandfather, Woods Lewis, was born in 1843 near Sallisaw, Oklahoma, which was then Indian Territory. His parents must have crossed on the Trail of Tears during the removal of the Cherokees from Georgia and the Carolinas in the late 1830s. But he fled the new territory after he killed a white man over a wagonload of corn, and joined the Fourth Cavalry, Union Army, in Tennessee. After the Civil War he married a Tennessee woman, and they migrated to Arkansas. He died in 1904.

I was born in Kansas City, Missouri, March 18, 1941. My father had come north from Arkansas when his father died. He was not quite twenty when he went to work in the stockyards for Armour. Over the years, he became a superintendent, and we were transferred to several cities. In 1954, when I was thirteen, my Cherokee grandmother died. I stayed in Indiana during her funeral. It had been seven or eight years since I had seen her.

During that time, my dormant heritage, my "Indianness," was rising slowly from inside.

I graduated from high school in St. Louis in 1959, and from the University of Missouri in 1964. I married. A son, David, was born in 1964, and a daughter, Jennifer, in 1967. In 1983, I finished my M.A. at Central State University in Edmond, Oklahoma. Now I am divorced and teach poetry and write.

I live in Tulsa, within a hundred miles of where my great-grandfather was born.

One of the first realizations of my dormant heritage came long ago when I was in school: I wanted a medicine bundle. I wanted to know what I would do. I began with a vision quest: a search for a feeling within me. And I returned with that feeling I sought as though it were a small object I had found within myself: a button or a coin. I had been given the written word, not all of it but a corner of the field, a small plot: poetry. And I knew I should stay with it no matter how often I felt pulled away.

I write in other genres than poetry, but everything I write is from the poetic perspective: not the old poetry with its emphasis on rhyme and rhythm, but the contemporary word art that reveals underlying meanings and relationships.

I wonder sometimes why I am drawn to words. Maybe because language is so much more than I am. Maybe words chose me because they would have such a challenge. I smile when I think of my grandmother who could not write.

But words are not alone by themselves. They carry meaning. I must have something to say and must say it well: I want to represent life with respect. I want to write about what I feel and think; what I experience and come to believe. I want to write about the dignity of the common man and the uniqueness of the ordinary moment. I want to have courage to face the wilderness within. It provides tension. And I want to have a sense of self as whole even though fragmented. It gives voice.

This is often where I struggle. Part of me came across the sea from Europe to Virginia, then west in a wagon to the Missouri/Kansas border where my mother's family settled. The other part of me walked 900 miles on foot during the forced migration of 17,000 Cherokees from the East to Oklahoma.

I do not know why the little storm of words falls upon me. But I hear voices in the grass: Two Dresses, they say with the wind. And truly, I have the feeling of being split between two cultures, not fully belonging to either one.

POEM #1

There are times you are Indian and Teehee the Little Piney laughs. You hear its voice and Waters move across the tongue of the large rock.

There are times you are not white and they look at you as though something were wrong. You are withdrawn, not interested in their program. No enthusiasm.

You are listening to the rock and watching the quavering trail of moss in the clear Waters. You see it goes nowhere but simply: Is. You say, Father, Great Spirit, and they mention your absurd speech. They shake you. Kick you a bit. Only to bring you to your senses.

You want to stay at the Waters and listen to the Spirit. But they call you to work.

The ends of four rakes rest against the back of a truck like teats on a cow's udder. Hayrolls of buffalo graze in fields like folded socks, and ponds are silver buttons on a soldier's uniform.

The past comes as captain, lieutenant, and horse soldiers, through blistering summers and a winter that smirks in corners of the field. You are outnumbered, overpowered, and there is nothing you can do.

After your defeat, they call you to themselves. Your one hand goes out to meet the other and in shaking you are a stranger to the two.

Poetry, for me, is storytelling: a dance of sound and sense which concerns the interplay between the concrete and abstract, the visible and invisible worlds. Poetry is the medicine bundle I carry. Not a pouch around my neck on a cord, but a feeling within.

In the old days, a young Indian man would go alone into the woods for several days and in thirst and hunger, possibly through a change in body chemistry, maybe by intervention of the Spirit, he would see a bird or animal or have some vision that would give him knowledge of his mission. He would carry a token which represented that vision around his neck. It was the source of power all his life, enabling him to go into battle, or lead his tribe or family through harsh elements, or counsel them.

I think that I had that sort of vision once, when I dreamed one night of an Indian campground under a wondrous purple-magenta sky. I think, possibly, it was my Indian heritage struggling for expression. Maybe because I am only part Indian, it must fight for survival. Out of my eight great-grandparents, only one was Cherokee. How can the influence of one be as strong as seven together? Yet in my writing, as well as in my life for the past several years, it is my Indian heritage that emerges again and again.

I find that the Indian, as well as poetry, stands between the visible and invisible worlds, between earth and heaven. The Indian, and poetry to some extent, has been rejected by society and is not at home here. Neither are we at rest in the spirit world. We are neither here nor there but in the midst of the journey. Part of one, part the other, revealing neither fully but indicating a struggle for reconciliation on the part of both.

Alone with my pencil and paper, a small pony with tinkling bells on a sash prances on the path between two worlds. And Two Dresses, the name I hear in the blowing grasses, takes on a deeper meaning: not only am I split between two races, but I am divided between two dimensions. I inhabit a body of flesh and I am also spirit.

The mind makes form of what happens around it: ordering the unordered events that come sometimes like a tomahawk. It also presents the world behind the world, giving us glimpses into the existence of the hidden one.

Poetry is a ghost dance in which one world seeks the other. Though the two worlds are opposed, they long to be united. Poetry is a road, a highway. Perhaps that is the reason I like to travel. Sometimes on a journey I feel disconnected from earth and caught up in the realm where buffalo still feed and Indians pass to winter camp. And over that is another something: a deep communion in which a healing unites the two worlds.

POEM #2

Sometimes I hear my voice
as it must have been before
the split

when two were one,
as maybe it will be again
in hunting grounds
when we remember the old earth
& how not speaking
we spoke
under the walnut trees.

Neither voice
now strong enough to reach
the other:
migrating Indians
split in two camps
to preserve the tribe
from attack.

> The chambered shells of walnuts
> pushed by footsteps
> into the bare ground
> by the backporch
> where we cracked their shells:
> tiny hoof-prints of prehistoric horses
> prancing under the walnut trees.
> Whee hay/they whinny.

> The night a chamber pot
> I remember from her house,
> a black moon nuzzling
> somewhere under the sky.

One voice from light / the other from dark
overlapped as when sun shines on moon,
speaking in two half-voices, and the two
sounding, sometimes, almost one.

I think I feel an affinity to poetry because I am part Indian and there is a link between them. It is the same also with faith. The Cherokee nation always was split between pagan beliefs and Christian faith. Even before the missionary, some of our beliefs were strikingly similar to those in the Judeo-Christian tradition, and there was speculation that the Cherokees were a lost tribe of Israel.

In the suffering Christ, certainly, is a likeness of the Indian. In fact, a vision of him was part of the ghost dances of the early 1890s on northern reservations. Maybe it was a message that the Indian would be prone to suffering in the modern world.

In my Christian faith, God is the Great Spirit, the Father. Jesus Christ is the son, the opening, the door. I see Christ standing on the prairie with his arms outstretched in love. A hole clear through his chest where his heart should be because this is what he lost when he was flesh in this world. When he was on earth, he was broken and fragmented like the Indian.

He is despised and rejected of men, a man of sorrows, and acquainted with grief, and we hid as it were our faces from him; he was despised, and we esteemed him not–Isaiah 53:3.

I think I am more aware of that hole where his heart should be because I am part Indian. It is for a migration of our spirit into the world beyond the temporal one. To stand alone on the prairie even for a moment fills me with wonder and I get gooseflesh to know I am one with the Spirit. I feel the millions of years the prairie lived in its glory and fierceness, and there is even wonder in recent history: the movement of wagons and the momentary anguish of the Indian tribes when they knew their way of life had come to an end and they were helpless against the terrible, awful wait for the end.

Terror must have devoured their hearts and limbs just as it must have Christ on his way to the cross.

I have had my own terrors, which make me more aware of the terrors of the doomed Indian tribes. I think these fears have been a tool for understanding my race. Maybe these fears, in turn, were augmented by my heritage. When I read Indian histories, I have the feelings to go with the knowledge of defeat. To suffer as a member of a suffering race gives a sense of belonging. In other words, I have a heritage to relate to, whereas, if I were only white, I might have had more of a feeling of alienation without any kind of recompense for my accidents.

At two, I fell down the steps of a train as we disembarked for a rest during a trip from Kansas City to California. The fall nearly cut my nose from my face. I was wrapped in a sheet and laid on a table while my nose was sewn back on my face. If anesthesia was used, I did not feel it in my terror. Only raw pain and the howling fear during attack as though a huge, black bear gnawed at my face and there was nothing I could do to stop it. Even as I write this, I feel tears burn in my eyes. Not long after that, I burned my legs to the bone when I knelt on a floor furnace to watch its fire in a corner grocery near our first house in Kansas City. After that, I jumped up in a chair which overturned into a glass bookcase and had to have pieces of glass removed from my head and eyebrow.

One carries memories like a hole in the place of one's heart. I knew even as a child I was marked for a different path. I could not walk like others, but was marked by that aperture in which the Spirit entered with his glory.

POEM #3 SOLAR ECLIPSE

Each morning
I wake invisible.

I make a needle
from a porcupine quill,
sew feet to legs,
lift spine onto my thighs.

I put on my rib and collarbone.

I pin an ear to my head,
hear the waxwing's yellow cry.
I open my mouth for purple berries,
stick on periwinkle eyes.

I almost know what it is to be seen.

My throat enlarges from anger.
I make a hand to hold my pain.

My heart a hole the size of the sun's eclipse.
I push through the dark circle's
tattered edge of light.

All day I struggle with one hair after another
until the moon moves from the face of the sun
and there is a strange light
as though from a kerosene lamp in a cabin.

I put on a dress,
a shawl over my shoulders.

My threads knotted and scissors gleaming.

Now I know I am seen.
I have a shadow.

I extend my arms,
dance and chant in the sun's new light.

I put a hat and coat on my shadow,
another larger dress.
I put on more shawls and blouses and underskirts
until even the shadow has substance.

(from *Scintillations*, Jasmine Press)

I think the fact that this poem was published by the Bensalem Women's Organization indicates that the Indian is certainly not the only race with a sense of doom. But, to me, our doom is not so much history as an ongoing sense that our way of life has been stomped out and we will never be in the mainstream of society. Maybe the blacks feel this way, with the difference that they are removed from their land, while we are left on ours as a constant reminder of what we had.

The modern world is difficult. There are taxes, insurances, repair and maintenance of self and possessions. Doctor, dentist, car inspection, license renewal and tags. Laws to obey, regulations, registrations. Inoculations, obligations, donations, tithes, responsibilities. Rent, utilities, bills and payments, groceries.

Often, I feel like I am fighting with bow and arrow, or counting coup, when everyone else has a repeating rifle. Hampered in spirit, I must face the rigors of family and job, must establish credit and be responsible and punctual.

But poetry sings against difficulties. It is a wonderful, vibrant song, a story in which sometimes language is plot and images are characters which theme unites. And we can speak against the gravity that holds us down.

Poetry is the dust-devil we often see twirling on the plains: part dust, part wind; transforming imagery, rhythmic language, and the message conveyed into a testimony against our fate.

Recently on a trip to a poetry symposium at the University of Alabama, I saw a chicken hawk fly above the highway. Its throbbing shadow crossed the pavement at the moment I passed. I saw maybe four flutters of its wingbeat, then it was gone. That happening went to the core of the Indian part of me.

I know what the hawk looks like, even though I didn't see it. I recognize its place in the nature of the universe. I saw its shadow on the highway, small because of its height above the road. Also, I remember what I saw and reflect upon it.

Such incidents open infinite possibilities and relationships of those possibilities for the poet. I can stand in the field of imagination and build any number of networks between the hawk and its shadow, the hawk and me, me and the hawk's shadow, my passing there at that moment, my intersection of the fixed relationship of the shadow to the hawk, my inability to actually intersect, and any thought, feeling, sensory perception, memory, and so forth, that can be woven into the incident. I can build from almost any direction into "poem."

Poetry should expose effulgence. Indian poetry, especially, should promote stability, precision, hope. It should be salve for the broken race which is enriched by its bloody suffering and permanent loss of a way of life. The Indian is a barn with the loft door open to the universe. Our poetry should rise from despair. We should use our special "sight." If our poetry is a vent for anger, it should also transcend.

POEM #4

Ah ney shuu shhh

he hears
my arrow pierce his heart.

On the prairie
I strip flesh from his face

teeth in his jaw bone
a white row of flowers

I use my scraping knife
beat the tomtom of his belly

The smell of animal piss
and coyotes staking territory

The gristle that won't tear
the muscle as though glued on.

At night
the pulsing star is a mouth:

His turn, it says.

Two Dresses
　　like stiff teepees

　　　　　　Black bear
　　gnarls them into one

The strings of flesh
the smell of rotting bone

　　　　　　Now I am like him.

Black web of birds are braids
　　　　　　above the fields.

The sliver of moon　an ear.

Added to the excitement of "poem" and all its possibilities with the basic units of image, the flight of sound, the thought or emotion conveyed, the poet can also hunt for diversity of form.

POEM #5 (FOR DAVID)

Your hightop basketball shoes unlaced
scars from lung surgery
the scar my father carried on his hand

the war paint on your chest
over a load of corn
your hair a roach when you run

son you carry your war cry well

agape like the moccasined feet of your ancestors
shadow of the wound your great great grandfather
the scar I carry

your gym shorts are breech clout
gave a white man with a branding iron
hackle feathers at your ankles

Poetry has a meaning-giving function. Our life has fled and has not come back. But the fragrance of the hay is smelled along the road when the hay is mowed.

POEM #6

I look into houses for one in which
to move like trees on their way from green
to bud again.
    –I ask
how the evening sun comes
through the trees & dies,
how it rises on the next day of its birth.
    –The leaves
when they have lost their green
wander like an overthrown race.

Early on a morning
I tell you of a dream in which
I have to get out of the way
    –a narrow dirt road
flush to a cliff,
a ditch on the other side.
A haytruck tosses up the road,
I see no way around it but there are saplings
on the side of the cliff.
As the truck nears
I take a branch & pull myself up
out of the way
but the driver fears he will hit me,
pulls away from the cliff.
The overloaded haytruck sways he tries to back up
but cannot–
the haytruck falls into the ditch.

You say it is omen
but all the places I look at
I am dissatisfied with,
not any of them
a space which gravitates like a small earth
around the sun.
    –Our arguments
foot soldier and Indian on a fresco
like Egyptian farmers with hoes,
this needle in haystacks we prick our feet
looking for a house in which to move.

Short of flour & milk
we beat moths from the garden
we have not found,
paste a white picket fence to the house.

Closed in pages of the family album
Orvezene, my grandmother,
stands barefoot at a gate,
her white dress printed
with pink rosebuds,
hands clasped at her lap,
    —but she is standing.
Sometimes she wears a white straw hat,
sometimes she holds it
and it holds water for birds
but none come.

I will not take this vacancy of hate
on our long march in exile
but will carry the family heirlooms of
lodge pegs & china dishes
& bud vases
into a new place.

Orvezene, my father's mother,
Jennifer, my daughter,
& you so much like my father who kept us
together.

This land hardens us,
packing crates of white dishes,
tiny rosebuds knocked about.
Foot soldier, you hold my rage.
I know this place I've looked for
is not found
in a month nor even a winter,
but stretches itself
over a farm pond
or a bird bath in a hat she holds.

    —Finally spilled hay
& a house
blessed with light on the glass
polished by a corner of the sun.

On the last day at the old place
we leave our voices
in the hollow rooms.
    —The prairie seems so large:
its vacancy is space in which my daughter,
singing,
& my grandmother's ghost
walk to the car with our clothes.

The winged buffalo from our heritage
wait in the long chest with glass doors
in the hall
beside the pewter & flowered china bowls:
this baggage we carry
from one generation to another.

In the yard
their shadows twine
    —my father's granddaughter,
my father's mother.

And you, foot soldier,
hold on when I cannot.
You fill the garden hose
with water
over tender rosebuds,
the picket fence,
the clear glass window rubbed with sun.
    —We move
past the fallen haytruck.

Leaves growl
when we brush them from the car
under the large tree.
    —You still hold me
when I am squaw
who stirs my anger with flour
& water from the white straw hat.
Still my grandmother holds it
in the album for me to see.
    —As we drive away
I do not forget her silent anthem I follow.

The lesson of this world is that it defeats us, yet there is a personal and racial dignity to be found. I want that assurance to be the underlying tone of my poetry.

Since history cannot be changed, I would like to say that dissolution of a way of life can be beneficial (though I wonder how truly I believe that).

Between the repetitious chants of "hey ye hey ye" and the bitter, contemporary Indian poetry that equates the reservation with barren moon imagery and curses the white man, there is a rich heritage broken open like milkweed to be explored for its variety and texture.

Who knows what will come of Indian poetry in the future? Possibly in its vivid imagery there is a message the world will need.

POEM #7

> hey ye hey ye
> > I hear your hawk jazz,
> > > chickenhawk,
> see you up there above the road.

> My car straight as an arrow
> > between you and your shadow.

> > tee hee
> > > you laugh.

> I do not come between you:
> > Your shadow passes over my car.
> > > Now I see
> you are the long flight of my tribe
> > & your shadow is my sorrows.

> > hey bird, way nuh,
> > over hardships
> > > I soar like you

hey bonay

ay tow!

I suppose the ultimate subject of Indian poetry, for me, is the freeing of variables in ourselves and our world, and their relationships and interactions. Our experience encompasses the span from the pitiful weakness of the derelict on the street to the medicine man who reaches into the universe. It is a long journey, indeed, but a migration of which the Indian and his art are capable.

SIMON J. ORTIZ

The Language We Know

Simon Ortiz (Acoma Pubelo) was born in Albuquerque, New Mexico, in 1941. He attended the
University of New Mexico in Albuquerque and the
University of Iowa Writers' Workshop, receiving an
M.F.A. in 1969. Ortiz has taught creative writing
and Native American literature at San Diego State
University; at the University of New Mexico; and
at Sinte Gleska College in Rosebud, South Dakota.
He lives in Acoma, New Mexico, where he is serving
as lieutenant governor of his pueblo. Ortiz received
a Discovery Award from the National Endowment
for the Arts in 1969, a National Endowment for the
Arts Fellowship in 1981, and the Pushcart Prize for
Poetry in 1981 for his collection of poems *From
Sand Creek: Rising in This Heart Which Is Our
America* (Thunder's Mouth Press, 1981). Although
he is primarily a poet, he has written extensively in
other genres. His collections of poetry include *Going
for the Rain: Poems* (Harper and Row, 1976), *A
Good Journey* (Turtle Island Press, 1977), and *After
and Before the Lightning* (University of Arizona
Press, 1994). *Woven Stone* (University of Arizona
Press), a book of poetry and prose, appeared in
1992 and *Men On the Moon: Collected Short Stories*
(University of Arizona Press) was published in 1999.
He edited the anthology *Earth Power Coming: Short
Fiction in Native American Literature* (Navajo
Community College Press, 1983), and his works
appear in many anthologies as well.

I don't remember a world without language. From the time of my earliest childhood, there was language. Always language, and imagination, speculation, utters of sound. Words, beginnings of words. What would I be without language? My existence has been determined by language, not only the spoken but the unspoken, the language of speech and the language of motion. I can't remember a world without memory. Memory, immediate and far away in the past, something in the sinew, blood, ageless cell. Although I don't recall the exact moment I spoke or tried to speak, I know the feeling of something tugging at the core of the mind, something unutterable uttered into existence. It is language that brings us into being in order to know life.

My childhood was the oral tradition of the Acoma Pueblo people—Aaquumeh hano—which included my immediate family of three older sisters, two younger sisters, two younger brothers, and my mother and father. My world was our world of the Aaquumeh in McCartys, one of the two villages descended from the ageless mother pueblo of Acoma. My world was our Eagle clan-people among other clans. I grew up in Deetziyamah, which is the Aaquumeh name for McCartys, which is posted at the exit off the present interstate highway in western New Mexico. I grew up within a people who farmed small garden plots and fields, who were mostly poor and not well schooled in the American system's education. The language I spoke was that of a struggling people who held ferociously to a heritage, culture, language, and land despite the odds posed them by the forces surrounding them since 1540 A.D., the advent of Euro-American colonization. When I began school in 1948 at the BIA (Bureau of Indian Affairs) day school in our village, I was armed with the basic ABC's and the phrases "Good morning, Miss Oleman" and "May I please be excused to go to the bathroom," but it was an older language that was my fundamental strength.

In my childhood, the language we all spoke was Acoma, and it was a struggle to maintain it against the outright threats of corporal punishment, ostracism, and the invocation that it would impede our progress towards Americanization. Children in school were punished and looked upon with disdain if they did not speak and learn English quickly and smoothly, and so I learned it. It has occurred to me that I learned English simply because I was forced to, as so many other Indian children were. But I know, also, there was another reason, and this was that I loved language, the sound, meaning, and magic of language. Language opened up vistas of the world around me, and it allowed me to discover knowledge that would not be possible for me to know without the use of language. Later, when I began to experiment with and explore language in poetry and fiction, I allowed that a portion of that impetus was because I had come to know English through forceful acculturation. Nevertheless, the underlying force was the beauty and poetic power of language in its many forms that instilled in me the desire to become a user of language as a writer, singer, and storyteller. Significantly, it was the Acoma language, which I don't use enough of today, that inspired me to become a writer. The concepts, values, and philosophy contained in my original language and the struggle it has faced have determined my life and vision as a writer.

In Deetziyamah, I discovered the world of the Acoma land and people firsthand through my parents, sisters and brothers, and my own perceptions, voiced through all that encompasses the oral tradition, which is ageless for any culture. It is a small village, even smaller years ago, and like other Indian communities it is wealthy with its knowledge of daily event, history, and social system, all that make up a people who have a many-dimensioned heritage. Our family lived in a two-room home (built by my grandfather some years after he and my grandmother moved with their daughters from Old Acoma), which my father added rooms to later. I remember my father's work at enlarging our home for our growing family. He was a skilled stoneworker, like many other men of an older Pueblo generation who worked with sandstone and mud mortar to build their homes and pueblos. It takes time, persistence, patience, and the belief that the walls that come to stand will do so for a long, long time, perhaps even forever. I like to think that by helping to mix mud and carry stone for my father and other elders I managed to bring that influence into my consciousness as a writer.

Both my mother and my father were good storytellers and singers (as my mother is to this day–my father died in 1978), and for their generation, which was born soon after the turn of the century, they were relatively educated in the American system. Catholic missionaries had taken both of them as children to a parochial boarding school far from Acoma, and they imparted their discipline for study and quest for education to us children when we started school. But it was their indigenous sense of gaining knowledge that was most meaningful to me. Acquiring knowledge about life was above all the most important item; it was a value that one had to have in order to be fulfilled personally and on behalf of his community. And this they insisted upon imparting through the oral tradition as they told their children about our native history and our community and culture and our "stories." These stories were common knowledge of act, event, and behavior in a close-knit pueblo. It was knowledge about how one was to make a living through work that benefited his family and everyone else.

Because we were a subsistence farming people, or at least tried to be, I learned to plant, hoe weeds, irrigate and cultivate corn, chili, pumpkins, beans. Through counsel and advice I came to know that the rain which provided water was a blessing, gift, and symbol and that it was the land which provided for our lives. It was the stories and songs which provided the knowledge that I was woven into the intricate web that was my Acoma life. In our garden and our cornfields I learned about the seasons, growth cycles of cultivated plants, what one had to think and feel about the land; and at home I became aware of how we must care for each other: all of this was encompassed in an intricate relationship which had to be maintained in order that life continue. After supper on many occasions my father would bring out his drum and sing as we, the children, danced to themes about the rain, hunting, land, and people. It was all that is contained within the language of oral tradition that made me explicitly aware of a yet unarticulated urge to write, to tell what I had learned and was learning and what it all meant to me.

My grandfather was old already when I came to know him. I was only one of his many grandchildren, but I would go with him to get wood for our households, to the garden to chop weeds, and to his sheep camp to help care for his sheep. I don't remember his exact words, but I know they were about how we must sacredly concern ourselves with the people and the holy earth. I know his words were about how we must regard ourselves and others with compassion and love; I know that his knowledge was vast, as a medicine man and an elder of his kiva, and I listened as a boy should. My grandfather represented for me a link to the past that is important for me to hold in my memory because it is not only memory but knowledge that substantiates my present existence. He and the grandmothers and grandfathers before him thought about us as they lived, confirmed in their belief of a continuing life, and they brought our present beings into existence by the beliefs they held. The consciousness of that belief is what informs my present concerns with language, poetry, and fiction.

My first poem was for Mother's Day when I was in the fifth grade, and it was the first poem that was ever published, too, in the Skull Valley School newsletter. Of course I don't remember how the juvenile poem went, but it must have been certain in its expression of love and reverence for the woman who was the most important person in my young life. The poem didn't signal any prophecy of my future as a poet, but it must have come from the forming idea that there were things one could do with language and writing. My mother, years later, remembers how I was a child who always told stories – that is, tall tales – who always had explanations for things probably better left unspoken, and she says that I also liked to perform in school plays. In remembering, I do know that I was coming to that age when the emotions and thoughts in me began to moil to the surface. There was much to experience and express in that age when youth has a precociousness that is broken easily or made to flourish. We were a poor family, always on the verge of financial disaster, though our parents always managed to feed us and keep us in clothing. We had the problems, unfortunately ordinary, of many Indian families who face poverty on a daily basis, never enough of anything, the feeling of a denigrating self-consciousness, alcoholism in the family and community, the feeling that something was falling apart though we tried desperately to hold it all together.

My father worked for the railroad for many years as a laborer and later as a welder. We moved to Skull Valley, Arizona, for one year in the early 1950s, and it was then that I first came in touch with a non-Indian, non-Acoma world. Skull Valley was a farming and ranching community, and my younger brothers and sisters and I went to a one-room school. I had never really had much contact with white people except

from a careful and suspicious distance, but now here I was, totally surrounded by them, and there was nothing to do but bear the experience
and learn from it. Although I perceived there was not much difference
between *them* and *us* in certain respects, there was a distinct feeling that
we were not the same either. This thought had been inculcated in me,
especially by an Acoma expression–*Gaimuu Mericano*–that spoke of the
"fortune" of being an American. In later years as a social activist and committed writer, I would try to offer a strong positive view of our collective Indianness through my writing. Nevertheless, my father was an in-
adequately paid laborer, and we were far from our home land for
economic-social reasons, and my feelings and thoughts about that experience during that time would become a part of how I became a writer.

Soon after, I went away from my home and family to go to boarding
school, first in Santa Fe and then in Albuquerque. This was in the 1950s,
and this had been the case for the past half-century for Indians: we had
to leave home in order to become truly American by joining the mainstream, which was deemed to be the proper course of our lives. On top
of this was termination, a U.S. government policy which dictated that
Indians sever their relationship to the federal government and remove
themselves from their lands and go to American cities for jobs and education. It was an era which bespoke the intent of U.S. public policy that
Indians were no longer to be Indians. Naturally, I did not perceive this
in any analytical or purposeful sense; rather, I felt an unspoken anxiety
and resentment against unseen forces that determined our destiny to be
un-Indian, embarrassed and uncomfortable with our grandparents'
customs and strictly held values. We were to set our goals as American
working men and women, singlemindedly industrious, patriotic, and
unquestioning, building for a future which ensured that the U.S. was
the greatest nation in the world. I felt fearfully uneasy with this, for by
then I felt the loneliness, alienation, and isolation imposed upon me by
the separation from my family, home, and community.

Something was happening; I could see that in my years at Catholic
school and the U.S. Indian school. I remembered my grandparents' and
parents' words: educate yourself in order to help your people. In that
era and the generation who had the same experience I had, there was
an unspoken vow: we were caught in a system inexorably, and we had
to learn that system well in order to fight back. Without the motive of
a fight-back we would not be able to survive as the people our heritage
had lovingly bequeathed us. My diaries and notebooks began then, and

though none have survived to the present, I know they contained the varied moods of a youth filled with loneliness, anger, and discomfort that seemed to have unknown causes. Yet at the same time, I realize now, I was coming to know myself clearly in a way that I would later articulate in writing. My love of language, which allowed me to deal with the world, to delve into it, to experiment and discover, held for me a vision of awe and wonder, and by then grammar teachers had noticed I was a good speller, used verbs and tenses correctly, and wrote complete sentences. Although I imagine that they might have surmised this as unusual for an Indian student whose original language was not English, I am grateful for their perception and attention.

During the latter part of that era in the 1950s of Indian termination and the Cold War, a portion of which still exists today, there were the beginnings of a bolder and more vocalized resistance against the current U.S. public policies of repression, racism, and cultural ethnocide. It seemed to be inspired by the civil rights movement led by black people in the U.S. and by decolonization and liberation struggles worldwide. Indian people were being relocated from their rural homelands at an astonishingly devastating rate, yet at the same time they resisted the U.S. effort by maintaining determined ties with their heritage, returning often to their native communities and establishing Indian centers in the cities they were removed to. Indian rural communities, such as Acoma Pueblo, insisted on their land claims and began to initiate legal battles in the areas of natural and social, political and economic human rights. By the retention and the inspiration of our native heritage, values, philosophies, and language, we would know ourselves as a strong and enduring people. Having a modest and latent consciousness of this as a teenager, I began to write about the experience of being Indian in America. Although I had only a romanticized image of what a writer was, which came from the pulp rendered by American popular literature, and I really didn't know anything about writing, I sincerely felt a need to say things, to speak, to release the energy of the impulse to help my people.

My writing in my late teens and early adulthood was fashioned after the American short stories and poetry taught in the high schools of the 1940s and 1950s, but by the 1960s, after I had gone to college and dropped out and served in the military, I began to develop topics and themes from my Indian background. The experience in my village of Deetziyamah and Acoma Pueblo was readily accessible. I had grown up within the oral tradition of speech, social and religious ritual, elders' counsel and advice, countless and endless stories, everyday event, and the visual art that was symbolically representative of life all around. My mother was a potter of the well-known Acoma clayware, a traditional art form that had been passed to her from her mother and the generations of mothers before. My father carved figures from wood and did beadwork. This was not unusual, as Indian people know; there was always some kind of artistic endeavor that people set themselves to, although they did not necessarily articulate it as "Art" in the sense of Western civilization. One lived and expressed an artful life, whether it was in ceremonial singing and dancing, architecture, painting, speaking, or in the way one's social-cultural life was structured. When I turned my attention to my own heritage, I did so because this was my identity, the substance of who I was, and I wanted to write about what that meant. My desire was to write about the integrity and dignity of an Indian identity, and at the same time I wanted to look at what this was within the context of an America that had too often denied its Indian heritage.

To a great extent my writing has a natural political-cultural bent simply because I was nurtured intellectually and emotionally within an atmosphere of Indian resistance. Aacquu did not die in 1598 when it was burned and razed by European conquerors, nor did the people become hopeless when their children were taken away to U.S. schools far from home and new ways were imposed upon them. The *Aaquumeh hano,* despite losing much of their land and surrounded by a foreign civilization, have not lost sight of their native heritage. This is the factual case with most other Indian peoples, and the clear explanation for this has been the fight-back we have found it necessary to wage. At times, in the past, it was outright armed struggle, like that of present-day Indians in Central and South America with whom we must identify; currently, it is often in the legal arena, and it is in the field of literature. In 1981, when I was invited to the White House for an event celebrating American poets and poetry, I did not immediately accept the invitation. I questioned myself about the possibility that I was merely being exploited as an Indian, and I hedged against accepting. But then I recalled the elders going among our people in the poor days of the 1950s, asking for donations—a dollar here and there, a sheep, perhaps a piece of pottery—in order to finance a trip to the nation's capital. They were to make another countless appeal on behalf of our people, to demand justice, to reclaim lost land even though there was only spare hope they would be successful. I went to the White House realizing that I was to do no less than they and those who had fought in the Pueblo Revolt of 1680, and I read my poems and sang songs that were later described as "guttural" by a Washington, D.C., newspaper. I suppose it is more or less understandable why such a view of Indian literature is held by many, and it is also clear why there should be a political stand taken in my writing and those of my sister and brother Indian writers.

The 1960s and afterward have been an invigorating and liberating period for Indian people. It has been only a little more than twenty years since Indian writers began to write and publish extensively, but we are writing and publishing more and more; we can only go forward. We come from an ageless, continuing oral tradition that informs us of our values, concepts, and notions as native people, and it is amazing how much of this tradition is ingrained so deeply in our contemporary writing, considering the brutal efforts of cultural repression that was not long ago outright U.S. policy. We were not to speak our langauges, practice our spiritual beliefs, or accept the values of our past generations; and we were discouraged from pressing for our natural rights as Indian human beings. In spite of the fact that there is to some extent the same repression today, we persist and insist in living, believing, hoping, loving, speaking, and writing as Indians. This is embodied in the language we know and share in our writing. We have always had this language, and it is the language, spoken and unspoken, that determines our existence, that brought our grandmothers and grandfathers and ourselves into being in order that there be a continuing life.

JOSEPH BRUCHAC

Notes of a Translator's Son

Joseph Bruchac III (Abenaki, St. Francis-Sokoki branch) was born in 1942 in Saratoga Springs, New York. He was educated at Cornell, Syracuse, and Union Institute of Ohio, where he completed his Ph.D. in 1975. In 1970 he founded the Greenfield Review Press, which is devoted to multicultural publishing as well as the *Greenfield Review*, an eclectic literary magazine. He has edited a number of anthologies of poetry and fiction including *Songs from this Earth on Turtle's Back* (Greenfield Review Press, 1983) and *Returning the Gift: Poetry and Prose from the First North American Native Writers' Festival* (University of Arizona Press, 1994). He has written more than seventy books of poetry, fiction, and drama for adults and children including *Squanto's Journey: The Story of the First Thanksgiving* (Silver Whistle, 2000), *Crazy Horse's Vision* (Lee and Low Books, 2000), *Sacajawea* (Silver Whistle, 2000), and *No Borders* (Holy Cow! Press, 1999). He is a professional storyteller and has won numerous awards including a Rockefeller Humanities Fellowship and a National Endowment for the Arts Writing Fellowship in Poetry. He lives in Greenfield Center, New York.

The best teachers have showed me that things have to be done bit by bit. Nothing that means anything happens quickly—we only think it does. The motion of drawing back a bow and sending an arrow straight into a target takes only a split second, but it is a skill many years in the making. So it is with a life, anyone's life. I may list things that might be described as my accomplishments in these few pages, but they are only shadows of the larger truth, fragments separated from the whole cycle of becoming. And if I can tell an old-time story now about a man who is walking about, *waudjoset ndatlokugan,* a forest lodge man, *alesakamigwi udlagwedewugan,* it is because I spent many years walking about myself, listening to voices that came not just from the people but from animals and trees and stones.

Who am I? My name is Joseph Bruchac. The given name is that of a Christian saint—in the best Catholic tradition. The surname is from my father's people. It was shortened from *Bruchacek*—"big belly" in Slovak. Yet my identity has been affected less by middle European ancestry and Christian teachings (good as they are in their seldom-seen practice) than by that small part of my blood which is American Indian and which comes to me from a grandfather who raised me and a mother who was almost a stranger to me. I have other names, as well. One of those names is Quiet Bear. Another, given me by Dewasentah, Clan Mother at Onondaga, is *Gah-neh-go-he-yo.* It means "the Good Mind." There are stories connected to those names, stories for another time.

What do I look like? The features of my face are big: a beaked nose, lips that are too sensitive, sand-brown eyes and dark eyebrows that lift one at a time like the wings of a bird, a low forehead that looks higher because of receding brown hair, an Adam's apple like a broken bone, two ears that were normal before wrestling flattened one of them. Unlike my grandfather's, my skin is not brown throughout the seasons but sallow in the winter months, though it tans dark and quickly when the sun's warmth returns. It is, as you might gather, a face I did not used to love. Today I look at it in the mirror and say, *Bruchac, you're ugly and I like you.* The face nods back at me and we laugh together.

The rest of me? At forty-two I still stand 6'2" tall and weigh the 195 pounds I weighed when I was a heavyweight wrestler at Cornell University. My arms and hands are strong, as strong as those of anyone I've met, though my two sons—Jim who is sixteen and 6'4", and Jesse who is thirteen and close to 6'—smile when I say that. When they were little their games included "Knock Papa Down." Each year they've found it a little easier to do. My physical strength, in part, is from my grandfather, who was never beaten in a fight. Like his, the fingers of my hands are short and thick. I hold them out and see the bulges in the knuckles, the way both my index fingers are skewed slightly and cannot completely straighten. A legacy of ten years of studying martial arts.

Do we make ourselves into what we become or is it built into our genes, into the fate spun for us by whatever shapes events? I was a small child, often alone and often bullied. I was different—raised by old people who babied me, bookish, writing poetry in grade school, talking about animals as if they were people. My grandfather joked when he called me a "mongrel," a mixture of English and Slovak and "French," but others said such things without joking. When I was seven I decided I would grow up to be so big and strong that no one would ever beat me up again. It took me nine years to do it. ("Be careful what you really want," a Tai Chi master told me. "If you really want it, you'll get it.") My junior year in high school I was still the strange kid who dressed in weird clothes, had no social graces, was picked on by the other boys, scored the highest grades in English and biology and almost failed Latin and algebra. That winter of my junior year my grandmother died. My grandfather and I were left alone in the old house. That summer I grew six inches in height. In my senior year, though clothing and social graces showed little evolution, I became a championship wrestler, won a Regents' scholarship, and was accepted by Cornell University to study wildlife conservation.

How can I now, in only a few pages, cover the next twenty-five years? How can I adequately describe five years at Cornell and the year at Syracuse University, where I held a creative writing fellowship? At Syracuse, told by an expatriate South African writing instructor that my prose was too poetic, I smashed my typewriter in frustration and burned everything I had written. (Carol, my wife of a year, looked out the window of our small rented student housing bungalow and wondered what kind of bear she had married.) What about the Vietnam protests and the Civil Rights movement, the march on Washington and that long walk in Mississippi where James Meredith and Martin Luther King, Stokeley Carmichael and Marlon Brando took water from canteens I lugged up and down the line while state troopers with shiny insect eyes took our photographs with Polaroid cameras, waiting for the night when their eyes would look out from under white Klan hoods? And what about three years spent in Ghana, West Africa, where I taught in a school by the Gulf of Guinea? The Thunder Cult's drum rumbled at night in the next compound and a mad old man asked me to join him in a visit to Mammy Water under the waves of the man-eating sea. It was in Ghana that our son James raised his arms to the brightness in the night sky and spoke his first word, *Moon!* (I fictionalized my Africa experience in a novel completed in the 1980s. In it a half-breed American teacher discovers himself and his own country through life in a foreign culture—which he finds less foreign than his white expatriate colleagues. It is called *No Telephone to Heaven.*) Then came ten years of teaching in American prisons, and a decade and a half of editing and publishing multicultural writing: my introduction to *How To Start and Sustain a Literary Magazine* (Provision House Press, 1980) is a brief autobiography of my life as an editor. And all of that was made richer and more complicated by twenty years of marriage and sixteen years of learning from two sons—whose accomplishments bring me more pride than anything I've ever done. There isn't space enough here for more than the mention of all those things.

I can only go onward by going back to where my memories begin. I was not a black belt in pentjak-silat then, not a Ph.D. in Comparative Literature, a Rockefeller Fellow, a published poet, a "well-known Native American writer," as articles about me usually begin. (Thoreau might have written his famous "simplify, simplify" for the average newspaper journalist. How easily a few ill-chosen words can be used to encapsulate an entire human life!) Then I was only a child, with few experiences and fewer scars. All that I had in common with the person I am now is a confused heritage and the house I lived in then and still live in today. It is an old house with grey shingles, built by my grandfather on the foundation of a house owned by his wife's parents before it was burned down in a feud. It sits on Splinterville Hill, named for the ashwood baskets once made here. Just to the north of us, the Adirondack Mountains of upstate New York begin. I look out the window of the bedroom where Carol and I sleep and see, below the blue spruce trees my grandfather planted, the yard where I used to play.

How many memories of my childhood are my own and not those someone else had of me and told me about when I was older? I know that the image of a fence taller than my hands can reach is my own. I can still feel the chill, slightly rusted surface of its wire mesh against my face, my tongue almost freezing to its surface as I taste it on a day when the frost has glazed its red weave to the shimmer of a mirror. Is that my first memory or does the litter of puppies in Truman Middlebrooks' barn come before it? A warm milk smell of small animals, the sharpness of their teeth, the gentle insistence of their mother's muzzle nudged between me and them, pushing me away to roll on my back in the straw while someone's adult voice laughs. I know I am not being laughed at, so it is my grandfather's laughter that I hear. I never heard my father or my mother laugh when I was a child, and somehow life seemed too serious to my grandmother for her to indulge in much humor, even though she won her battle to keep me from my parents – that battle which I cannot remember but which has been replayed for me from the reluctant memories of those older than I. My grandfather, though, was often joking, often teasing. When he was serious it was a seriousness that no one laughed at.

The memory of me climbing the ladder, unafraid and right behind the old man, all the way to the roof forty feet up when I was only two, was my grandfather's. But it was recited about me so often that it became inseparably associated with my thoughts of my childhood. I know that I always dreamed of flight. I still do fly in my dreams. Its secret is simple – just lift your legs when you're falling and you'll never touch the ground until you're ready. To this day I don't understand why I can't continue to do it in the seconds after I wake from such dreams. But I have faith that eventually I will solve that problem one way or another and float away, with my body or without it. And though I've had some spectacular falls – at least one of which I should never have survived – I still love high places, cliffs and trees and resounding waterfalls. I inherited that fearlessness about high places and dying from my grandfather, just as I inherited certain stories. Here is one of them which is as much a part of my own fabric as if I had been there when that day was being woven:

I only went to school until I was in 3rd grade.
What happened then, Grampa?
I jumped out the window of the school and never came back.
Why?
I got in a fight with a boy who called me an Indian.

My grandparents raised me. I grew up only a quarter of a mile away from my mother and father's home on what we always called "The Farm," a plot of ninety acres with several outbuildings, which had been the home of my grandparents when they were first married. My grandfather gave The Farm to them after they'd been married a few years and were still living with my grandparents. The room where I type this was my parents' room when I was a baby. They moved to The Farm with my younger sister, and I stayed "for a while" with my grandparents. I sat with my grandfather in the wooden chairs he had made and painted blue and placed in front of his general store: Bowman's Store. I was wearing shorts and my toes couldn't touch the concrete as I dangled them down, using a stick to keep my balance as I stayed in the chair. There was a shadow in front of me. My parents. My grandmother took my hand and led me back into the house. "Get to your room, Sonny."

There my memory is replaced by that of my other grandmother, the Slovak one who lived three miles away up the South Greenfield road.

Your fader, he vas ready to leave your mother. Dere vere so many tears, such crying about you. Ah. Den your fader and mother they come and say they vill take you back, now. Dat is ven your grandfather Bowman, he goes out of the room. Ven he come back it is vith the shotgun. And he hold it to his head and say take him you vill never see me alive again.

Though I did not hear that story until after I was married, I knew that I was important to my grandfather. I realize now I must have been, in part, a replacement for my mother's older brother, who died at birth. I was always close to my grandfather. He delighted in telling how I was his shadow, how I carried my stick just like a spear and followed him everywhere. But, close as I was, he would never speak of the Indian blood which showed so strongly in him. I have a tape recording we made soon after we returned to live with him, back from three years in West Africa to the old house on Splinterville Hill with our new son, his great-grand-child, whose life would start the healing of wounds I had caused by simply being wanted.

Are you Indian, Grampa?
No.
Then why is your skin so dark?
Cause I'm French. Us French is always dark.

Yet I was conscious of the difference, of the way people looked at me when I was with my grandfather. When I was a freshman at Cornell University he came to visit, bringing two of my friends from high school, David Phillips and Tom Furlong. They spent two nights in the dorm, all of them sleeping in my room. My grandfather told everyone that David was my younger brother. They looked at my grandfather and then, more slowly, at me. David was black. When they asked me if it was true, I said, "What do you think?" When the fraternity rushing week came later that semester, I was on more than one "black list."

O my God, Joe, that's Grampa sitting there by the coffin!

I looked at the old man sitting in the front row in Burke's Funeral Home, right next to my grandfather's casket, and my own heart clenched its fist. Then the man looked at us. His face was younger and slightly less dark than that of his last surviving older brother. It was Jack Bowman. Though he lived in Lake George, the home of a more or less underground community of Abenaki Indian people even today, we had never met him before. In the year we had to get to know Jack before his own heart found a weak aorta less strong than his love for the land and his wife of fifty years, we heard more stories about my grandfather and his family. We also heard some of the denials of Indian ancestry, even though Jack offered no more of an explanation than his brother had for my grandfather's cutting himself off from his own side of the family after he married my grandmother, a woman of high education with degrees from Skidmore and Albany Law School, whose marriage to a semiilliterate and dark-skinned hired man of her father's sparked scandalized comment in Greenfield and Saratoga. In the face of those denials I felt, at times, like one who looks into a mirror and sees a blur over part of his own face. No matter how he shifts, changes the light, cleans the glass, that area which cannot be clearly seen remains. And its very uncertainty becomes more important than that which is clear and defined in his vision.

After Jack's death his wife Katherine fessed up. Yes, she said, Jack and Jesse were Indian. Everyone knew the Bowmans were Indian. She put it into writing and signed her name. It is the closest thing to a tribal registration that I will ever have. But it is enough, for I want to claim no land, no allotments, only part of myself.

There are many people who could claim and learn from their Indian ancestry, but because of the fear their parents and grandparents knew, because of past and present prejudice against Indian people, that part of their heritage is clouded or denied. Had I been raised on other soil or by other people, my Indian ancestry might have been less important, less shaping. But I was not raised in Czechoslovakia or England. I was raised in the foothills of the Adirondack Mountains near a town whose spring waters were regarded as sacred and healing by the Iroquois and Abenaki alike. This is my dreaming place. Only my death will separate it from my flesh.

I've avoided calling myself "Indian" most of my life, even when I have felt that identification most strongly, even when people have called me an "Indian." Unlike my grandfather, I have never seen that name as an insult, but there is another term I like to use. I heard it first in Lakota and it refers to a person of mixed blood, a *metis*. In English it becomes "Translator's Son." It is not an insult, like *half-breed*. It means that you are able to understand the language of both sides, to help them understand each other.

In my late teens I began to meet other Indian people and learn from them. It seemed a natural thing to do and I found that there was often something familiar about them. In part it was a physical thing—just as when I opened Frederick John Pratson's book *Land of Four Directions* and saw that the Passamaquoddy man on page 45 was an absolute double of photographs of Jesse Bowman. It was not just looks, though. It was a walk and a way of talking, a way of seeing and an easy relationship to land and the natural world and animals. *Wasn't no man,* Jack Bowman said, *ever better with animals than Jess. Why he could make a horse do most anything.* I saw, too, the way children were treated with great tolerance and gentleness and realized that that, too, was true of my grandfather. He'd learned that from his father, he said.

Whenever I done something wrong, my father would never hit me. He never would hit a child. He said it jes wasn't right. But he would just talk to me. Sometimes I wisht he'd just of hit me. I hated it when he had to talk to me.

The process of such learning and sharing deserves more space than

I can give it now. It involves many hours of sitting around kitchen tables and hearing stories others were too busy to listen to, and even more hours of helping out when help was needed. It comes from travels to places such as the Abenaki community of Swanton, Vermont, and the still-beating heart of the Iroquois League, Onondaga, and from realizing—as Simon Ortiz puts it so simply and so well—that "Indians are everywhere." If you are ready to listen, you'll meet someone who is ready to talk.

This short sketch of my early years, which I shall end here, represents only the beginning of a long apprenticeship I've been serving (*forever*, it seems). I seem to have an unending capacity for making mistakes just as my teachers seem to have an unerring ability to turn my mistakes into lessons. But the patience, the listening that has made it possible for me to learn more than I ever dreamed as a boy, is also the lesson I've begun to learn.

The most widely anthologized of my poems describes one lesson I was taught in the way most good lessons come to you—when you least expect them. Let it represent that part of my life which has come from continual contact with Native American people over more than two decades. Because of that contact my own sons have grown up taking such things as sweat lodges and powwows and pride in Indian ancestry for granted. The small amount that I have learned I've tried, when it is right to do so, to share with others.

BIRDFOOT'S GRAMPA

The old man
must have stopped our car
two dozen times to climb out
and gather into his hands
the small toads blinded
by our lights and leaping,
live drops of rain.

The rain was falling,
a mist about his white hair
and I kept saying
you can't save them all
accept it, get back in
we've got places to go.

But, leathery hands full
of wet brown life

knee deep in the summer
roadside grass,
he just smiled and said
*they have places to go to
too*

(from *Entering Onondaga,*
Cold Mountain Press, 1978)

The Personal Statement

of Barney Bush

Barney Bush (Shawnee) was born near the end of World War II. His books include *My Horse and a Jukebox* (American Indian Studies Center, UCLA, 1979), *Petroglyphs*, with drawings by Meenit Tatsii (Greenfield Review Press, 1982), and *Inherit the Blood: Poetry and Fiction* (Thunder's Mouth Press, 1985). Most recently he has written poetry set to music in collaboration with the English composer and performer Tony Hymas. Recordings of this work include *Remake of the American Dream* (NATO Records, 1992), *Left for Dead* (NATO Records, 1994), and *A Sense of Journey* (Qualiton Imports, 1995).

.,.,"

Usually, I say that I am from Oklahoma, which is true in the tribal sense that my relatives who remain strongly attached to our identity live there. And like any native person who has not been severed from family since birth, I could fill volumes with stories of dislocation, feuds, intermarriage with white captives, attempts at assimilation, fur-trapping trade, relatives who hung at the edges of frontier mentality in Kansas, Oklahoma, and Missouri, not to mention the area where I was born in southern Illinois; and there are, of course, the horrendous stories of boarding schools, and some of my grandmother's sisters who climbed to the height of the Anglo-Indian social ladder in the late eighteen and early nineteen hundreds by casting their lot with the BIA education system. Yes, I could fill volumes, and by doing so cast a fresh fuel on old disputes that yet smolder beneath emotional scars.

The families from which I descend are so large that there are first cousins, second cousins—traditionally brothers and sisters—that I have never met, but they spread the bloodlines from the Northwest coast to the Southeast. Although the primary remnants of my own cultural up-bringings are Shawnee, other tribal bloods run through my veins as well as the "captive bloods." World War II had not run its course when I became the firstborn to my mother's and father's blood, followed by Fred and John and eventually Blueberry, Bobijack, Richard, David, Lance, Joe, Bernard, Johnny, Betty, Barbara, Joy, Phil, and ole Ed—some from different tribes, but in our way they cannot be separated to the satisfaction of the European statistical thought. And even with this, there are more brothers and sisters, grandparents, the whole gamut of kin, than one can name to fill the pages. And I have two sons, Phil Dayne and John Colin.

My first memories are relatives, leaves, and hunting dogs—and there were ceremonies within our clan that seem to be neglected now that so many of our kin are marrying people attached to soap-opera mentality.

My second memories are attachments to the land, and the bluffs of the Ohio River country, just a few miles up from where it blends with the Mississippi River. The next memories are beatings at the Southern Baptist-oriented grade school—where I first became aware that my ancestors were defined as savages—especially by the male teachers. None of us, I believe to this very day, has figured out what they meant by their language or their system. My memory tries to fade when I think of so many of my childhood brothers and sisters who are no longer alive—cirrhosis, car wrecks, gunshots, and the "mystery" deaths.

PROSPERITY

    coal claims 1981
    a young brother

He lay head upturned over
the window   rain
pouring down radio
blaring acid rock My
eyes painted fingers still
wrapped to aluminum
Life poured from his
mouth through mud
funneled its red stream
down the side of the car.

(from *Petroglyphs*)

This one female teacher that I had for the first four years taught me a lot about art and allowed me to experiment with colors and with words. I learned the vulgar words rapidly, and was punished harshly for using them. It was difficult for me to understand that such simple words for bodily functions could bring such severe beatings for having written them down or said them aloud. Dominance is the key to a culture's use of language. Simply, the English speaker's government is in control of lives here in our country—and we must give respect to their language whether it makes sense to us or not.

The next four years in the same room of the same school were spent with a different teacher, a male from whom the only kindness I can remember is his having given me a stone axe head that he had found when he was a child—a strange act for someone who wielded the razor strap with such fury against me. I look back now, and I think maybe he thought it was his god-given task to bleed the savagery out of my pores. I never saw him attack other students with such cruelty, although he did whip others. Near the end of the eighth year came the stripminers—another of that world's great war machines against nature and humanity.

THE MOST BEAUTIFUL SIDE OF OURSELVES IS OUR LOVE FOR OUR HOMES—THE UGLIEST SIDE IS HAVING TO DEFEND OUR LAND FROM THOSE WHO DESTROY IT

Beware   earth destroyers
You have stolen   stripped
sold   bought   stolen the
land you could have lived on
in peace
All prices are paid
Creator   give us strength
to surrender our vengeance
our sorrow   so that
you may accept it as pity on
all of us   and
return to us wearing the
plume from under the eagle's
tail   so that
your children may recognize
you
Earth destroyers do not
recognize eagles' plumes
do not know that the
earth will turn
upon them.

(from *Inherit the Blood*)

The stripmines, the horror of their destruction, the move from our valley, the entrance into a primarily white high school in southern Illinois are all massive scars in my memory. There were teachers who were kind to me, perhaps more tolerant than kind—and others who were bigoted, angry with life that had cast them into the role of smalltime teachers in a smalltime town, the kind of stuff that American writers make into good trash novels. I had one English teacher in high school—there were others, but their hearts were not into being teachers. I wish to speak this good woman's name—Bernice Patterson. She never married and was into the years when I came to her my freshman year. She spotted me out right away—by my language first, "Backwoods, my dear, backwoods." She had taught Indians before in Colorado; in fact, we later learned that she had also taught English to my own mother. My mother spent hours with me, up by kerosene lamp—like Abe Lincoln, aieeee!—into the night with dangling modifiers, objects of the preposition, and sentences to be diagrammed. This was real horror but one that branded itself positively into my brain—meaning that it has been important in speaking and using the English language. Nowadays, I hear Indian people speaking all this proper English language, and white people, even on news broadcasts, totally devastating this language.

There were other humiliations in this small town. Some were racial—in fact, most were racial, although if its citizens were asked if they discriminated against Indians, their reply might be, "Hell, no, my great-grandmother was a Cherokee, and we live right next door to coloreds." There must be some endurance in my relatives that was not genetically passed on to me. I couldn't live where I couldn't be free with who I was/am. It doesn't seem to bother them a whole lot—at least outwardly. All my male relatives continue to hunt and fish, and the female ones take care of houses, gardens, primary child rearing—and generally instigate feuds.

Following high school, I took off hitchhiking around the country, going to powwows—which we were not allowed to do as children—took to alcohol, generally an investigation into the life-styles and mores of white America. Aieeee, we keep saying that some Indian writer is going to do this book.

NORTHWEST NOON

It was after the
mating season of the elk
and the road was
covered with brown leaves
remnants of high country's
heavy frost
He woke up shivering ice
had formed on the blue
plaid coat where he

spilled wine last night and
where was Rita or had he
simply dreamed her into
that world above the
railroad tracks
She had said her name
was Rita thinking of her
had kept him from freezing
He pulled and blew crusts of
dried blood from his
nose took a ceremonial
piss beside two ponderosas that
grew together
Sun was warm but wind
moaning bit sharply around
his shoulders
Walking instinctively to
someplace he looked about at
dried up corn patches
raised by
whitemen He knew the
feeling of this time somewhere
long ago in Oklahoma when
Old Mable had given
him a Bible with his name
stamped in gold
Image distorted he shook
it from his head and
walked toward the road

It was a northwest noon dogs
slick
in wind broken crevasses
drowsed under the last warm
sun acid coffee
rivuleted muddied corners of
his mouth
Truckers stopped here to eat on
their way to Seattle Boise
Helena or on to Minneapolis
Harvesting was long over he
was thinking of maybe
wintering out with this

one Pueblo girl near
Albuquerque
He washed his face   ritually
a last season in this damned
stinking toilet
With wet fingers he combed
shine back into his dark
sunburned hair   a quick
glance in the yellow
mirror   ah hell
he resigned
It had always been this way
no one to talk to about
leaving
Whenever he heard train whistles
or saw wind turning buffalo
grass a certain way   his
friends suddenly became
married to silence of the
autumn sky
Down the road he started
walking until he was no
longer around there anymore
He sang his grandfather's
hunting song   flushed a
covey of quail from
roadside sagebrush   watched
them light smoothly out of
range   Dusk
there was a car but
he never saw who was driving
Hands in his pockets his
eyes were on the road and
silvery flashes of pine needles
swaying   in the last light of
day.

(from *Petroglyphs*)

Up to this point, I have written in a very broad sense of my early
life; each segment is a story in itself. My education after high school is
no less a number of stories. After several attempts at a junior college in

southern Illinois, I managed to complete two semesters and transfer to Ft. Lewis College in Durango, Colorado. There, a large number of the students were my own people from many tribes. It was a good time, and I got a degree in art–and, I believe, history–in 1972. I spent some time studying jewelry-making at the Institute of American Indian Arts in Santa Fe, New Mexico, and later taught two courses, folklore and literature. Afterward, I went back to Oklahoma and helped start a school for our Cheyenne relatives at Hammon. Several of us, because of injustices, became involved with the American Indian Movement and the National Indian Youth Council. There were a lot of crazy things happening in those days. Maybe I will write about them someday, but not now. I don't believe the general American public could emotionally handle the atrocities that their own system secretly perpetrates. Their colonial government has a way of making the public feel comfortable by making those of us who want justice look like criminals. Since our own dignity and sense of right and wrong have started following the course of the brainwashing in the churches, schools, and television, we do have criminals among us.

During these early years of 1968–72, I began to take perceptions of personal experiences in a literary sense as a last resort to making known to those people in places of social power our spiritual sense of balance with all life–known and unknown–hoping that this might make a difference to indifferent lawmakers.

Following what contributions I could make to the Cheyenne school in Hammon, I was offered a job as a "Native American Specialist" at the University of Wisconsin in Milwaukee. I, of course, had no idea what this title meant. Several jobs were to follow in which I taught courses related to Native American literature, history, and art–several colleges and institutions temporarily pacifying the recurrent interest in the "plight of America's first people." During this time, my eyes are starting to open, to see that people are indeed being influenced by my poetry–our poetry–or at least I thought they were. I was invited to the Southwest Poetry Conference at Navajo Community College in 1971 where I gave my first public reading. There were other people there, some that I had never heard of–Gary Snyder, Gene Frumkin, Anglo people who have become gurus of American poets. Then there was my old friend Simon Ortiz, of Acoma Pueblo, who was beginning to be heard as a voice that spoke for native relationships to this earth; and Soge Track from Taos Pueblo, whose poetry spoke so beautifully and full of strength that I believe it made the non-Indian people uncomfortable; and Tony Schearer, Lacota traveler and poet–who had in previous years given me a ride when I was hitchhiking–his poems at the time were a bit esoteric for my untutored mind–but it was good to be in his presence.

AMERICAN JOURNEY: The White

Man's Educational TV Approach
to Freedom for All

Sometimes you win whiteman
and i forget it is you who
smiles when i am broken whe
n i panic thinking where
will i get money to pay rent
or phone bill or my nation
al defense student loan
Sometimes you win on tv and
i become angry watching the
educational channel
American Journey a whitema
n retracing steps of de Tocq
ueville concluding that
    Americas experiment with
    democracy has been succe
    ssful
and last scenes are despair
in native Alaskan fishing vi
llages
Yes whiteman sometimes yo
u win but we are yet here
on our native soil all the
way to Tierra del Fuego
blood quickly seeping into e
arth in democratic splendo
r clearing way for your m
aster plan

We are still here and some
times you win even as you
bootlick black folks for
their votes promising the
m a place in paradise

Blacks win too as pockets fi
ll with ransom money to aid
you in destruction   you bre
athlessly pray
We are still here   with suc
cessful part natives running
stoically with stars and str
ipes in one eye   dislocatio
n in the other   Sometimes y
ou win and i become angry be
cause your destruction is pl
ugging into every household
on the planet   bringing fre
edom and fast food   You hyp
ocrites   Freedom and food
were already here   but you
were not the distributors   y
ou know who was   You loom a
s a great shadow between ear
th and sun   When suns power
wanes   you are there with gl
eam of gold painted gods   Yo
u are death   painting your
color onto faces of millions
death that lays waste to all
of nature   and you call our
great patriots   blood thirs
ty savages   and make outlaw
s out of your own people who
love children
Yes   whiteman   sometimes yo
u win   gloat in your americ
an journey   allying with su
ccessful majorities   depic
ting drunken natives crawlin
g from beneath automobiles
Yes you win   Native people
win too   win the competitio
n   the finish line   for th
e most suicidal on earth an
d successful white writers a
dvise me to

Avoid the Indian trip
and just write poetry
Hoh Wah***************

It is a morning
Sun breaks into autumn frost
There is a silence as if the
whiteman has come and gone
Our windows steam from boil
ing choke cherries and
coffee This morning i
light cedar pray that my
son who walks knowingly this
blood drenched earth to
your school will replace
your american journey with a
human one.

(from *Inherit the Blood*)

As the years have gone by, I have given readings at many locations throughout North America, doing so because I believe it is right to speak as we do—perhaps influencing individuals rather than the masses who have the voting power. My ideas are constantly changing, even my concept of myself as a Shawnee, a singularly tribal person. It is strange—when I am at home, there is trouble because of my influences from the outside; I feel like I have let everyone down and that I have truly alienated myself with habits that I can't see. Then when I am gone from them, relatives my own age tell me how well my older relatives speak of me. There are mysteries about being who we are that have no definition, at least to me.

In 1978, I headed up to the University of Idaho to work on a master's degree in fine arts and English. Those Northwest Indians were sure different. My old friend Ed Wapp was teaching and working on another degree over in Seattle, so we would often rendezvous, either in Seattle or in Pullman or Moscow (Idaho), and present a formidable barrier to those Northwest Indian ways. They may say, "Ohh, yeaahh," but they know. Ed, who is Comanche from Oklahoma, and I often crossed trails around the country. He is one of few traditional flute players who have the power of that flute passed on to them. He has taken some of the spirit from my poems and composed pieces for that flute. When one hears the performed poetry and music together, the power from the flute, it makes everyone in the room feel the medicine of our existence on this earth.

Fresh cut kindling
    snaps and cracks
    in the fireplace
The house has that
    warm feeling that
    is always good
    during a snowstorm
Only does the fire
    keep me thinking
    about you heading
    north for the reservation
    snow coming down
    so heavily like the
    feelings you left with
The wind cuts through
    this dark night
Known only to me
    I hesitate to
    shift the blankets
    remaining exactly as
    we left them this
    morning
The small dirt streets
    are barely passable
    and I wonder if you
    are standing by the
    wood stove in your
    mother's house staring
    quietly out the window
I wish I were helping
    you feed the cattle
    this evening
There in the smell of
    loft dry hay the
    mountain wind is
    whipping snow through
    broken planks and
    a log roof long in need
    of repair

The walk back and
    a moment to linger
    by the creek where
    fluteplayers share
    their loneliness and
    dream in the mountains
But you are far away
    fading into the storm
    wearing that spotted blue
    blanket
    into the storm far away.

(from *My Horse and a Jukebox*)

After graduating in 1980 from the University of Idaho, amid controversy over some crazy things that happened while I was there, I was called home by my grandparents. They were getting ready to die. Within a year they had gone on and had left me stunned that another era of our being had passed into physical absence. Many personal things occurred afterward—much thinking over what I was going to do. What I thought I would like to do was to become reacquainted with all my relatives in Oklahoma and to let them know that I never intended to speak English again; I would stay out in the hills and do craftwork, hunt, fish, and raise a garden, alone or with my sons, but go to stomp dances of course. I started drinking more seriously, seeking refuge, seeking death actually, from a world that was feeling more and more unnatural to me. Jack Davis, a friend, and my major professor in English at the University of Idaho, once told me that he felt I had a touch of the "messianic complex" about me. I wasn't quite sure what he meant then. I think, now that I understand the term, that all of us who seek what is right for our existence, our earth, possess a touch of the "complex." I think that all who struggle to remain faithful to our Creator's gift must possess a great deal of this complex in order to survive and be examples to the younger ones, and to the ones who have given up the spirit. Following a painful accident related to drinking, I finally realized that I must decide whether I wanted to follow my grandparents or to truly take up this life. Circumstances that followed led me to choose life. The drinking had to go—and many other ways that were attractive to me. Now I am learning to speak more clearly, and this brings me to my present way of thinking.

    I am a writer simply because America stresses the written word as the primary establishment of truth. If it is not written down, then one has no "proof." I am a writer because I respect this earth, all the universe, all that is known, and that which is unknown. I respect all who acknowledge this interrelationship and pity those who squander their lives attempting to destroy it or steal its power.

We are exposed at the earliest ages to colonial America's truths, which are truths only as long as a group of their people have sat, debated, and philosophized long enough to satisfy themselves that this is indeed a profitable truth; therefore, they conclude, "Let us declare to all of mankind our discovery." If mankind were not making war against life, then I would redirect the power of words to sculpture, paint, beadwork, swimming, planting and caring for our gardens, and traditional observances alongside the smoke-scented bodies of my people.

TRUTH

Wrapped in
blanket in
tobacco smoke from
my pipe i am here
somewhere like a ghost
a phrase from a history
text sitting at the
window eyes crossing hills
looking for relatives
relatives who know
that we are the
way of this
land Whites
know it too wanting
an identity but cannot
find in this land what was
left in europe but yet they
search stripping and tearing at
the earth devastating native
lives in whose eyes yet lurk
the seven cities of Cibola
They see us but cannot
hear They read

that we stood
and fought
endured
all the genocide
bullshit for homes
families survival and
they know cowardice how
they fled europe becoming
traitors using freedom and
religion as passports but it
is greed that all this dying has
been about Strange you white
man what you die for strange lies
you tell your children They
would know truth if your
hearts were in this
land There is
always truth
at the
source.

(from *Inherit the Blood*)

Those who hunger for monetary power and world control have used words more effectively than anyone else, including all the combined writers and artists of the world who would have it otherwise. Smugly, they play games with words while human, animal, and plant life, water life and air, are being tortured and destroyed. Even now, that pitiful power looks beyond earth for expansion of areas in which new means of destructive planning can be enacted. Words hypnotize, and deceive everyone at one time or another, but these hypnotic words cannot last long in the hearts of true warriors. And I don't mean warrior in the way we have allowed the whiteman to define it for us. Real warriors might take different paths and more than often do. However, no matter what road is taken, it is always the road of truth. It is one that has been sought, perhaps by praying and fasting; it is the road that cannot be bought with money or evil power, though it is commonly overgrown with weaknesses that approach us in numerous disguises.

HE WANTS TO BE A WARRIOR

For Dean

He wants to be a warrior
buried in crimson cloth body
painted with honors borne by
spotted horses relatives trailing
singing his exodus
He looked in the mirror one last
time Hidatsa eyes staring back
bloodshot from one wild night cliffs
above Albuquerque
Long time since we had seen each
other weep eyes logging old
times hiding in snowstorm butchering
illegal Colorado elk panicked eyes
but invisible to wardens on horseback
We protected each other winter
jail New Mexico Tierra Amarilla
Ft. Lewis Indian club bail fund $1.17
our friends spent on wine
We laughed him three days out of
the army first day drunk hunting
rifles hocked at Isleta gave his
new Olds the Indian car look
I had to drive back in braille
Cigarette up in air ashes flipped to
morning sun he spoke without words
dreaming backroads to North Dakota
Sorry Dean again Cant go this
time eyes squinting in that same
sun coming leaving forever last
times flying in dreams childrens
hair scruffly combed sitting eternally
in tintypes
He broke my road stare wanting me to
stop His northern face of open
plains swept summer clouds eagle tail
fanning days gone by He said
I want to be a warrior Lightning
struck inside my belly Heed left the

beer stench   snapping barbwire strands
around Sandias
I heard those words again
   I want to be a warrior.

(from *Petroglyphs*)

When the Great Spirit put us on this earth, he gave us as tribes, individual roads to follow. They were given to all people, and the roads are all from the same source. Each group of people had different ceremonies because the land was different. Respect has to blend with our homeland. The white world worships an image of itself, one that it has created for its members to follow if they want to be rich, powerful, and sexy. This has set off chain reactions around the world, causing naive societies to believe that this religion of wealth and power is theirs for the asking, and that there is no price to pay but surrender and hard work. The devastated earth, the air, water, the extinct species of mankind, animalkind, and plantkind, the drugs, suicides, family separations–these are all the results of false ceremonies. Listen to both voices! The whiteman will twist good words into philosophical thought that attributes the desire for freedom to some primitive longing for the past. We must listen to how the white people use their language. They use their language sometimes with good meaning intended, but to follow its instruction is death. The few white people with whom we share our feelings of frustration realize that something is wrong with language–the voice and the heart are not working together.

Some of our "famous" chiefs heard very clearly what was taking place. D'akoomsah (Tecumseh) spent years traveling from what is now eastern Canada to what is now Florida, to the Mississippi River, talking with all who would listen about what were the intentions of the white worlds. Some historians say it was the whilte folks' military superiority that spelled doom for native peoples; some write that it was the native lack of understanding about ownership of the land; some say it was the warfare that already existed among native people, thereby renewing old feuds in competition for the fur trade; some say it was the alcohol; some say it was the whiteman's religion; some say it was increased dependence upon guns, steel knives, hatchets, kettles, cloth, wool blankets, and intermarriage with whites. D'akoomsah believed it was all these things plus one: Our people were not listening closely enough to what the white folks were saying, since in our cultures a person's voice was the sound of the heart–so we come back to the old concept of the "forked-tongued ones." By the time a majority of our leaders had learned what this meant, we were already hearing of the murdered and frozen bodies at Wounded Knee.

LISTEN

to the greedy world capturing
our thoughts
Listen through the iron
windows inside our eyes
Listen in the crack of
summer   when spirits
come from beyond autumn
to touch our shoulders
Listen
They hold the ropes to
pull the bars away from
the windows
Listen.

(from *Inherit the Blood*)

So why do I write? It is difficult for me to encourage writing, and even more difficult to discourage writing. We already have our tails in the snares of the European school system, which reflects this rabid philosophy of "take it or kill it"; teaches us to speak their language but, obviously, does not or cannot teach us to understand it. Continually I find concepts that I had formally incorporated into English thought only to find out later that this was not the way it was used at all. How English speakers must laugh when I turn my back. Will speaking the language fluently make us more like them or will it help us to understand where they are coming from, enabling us to pity them as we should be able to do, and to perhaps find ways to teach them how to live on this planet? Teach them how to treat their children? How to treat our children? There are so many from the "power hungry" who share that same sense of racial and cultural superiority that they take our children, whom they have stolen or adopted, and attempt to perform the same kind of brainwashing techniques on them as is attributed to the most extreme religious cults that lure spiritually deficient victims into their power. When these children, who come from a totally different consciousness of what determines dignity and self-respect, fail to find purpose in the designs of well-intentioned(?) adoptive parents, or groups who seize children, these people often submit the children to psychiatric care. Once this fails, the children wind up in foster homes, in correctional centers, and on the streets. Either way, the result is the same and includes sexual abuse, humiliation, and death. It is truly among the most shameful of world inhumanities, to rob human beings of our special unique qualities given to all of us by the Creator. And I do understand that there are some families who can come forward and say, "These are our adopted Indian kids. See what we've done for them: They have survived well and with complete awareness of their heritage." Oh yeah, well–okay.

A SINGLE PROSELYTE

Long sunburnt hair matted to
sweat on his cheeks   He was
yet walking at summers edge
still going home somewhere
before winter set in
It was america   but he was
not an american though born in
blood of this earth
Prisons were everywhere
In them he had seen his face a
thousand times over   seen
headless bones of ancestors
scattered over hillsides   over
stripmine dumps   left by
looters who sell even the
fleshless skulls
In sprawl of urban bars
blueblack fleshfilled nights
stirred with razor edges
used on his own blood
Short term prison for killing
one of his own   even though
he pretended they were white
He woke up that last morning
lips puffed   slivers of
glass in his teeth   hands
too unsteady to grasp the
tiny thorns of the beer bottle

Gazing at the faceless body
lying next to him wondering
if he had been kissing on it
he laughed at himself
Survival was still with him
even more when he sees bodies
of those who lost it for
whom dreams were not enough
nor religion held together by
witchcraft and white gods or
elders who sip their bottles
beside the drum
As he walks he shakes his
head at whites who call earth
a savage wilderness and their
cities civilization whose
infertile bodies infertile
minds steal adopt native
children send them to mental
institutions when they cannot
imitate when they cannot
turn from their own blood
His head shakes until he feels
his brains ready to explode
when he hears white leaders
condemning atrocities pleading
for humanity with ears and
hearts closed when his own make
the same pleas to americas
leaders
He stares at the golden rods and
sweet william grandparents
memory somehow attached searches
back to when stone was made
smooth to fit the hand
It is enough he thinks
holding round stone from
Old Town in his palm
pinches out a bit of ancient
tobacco
Hot hazy sky clouds with
autumn wind Balsam limbs

whine   Shadowy figures
circle the white drum   sing
in presence of White Plumed
Spirit   seen by ones
created from this earth
He walks   listens for
voices of relatives   listens for
songs   listens for
thundering of hooves   listens for
wailing behind prison walls
wailing of power hungry spirits
spilling from carcasses of newly
born
He listens until he hears cracking
of silence   smells the
bowels of earth   and
downpour of rain causes the bear to
stand upright.

(from *Inherit the Blood*)

For me, writing has become prayers that say, "Great Spirit, return to us our freedom, our land, and our lives. We are thankful for the present from which to learn how to be thankful for the past, and how to be hopeful for the future." And at other times my writing will say, "Listen to these voices, white people, listen . . . you of all the people on this earth need to listen—with your hearts—until you can truly distinguish right from wrong, and be strong enough to uphold your portion of what is right among all peoples. Your original religion comes from the same source as ours—the good one. Pray for the truth to live among us." And my writing says that there are many voices that are links connecting with all that extends from the source. These voices sometimes speak personally to our own tribal relatives: "Don't give up. This is the world that the Creator gave us. He will not let us down, if we remember what He and His good spirits have given us—if we remember that when we are weak, we aid the Earth Destroyers. The Creator told every one of us in our tribal beginnings to look after our ceremonies, and each other."

Praying to seek a vision, to seek truth, is always right. Truth builds upon itself—as the true mark of a warrior who conducts himself/herself accordingly—so that its beauty may shine in the faces of our children. Our Creator makes available to us, all that we need. It is an honor to go out and gather it. We must remember to say, "Thank you." It is honorable to give away, to show our gratitude – and to let the children see this. I try to say this with all the emotions in these voices, the poetry and stories, "Let us calm down. Be patient. Be silent and imagine what is right . . . its signs shall be all around us."

LINDA HOGAN

The Two Lives

Linda Hogan (Chickasaw) was born in Denver, Colorado, in 1947. Her books of poetry include *Calling Myself Home* (Greenfield Review Press, 1978); *Seeing Through the Sun* (University of Massachusetts Press, 1985), which won an American Book Award from the Before Columbus Foundation; *Eclipse* (American Indian Studies Center, UCLA, 1984); *Savings* (Coffee House Press, 1988); and *The Book of Medicines: Poems* (Coffee House Press, 1993). She has also published three novels—*Mean Spirit* (Ivy Books, 1990), *Solar Storms* (Scribners, 1995), and *Power* (W. W. Norton, 1998)—and is currently completing a fourth. Her other works include *Dwelling: A Spiritual History of the Living World* (Touchstone, 1995) and *The Sweet Breathing of Plants: Women Writing on the Green World* (North Point Press, 2001), which she edited with Brenda Peterson. She also collaborated with Peterson on *Sightings: The Gray Whales' Mysterious Journey* (National Geographic Society, 2002). A full-length autobiography *The Woman Who Watches Over the World* (W. W. Norton) appeared in 2001.

November 13, 1984. Today the newspaper contains the usual stories: two countries negotiating money and peace, a space shuttle penetrating the sky, the U.S. government preparing to invade Nicaragua, thousands of Minneapolis teenagers in line to purchase tickets for a Prince concert, an infant girl rejecting the transplanted heart of a baboon. Children are being abused and raped in their families and schools, and by their protectors. There has been a sniper shooting. Two large scorpions guard jewels in Bavaria. Coal miners and other worker struggles are in resistance against governments and police. Microwaves and diamonds are on sale.

In the face of this history that goes on minute by minute, the oppression recorded in the papers, human pain and joy, it is a difficult thing to think of autobiography, that telling of our selves or our lives or innerness.

I tell parts of my stories here because I have often searched out other lives similar to my own. They would have sustained me. Telling our lives is important, for those who come after us, for those who will see our experience as part of their own historical struggle. I think of my work as part of the history of our tribe and as part of the history of colonization everywhere. I tell this carefully, and with omissions, so as not to cause any divisions between myself and others. I want it to be understood that the opening paragraph, the news of November 13, 1984, is directly connected to this history, to our stories, to the continuing destruction of Third World and tribal people, and the exploitation of our earth.

I come from two different people, from white pioneers who crossed into Nebraska plains and from Chickasaw Indian people from south central Oklahoma.

Of the pioneers I know very little except for a journal I have that was written by my maternal great-grandfather during the Depression, in 1934. It is a spare book, though it spans the years from 1848 to 1934. His words cover a great movement across the American continent.

The journal describes pre–Civil War 1861 when my maternal great-grandfather, W. E. Bower, hoed broom corn, working from dawn to night before he walked home three miles. In 1862 he moved to where a railroad was being constructed, near the Wisconsin River, for hauling wheat. They used wood as fuel for the engines. He cut and hauled wood. At night he worked with his father making shoes until an accident occurred in which the elder Bower was dragged by horses and injured. The younger man then went to work full time for the lumber industry. In three years (1872) he went to Nebraska to homestead. The crops and trees were all eaten by grasshoppers. I have seen this in my own life, so I know it is true. My father tells of seeing plagues of grasshoppers that ate everything made of wood, even shovel handles.

Desperate after crop failures, Bower began hunting buffalo in order to sell the meat. The settlers were starving, according to his journal, and the government was sending soldiers out to shoot the buffalo. They also hunted beaver and antelope. He was followed once by hundreds of coyotes and was afraid at night.

I see from these words how closely destruction of the land and animal life are linked to the beginning American economy. This continues to be true. I see also how desperate the struggle for survival was for the new white Americans in those days. Their lack of regard for the land and life came out of that desperation. It continues today out of that tradition, but does not work in the service of life.

Bower writes about a Railroad section boss who refused to give him and his cohunters water from a well and refused them water for their horses, and how the hunters went for their revolvers before they were allowed to drink.

I believe he commented upon this cruelty because it surprised him. Historically, the incident took place at a time when major acts of genocide were being committed against tribal people across the country, when Mission Indians were being moved and moved again as settlers began to take over the California lands, when southern tribes were just removed to Indian Territory (Oklahoma), and when numerous other tribes from the North were being forced into the South, many in resistance. It was a continuing time of great and common acts of cruelty and violence.

Bower commented that he saw Indians and they looked friendly. I
made this into a poem:

OLD MEN AT WAR, OLD WOMEN

Be silent
old men who live inside me,
dark grandfather that was silent
though I was his blood
and wore his black eyes.
He's living in my breath
when it's quiet,
all his people are walking
through my veins without speech.

And blonde grandfather
fishing the river for Chubs,
many hunts
to sell buffalo who stood quiet
trusting the settlers
starving in Nebraska.
His words:
    We saw Indians but they seemed peaceful.

Red River,
I'm at the red river
and it's going dry,
all of us,
we are here,
and I'm drinking your wine for you,
the color of dawn
heading for light
heading for one light.
I'm wearing your love and hate
like silver
and blue stone.

This face
this body
this hair
is not mine.
This war inside me
is not mine.

I've been waiting,
where are the women?
Are they listening to this
beneath all the soft layers of my skin.
Are they listening.
Are they loving each other?

(from *Eclipse*)

During the time Bower traveled the continent, my Chickasaw people were trying to make a life in Oklahoma after having been moved forcibly over the Trail of Tears, that trail they began unwillingly and with great sorrow, from our homeland in Mississippi in order that settlers there could have the rich southern lands. That was the trail where soldiers killed children in order to make the journey quick, where women were brutalized, men murdered, where the bodies of living people were left to die as markers along a trail of history, pointing the direction back to our homeland.

After Removal, Chickasaws, many of whom had cooperated with whites and been slaveholders in the South before the Removal Act, were told to fight for the South in the Civil War. It is surprising that anyone thought Indian people might want to take up white wars after Removal, which politicized tribes, which Geary Hobson once said was a travesty that turned any white blood running in our veins red.

In a November blizzard those Indians who refused to fight were sent into Kansas without rations, horses, shoes, or clothing. Most died, and it was planned that way. As Joy Harjo has said, there are those of us who have survived who were never meant to survive.

This was followed by the Dawes Act, by other wars, by one tragedy laid down upon another, by land loss and swindles during the oil boom and the Depression, by continuing struggle, poverty, and loss.

My great-grandmother Addie was the granddaughter of Winchester Colbert, head of the Chickasaw Nation. She married Granville Walker Young, a rancher and politician of French-Indian (*métis*) ancestry and as such, in Indian Territory, was considered to be white. As a white intermarried citizen of the Chickasaw Nation, he was given land, and later a place on the Chickasaw legislature, and they built a large home. It is said that as a commissioner of lands, he managed to accumulate money from the tribal holdings. I would like to think this is not true and that

I've been misinformed, but historically, it sounds correct. It is not that different today with some Indian leaders.

Their daughter, Lucy Young, was my grandmother. When she married a Chickasaw named Charles Colbert Henderson, her father disowned her, as he did another daughter.

My grandmother graduated from the Bloomfield Academy for Chickasaw girls in 1904. In school, she learned to play the violin and the piano. She learned the manners of white upper-class southern women, for this was what the teachers valued in Indian girls, yet when I was a child, she and my grandfather lived in southern poverty, without water or lights, with horse and wagon.

That is the history of most of the southern tribes. I believe that when I say the truth, many of my family will feel defensive, as if I am saying that there was something wrong with my grandparents or family that we did not have money. But it is a shared experience. Some Indians built ranches, farms, or nearly comfortable lives only to lose them and return to poverty. We are landless Indians. Most of us continue to live below the poverty level defined by the U.S. government. We often dislike ourselves. We are made to believe that poverty is created by ourselves and not that it is an economic problem existing within the history of the American way of exploiting the colonized.

I come from people who have not had privilege. This is because of our histories. Those who are privileged would like for us to believe that we are in some way defective, that we are not smart enough, not good enough. In fact, it may seem that way because we speak separate languages and live a separate way of life. Some of us learn their language, the voice and ways of the educated, and we are then bilingual or trilingual and able to enter their country in order to earn a better living. But seldom do any of them understand our language, and our language goes deeper than words. It goes all the way to meaning and heart.

We have not valued the things that are desired by the privileged. We do not assume that we will go to college, or that there are places for us out in the dominant and dominating world, or that if we do certain things we will be taken care of. We generally do not know these "skills," and we often settle for very little because it seems like so much to us. We do not often fight for our rights, nor do we know what they are. We assume we are lucky to be doing so well. Plus, we are accustomed to a "system" that removes small liberties from us when we ask for what we deserve. My ex-husband's father, a non-Indian, worked in Oregon for a grocery firm for less than standard wages. He tried to organize his fellow workers to strike for decent pay and the company threatened to close down. The men, who had no other source of income and lacked also the means to move, had no choice left but to work for substandard wages. And it has been even harder for minority people.

For me, when I was a child, two lives lived me. In Gene Autry, Oklahoma, where my grandparents lived, they still went to town in a horse and wagon. They had no water. I wrote a poem about my sister and me in the 1950s in Indian Territory, Oklahoma:

> Already you have a woman's hip bones,
> long muscles
> you slide your dress over
> and we brush each other's hair
> then step out into the blue morning.
> Good daughters,
> we are quiet
> lifting empty milk cans,
> silver cans into the wagon.
> They rattle together
> going to town.
>
> (from "Going To Town," *Calling Myself Home*)

There was no water, electricity, or plumbing but when we were there we did have Coke, orange soda, and spoonfuls of white sugar. We bathed outside in a galvanized steel tub with Lava soap and water our grandmother heated on the woodstove. Our water came from the pump in town, over the few miles by wagon. My grandmother cooked dozens of eggs in the morning. She raised chickens. She rose from bed before daylight in order to brush her floor-length hair. When I was there, I got up early to help brush out her hair. I have felt this life deeply to be mine; though I lived in many other places and was born in Denver.

Outside of Denver, Colorado, in what was then a rapidly changing rural area called Lakewood, my father worked as a carpenter. That place is now city suburbs, but then we lived near a turkey farm. My mother took me a few times on a bus into the city to Woolworth's, and there was a legless man outside on a cart selling red paper poppies. My mother bought me ice cream. Here is an excerpt from around this time. It is from a short story called "Ain't No Indians in Hell" (*13th Moon*) and is about our first move into a neighborhood at the time our father was gone to the Korean war:

We were going to talk to my father and we were having a television delivered, all in one day. One of my father's checks had come through and mom's ironing money went for a down payment on the console and the rabbit ear antenna.

The television arrived first and we watched the Fred and Fay show with the clown and just heard Fred say, "You know, boys and girls," when mom shut off the picture.

We all walked together toward the church by the park.

A man with only one leg passed us. I turned to watch him. "Quit staring," Marnie said. "It isn't nice."

In the basement of the church was a large radio with a brown speaker. There were funny sounds coming through it and we waited while a voice took shape in there. The voices were stale and static. A woman standing in front of my mom spoke to the voice and left, crying. Then it was our turn and my mother spoke to a voice she said was my father. "I love you, honey," the voice said. And she told him we had seen grandma, that we had gotten one of the checks, and that the tomatoes were fine but the worms were eating us out of house and home. Marnie told him about the elephant she rode, and said also, "Gracie wouldn't ride him. She was plum afraid." I stared at the box and couldn't speak to it except to say, "Hello" and "Fine."

We walked back home, silent. Mom changed back into her large blue dress and went outside with the rusted rake and began to rake the place where there wasn't even any garden or dry grass.

She raked until it was dark and then she stayed outdoors. Marnie and I had stared at her through the window, raking at nothing, and then we saw her lie down on the grass to watch the stars begin to emerge.

Marnie tucked me in. "Okay," she said. "On the floor is the Kingdom of the Alligators. If you put a foot down there or get out of bed, they will eat you."

When I woke up later, the light in the corner was still lit and there was a small circle of gold on the wall. Marnie was asleep, her arms neatly and perfectly on top of the sheet. Mom was in the living room watching television and ironing. She lifted the iron and placed it back down again and moved rhythmically.

I turned around in my bed so that my head was at the bottom and watched the television. The room was doorless so no one could close me in or out. I heard a sound, a chirping in the bedroom, and followed it. I stood on the bed, careful to not fall into the Kingdom of the Alligators. It was a small green cricket up on the doll shelf. It was rubbing together a wing and leg, over its head. In this way it started a jungle or a fire, and I stood, forgetting the heat and watched it sing with its body, hearing the song of the night.

After the Korean War, when my father returned to us and I was eight, my parents moved to Colorado Springs to live in a housing project called Stratton Meadows, a name that signified that the land there was once beautiful. It was near the Fort Carson army base. This was a mixed-race area, and working class. There were a lot of "Spanish" as Mexican-Americans used to call themselves out of their own sense of self-dislike. I wrote a story called "Friends and Fortunes" about Stratton Meadows. One time a woman from National Public Radio read this story and said, I always knew there must be people like this, but I have never read about them. By "them" she meant the Others, those she had never been. She did not understand that I was one of them, alive and breathing, standing before her.

Where I live, people do things outdoors. Out in the open air, they do what wealthier and more private people hide inside their homes. Young couples neck beside the broken lilac bushes or in old cars parked along the street. Women knead bread on their steps, and sometimes collapse in a fury of weeping on the sidewalk. Boys breaking windows do not hide in the darkness of night.

We are accustomed to displays, so when Mr. Wrenn across the street has the DTs in front of his house, conversations continue. *What will be will be, and life goes on,* as my mother is fond of saying. The men who are at home go over to convince Mr. Wrenn that the frogs are not really there. If that tack fails, they kill off the frogs or snakes with imaginary machetes or guns. While they are destroying the terrors that crawl out of the mind, the rest of us talk. We visit while the men lift their arms and swing, aiming at the earth, saying there are no more alligators anywhere. "Lovely day, isn't it?" someone says.

I am grateful that I have learned how to analyze what happens to us on a daily basis in the form of classism and racism. Otherwise, like many others, I would have destroyed myself out of frustration, pain, and rage. Several times, like so many others, I have bordered on that destruction. We do it with alcohol, suicide, insanity, or other forms of self-hatred: ways of failing in our good, strong living.

It is sometimes easier to stay where we are, where we know our place, can breathe, know the language, but for the fact that we are largely powerless there to make any change for ourselves, for others, for our children.

It is difficult for us to gather our human forces together because our circumstances force us into divisions and anger and self-destruction.

From childhood I believed that oppression (I had no word for it then) was wrong; that the racism I heard daily—all sorts from without and from within my own family—was wrong; that cruelty, all forms of violence and destruction of earth and life, was wrong. I learned every single thing that I know in order to fight these wrongs, and I have not often bothered to learn other things. I began fighting against brutality and oppression when I was still only half-formed in my ideas and language, and sometimes at great risk to my own self. With great courage I began a fight toward growth and integrity, and I am very proud of that young woman I was who believed so strongly in life and had so much hope of change that she found energy and courage and was politicized rather than paralyzed by the struggles.

When I began to write, I wrote partly to put this life in order, partly because I was too shy to speak. I was silent and the poems spoke first. I was ignorant and the poems educated me. When I realized that people were going to read the poems, I thought of the best ways to use words, how great was my responsibility to transmit words, ideas, and acts by which we could live with liberation, love, self-respect, good humor, and joy. In learning that, I also had to offer up our pain and grief and sorrow, because I know that denial and repression are the greatest hindrances to liberation and growth. Simon Ortiz has said that denial is the largest single factor working against us in this country.

My life has been a constant effort at self-education, a constant searching and re-searching what was important for me to learn. I went to college as an older student. I had years of work experience behind me. I started work at fifteen as a nurse's aide in Hill Haven Nursing Home, where there were rats and where we aides laundered the sheets and diapers of the patients at 4:00 A.M. I felt fortunate to have this 75-cents-an-hour job. I did not know how many other girls prepared for college at that age, did not work full time. It was never mentioned to me that I might go to college, although my mother did try to convince me not to quit high school. I was engaged young and I wanted to get married. I didn't know anyone who went to college, or even what it was.

I worked many jobs like this. I worked for a dentist at $1.05 an hour. When he praised me for learning to mount X-rays after only one lesson, it made a great difference in my life that he thought I was intelligent and mentioned it to me on several occasions; but in spite of that encouragement, I worked at many other low-paying jobs, in nursing homes, in dental offices, and filing for a collection agency where I occasionally threw away the files of people who called to tell how hard their lives were. I believed them, although the owner said they would manipulate the collectors with their lies about death, poverty, or illness.

The poor tell terrible stories, it is true.

The last job I had before I went to college was working for an orthodontist who believed Ayn Rand's philosophy, received her *Objectivist Newsletter,* believed I was inferior because I worked for less than his wife's clothing budget or their liquor bill (I paid their bills at the office), and who, when I received money to attend night school and was proud, accused me of being a welfare leech and said, during the first space flight which cost lives in money, that I should be ashamed of myself. He fired me shortly after that for missing a day of work. I yelled at him as I left the office. It was the first time I fought back for myself.

That fighting back was an act of strength and self-respect, though I felt badly about it at first. Again, I look back through the years with great love for who I was, for knowing something was wrong, even though it was years before I had words for what it was:

Tell them all
we won't put up with your hard words
and low wages one more day.
Those meek who were blessed
are nothing
but meat and potato eaters,
never salsa or any spice.
Those timid are sagging in the soul
and those poor who will inherit the earth
already work it
so take shelter
take shelter you
because we are thundering and beating on floors
and this is how walls have fallen in other cities.

(from "Those Who Thunder")

When I say that I spent my life in self-education, I want people to know that part of this was done even when I went to college. I was a commuter student, attending night classes until my last year or two. There were no classes that made any connection to my own life experience or perception of the world. The closest I came to learning what I needed was in a course on labor literature, and the lesson there was in knowing that there were writers who lived similar lives to ours.

This is one of the ways that higher education perpetuates racism and classism. By ignoring our lives and our work, by creating standards for only their own work.

Education can be a hard process for minority and women students who have already learned too much of what we don't need to know. As an educator now I use books that are significant for us and are not often found in the university.

I find this especially necessary because I am aware of the fact that as a light-skinned Indian person I am seen as a person of betweens, as a person of divided directions. Non-Indians are more comfortable with me than they are with my darker sisters and brothers, for they assume that I am similar to them, or somehow not as real as other Indian people. This preference for light skin is true of other minorities also; the light ones, the mixed ones, are seen as closer, in many ways, to the dominant culture. But I want to point out how exclusion works in a divided society and how color affects us all. To be darker means to experience more pain, more racism, less hope, less self-esteem, less advantage. It means to be vulnerable to attack by police, to be left untreated more often by physicians, to be more vulnerable to rape and other forms of violence and abuse, and to have less of resources or assistance. I know women who have been raped by police (the protectors of life and property). A young boy I know was stripped naked by the police in Denver and let out of their car to walk home across town with no clothing. He had not committed a crime. He looked suspicious because of his dark skin. These are not isolated or unusual incidents. They happen most often to darker people.

My teachers have been those who before me found the first ways to speak of these things. Writers like the women in *This Bridge Called My Back,* Audre Lorde, Meridel Le Sueur, Tillie Olson, and D'Arcy McNickle, a Flathead Indian writer who documented the truth, as did Gertrude Simmons Bonnin, Zitkala Sa. I have been deeply interested in the work of many writers of the 1930s, and of writers from other countries who are engaged in struggles for survival. I continue to read books from contemporary radical and alternative presses, for those are the books that talk about our lives. I wonder why it is that to be working class or a woman of color in America and to write a book about it is a radical action and one that must be published by the alternative presses. Why is it that telling our lives is a subversive thing to do? Perhaps it is again that burden of denial and of repression. Still, it seems that the covering-up of the truth is the real act of subversion.

I read books of feminist theory and often relate that to culture and class. The experience of being a woman has the same elements as being Indian, black, and poor, even though some of the strongest divisions seem to be cultural ones, and some of the most difficult forms of exclusion and misuse that I have felt have come from white women in the women's movement and in the academy where some women have, by necessity and for their own survival, perfected the language of dominance and entered into competition with one another. I believe in the women's movement as another resistance struggle, not as an entering into the ways of the bosses. For many women, their movement is not resistance as much as infiltration. As Audre Lorde has said, "The Master's tools will not dismantle his house." My own efforts have gone into new tools, the dismantling, the rebuilding. Writing is my primary crowbar, saw, and hammer. It is a way of not allowing ourselves to be depowered by disappearance.

When I was a child, I knew that my journey through life was going to be a spiritual one.

I mention this here because I have met many people on this journey and I know there are those who will find this useful. I am hesitant, however, to go too deeply into it because of the misuse of Indian spiritual beliefs and traditions by those non-Indians who are in spiritual crises, and who hope to gain from the ways of other cultures because they do not find their own ways to be valuable. Searching out "ways" may be a problem in itself, since we are all part of the same motion of life, our work being to serve the planet and its people and creatures, whether we show respect to the life energy through ceremonies or through other kinds of services or through the saying of mass. It seems like people search for ways instead of integrating meaning. North Americans emphasize what they call "method" and "analysis" but do not often get into the center core of living.

Also, many spiritual traditions would have us believe so completely in a caste system that we may come to see the paths of others as superior or inferior to our own. Again, it is because we learn to measure the weight of our accomplishments without learning to love our inner lives. We must learn to see those measurements as meaningless, and to honor that innerness as real and as sacred. Here is a poem I wrote about traveling to Chicago:

EVOLUTION IN LIGHT AND WATER

Above gold dragons of rivers
the plane turns.
We are flying in gravity's teeth.
Below us the earth is broken
by red tributaries
flowing like melted steel,
splitting the continent apart
and fusing it
in the same touch.

It is easier to fall
than to move through the suspended air,
easier to reel toward the pull of earth
and let thoughts drown in the physical rivers of light.
And falling, our bodies reveal their inner fire,
red trees in the lungs,
liquids building themselves
light in the dark organs
the way gold-eyed frogs grow legs
in the shallows.

Dark amphibians
live in my skin.
I am their country.
They swim in the old quiet seas
of this woman.
Salamander and toad
waiting to emerge and fall again
from the radiant vault of myself,
this full and broken continent of living.

(first published in *Denver Quarterly*, Winter 1985)

That amphibious woman, the light and dark of myself, the ancient woman I am, comes to be viewed in another way in a later poem that realizes the essential value and strength of humor as one of the tools the masters have not used in the building of their houses:

And there are days
the old women gossip and sing,
offering gifts of red cloth and cornbread
to one another.
On those days I love the ancestors
in and around me,
the mothers of trees and deer
and harvests, and that crazy one
in her nightgown
baring herself to the world,
daring the psychiatrists to come
with their couches and theories and rats.
On those days the oldest one is there,
taking stock
in all her shining
and with open hands.

(from "It Must Be")

    Those on spiritual journeys are often seen to be, or afraid of being, crazy. Contemporary analysis, and I call it that on purpose, has not given people the strength they need, or fed the inner being, the spirit. It has failed to connect people with the world and yet has somehow managed to judge and categorize people who must travel that way, toward connections. I notice how seldom we find it strange that a person decides to specialize in an unusual scholarly career—studying Gawain, for instance—or how little we disdain scientists who perform animal experiments in the name of science, or how we do not find it abnormal that some persons devote their lives to selling insurance or cars or light fixtures. And yet spiritual people are unacceptable in many ways.

    The poem mentions psychiatrists. It is interesting to note here how many institutionalized people are at poverty level, female, minority, or are men who have verbalized belief systems or religious views that professionals find inappropriate. I think of Nijinsky believing his body was god, and it was, and I think of him dancing "Guernica" in silent protest of war and how that dance made the audience "uncomfortable" and how he died in a mental hospital. He behaved in an insane manner while the sane were enlisting to kill one another. The doubleness of this is intensified in the fact that to be conscious and aware often does make people broken in their Selves.

All of the work I do is part of a spiritual journey. "Spirituality is your inner self," a medicine person in New Mexico told me. It is in being. It is in seeing the world, in breathing, talking, cooking. Poetry is a large spiritual undertaking. So are stories, in the telling and the listening. So is being a mother and a caretaker of animals and trees. Doing dishes or painting a wall. More recently, teaching.

I have learned that to be spiritually conscious means to undertake a journey that is often a political one, a vision of equality and freedom. It is often to resist, to be a person who has not cooperated in giving up the Self or in joining up with the world that has denied us our full lives and rights. It is to assist others in the first steps of the journey, and to *not* offer assistance where it interferes with growth. It is to pray as well as to fight for the animals, the waters, against all wars, violence, and division. It is to learn clarity and to act out of kindness and compassion. It is to not be involved in conflict except when necessary to grant human and civil rights, animal rights, or to protect the earth from intrusion, poison, or other destruction. It is to pray and offer our breath and songs back to the world.

It is a paradox in the contemporary world that in our desire for peace we must willingly give ourselves to struggle. When once the spiritual people could advocate the path of least resistance, now the road to peace is often a path of resistance. This is why we find that in the past years many spiritual people have entered into civil disobedience, have retrained themselves from their previous concepts of religion as a sort of "separate" peace, an *isolated* inner experience, a motion toward acceptance of all things as the will of a creator. We now know that if we want rights we can neither only pray for them nor request them from those who have denied them to us. We know that civil rights and human rights are the same. The struggles of Indian people in Guatemala, El Salvador, Nicaragua, and other countries are the same as our own have been, and we must interfere in the genocide of those living beings that share our continent. We know that the struggles of the hungry are our own. And while we advocate kindness, we also know that for us to continue to practice kindness to oppressors is to act in a way that deprives us of the right to defend ourselves in a situation that remains one of war between nations. It is to cooperate in the violations of our own rights. We are only learning this, and now non-Indians also are learning to recognize the sanctity of all life.

For my inner growth, it is best when I remember to say "Thank you" to every living thing that graces my eyes or whose sound fills my ears. It is best if I return some of my richness to the spirit world and to the earth, if I feed the birds and carry love into the world. This is all that is required, not elaborate rites and ceremonies, just the need to *be* and to live fully. The healing ceremonies only return us to our being when the busy life and fast world have broken down our inner ways. They return us to our love and connection with the rest of creation. That is their purpose. They remind us of where we are within the framework of all life.

Other means that are consciously and actively used for this return to creation are the labor of service, basic and daily work, a strong consciousness of our moment-by-moment living. It is with great meaning that we live, every minute of our lives, but too seldom do we consider that meaning and the significance of our actions and words.

The stories of my life are many. I have omitted the small stories here in favor of the larger story that lays itself down with those of others. The stories of my life:

I have loved the songs of the first frogs in springtime, the red light of morning, the red earth, the heartbeat of trees and waters. I have been comforted by human and animal closeness and I have given comfort to the living and to the dying. I have taken care of the bodies and hearts of the sick. I have cooked meals, laid linoleum, cut wood, fixed roofs. I have bathed children, woven wool, made jewelry, painted pictures, and made music. I have lived with old people and with children, with no one too easily. I have worked as a fry cook, a waitress, a nurses aide, a teacher's aide, a secretary, a dental assistant, and in numerous other jobs. I have protested cruelty and other wars. I have not been afraid to offend the offensive, disturb the disturbed, nor to be kind and loving to the gentle. I have fought and I've given up easily and wondered if I could live one more day, and lived. I have been careless and made separations through my words and actions. I have made healing unions in the same ways. I've listened to the songs of night. I have hated death and taxes and I still do. I never once believed, not for a minute, that there are any two things you can't avoid:

I am the big woman with black eyes and a quiet face. I have a slow walk except when the breeze whistles at me like a cop after loiterers. I wear my white skirt wrapped over my big hips and walk through town laughing. I have a sailor in every port. I'm greedy, I drink all the coconut soda, and eat plum jam I never offer to guests, even to you whom I like.

Every day about this time when the world is coming to life, I think about death and I weep, laugh, and am silent. Once silent, I remember the smell of whiskey so I go to the water with my blue bucket and taunt the fishermen who have drunk too much the night before and who are baiting for something under the surface of the world. I say, "You don't even know what you might pull up from the water; an old shoe, a tire, or a snapping turtle. And you call yourselves fishermen." Then I wade out by the rocks and reach in with my bare hands. When I am through, my catch is the best, silver fish the size of my pan. I don't give them away. It pays a woman to be greedy. It is a heavy price we pay for what we give too easily.

Sit still now, the miners are passing by and we will wave at them from the window. Sometimes they are small men, but it is big work they do. When we women wave, it reminds them to be large. See their poor faces, dark with the coal in their lungs? Their souls have vacated the premises so they won't have an inner revolution when they listen to their own voices say, "Hey, the bosses are getting rich and my family is still hungry, my back hurts, and my lungs are half gone, and the president of this country has cut my pay, so the hell with this place *and* the war tax."

(from "The Big Woman")

WENDY ROSE

Neon Scars

Wendy Rose (Hopi-Miwok) was born in 1948. Her father is full-blood Hopi, her mother Anglo-Miwok. She has a degree in anthropology and has published the anthropological study *Aboriginal Tattooing in California* (Archeological Research Facility, University of California, Berkeley, 1979). Her many books of poetry include *Hopi Roadrunner Dancing* (Greenfield Review Press, 1973); *Lost Copper* (Malki Museum Press, 1980), with an introduction by N. Scott Momaday and illustrations by herself; *Long Division: A Tribal History* (Strawberry, 1981); *The Halfbreed Chronicles and Other Poems* (West End Press, 1985); *Bone Dance: New and Selected Poems, 1965–1993* (University of Arizona Press, 1994); and most recently *Itch Like Crazy* (University of Arizona Press, 2002). Rose teaches in the American Indian Studies program at Fresno City College.

I hate it when other people write about my alienation and anger. Even if it's true, I'm not proud of it. It has crippled me, made me sick, made me out of balance. It has also been the source of my poetry.

Writing this autobiographical essay has been the most difficult, most elusive task I have faced as a writer. I work hard to be less self-involved, less self-centered, less self-pitying. As readers and listeners have noted the angry or somber tone of my poems, I have struggled to lessen these things or, at least, keep them in proportion. I work toward balance and attempt to celebrate at least as often as I moan and rage. Everything I have ever written is fundamentally autobiographical, no matter what the topic or style; to state my life now in an orderly way with clear language is actually to restate, simplified, what has already been said. If I could just come right out and state it like that, as a matter of fact, I would not have needed the poetry. If I could look my childhood in the eye and describe it, I would not have needed to veil those memories in metaphor. If I had grown up with a comfortable identity, I would not need to explain myself from one or another persona. Poetry is both ultimate fact and ultimate fiction; nothing is more brutally honest and, at the same time, more thickly coded.

When I speak of bruises that rise on my flesh like blue marbles, do you understand that these are real bruises that have appeared on my flesh? Or has the metaphor succeeded in hiding the pain while producing the fact, putting it in a private place just for those readers and listeners who know me well enough to have seen the bruises? I live with ghosts and like anyone who lives with ghosts, I am trapped inside their circle. I long for someone to siphon off the pain, someone to tell it all to, someone to be amazed at how well I have survived. There is both a need for and a revulsion from pity. More than pity, I have needed respect. More than respect, I have needed to be claimed by someone as their own, someone who is wanted. I have survived—and there is pride in that fact—but is my survival of any value? Is my survival different from the millions of survivals in the world? Or is its kinship with them the truth of the matter—that we are growing, reproducing, living together as relations? Is my survival the final proof I have needed that I belong here after all? Will I be missed someday?

When I was first approached for this essay, my response (which lasted for several months) was simply to insist that the editor take some body of my poetic work and let it speak for me. I must have decided that there is some reason to make my pain public, although I am enough of a coward to keep the greatest pain (and the greatest pleasure) to myself. Would releasing the secrets let loose a passion so great and so uncontrolled that it would destroy the poetry? I am told that I take risks. When I am told that, the tellers mean that I take risks artistically, in style or technique, in placing the words on the page just so in a way that other poets would have the sense or the training not to do. It is usually meant as a compliment.

Do you know what is the greatest risk of all? Someday I may be forced to see myself as in a sweat vision, wide open to the world. I may find that I am only that one I saw in the vision, no more, no less. I am only what you see. The vision is naked and cannot be tampered with. Is it enough? Will the voices that have always said I am not good enough be quiet? Is this worth the pain and the poetry? Will you be satisfied?

Facts: May 7, 1948. Oakland. Catholic hospital. Midwife nun, no doctor. Citation won the Kentucky Derby. Israel was born. The United Nations met for the first time. It was Saturday, the end of the baby boom or the beginning. Boom. Stephen's little sister. Daughter of Betty. Almost named Bodega, named Bronwen instead. Little brown baby with a tuft of black hair. Baptized in the arms of Mary and Joe. Nearly blind for ten years. Glasses. Catholic school. Nuns with black habits to their ankles. Heads encased in white granite. Rosary beads like hard apricots—measuring prayers, whipping wrists. Paced before the blackboard. Swore in Gaelic. Alone. Alone at home. Alone in the play yard. Alone at Mass. Alone on the street. Fed, clothed in World War II dresses, little more. Mom too sick to care; brother raised by grandparents. Alone. Unwatched. Something wrong with me; everyone knows but me. They all leave me alone. No friends. Confirmation. Patron Francis of Assisi. He understands. Public high school. Drugs, dropping out. Finally friends. Getting high, staying high. Very sick, hospital. No more drugs, no more friends. Alone again. Married at eighteen. Tried to shoot me. Lasted three months. Again at nineteen. Lived in basement, then in trailer. Worked in Yosemite. Sold Indian crafts. Went on display. Drinking, fighting, he tried to burn down the house; he gave me the name Rose. Starved in Nevada; nearly died. Home. Eating again; got fat. College. Graduated in ten years. Went to grad school. Alone again. Met Arthur. Fell in love, still happy. Another ten years. Live in a nice house. Fresno. Have a swimming pool. Air conditioning. Have an old cat. Rent a typewriter. Teach. Work on doctorate. Two of us now. Moved to another planet, home.

Healing.

I am probably my mother. She bears my face but is lighter in complexion, taller, long-legged. She was thin enough as a girl to have been teased for it. Her eyebrows each come to a point in the center, little tepees at the top of her face. My brother inherited these, while I got her upward-turned nose and hair that thins at the temple. From my father I have coarse dark hair, a flatness of face and mouth, no waist, a body made of bricks. At different times, I have resembled each of them. I see myself in old photographs of my mother as a short, stocky, dark version of her, and others have seen my father in me, thinner, younger, lighter, female.

As much as I have come from them, the two of them threw me away. I am the part of them that they worked long and hard to cut off. I have never depended on them. I have floated into the distance, alone.

I have heard Indians joke about those who act as if they had no relatives. I wince, because I have no relatives. They live, but they threw me away—so, I do not have them. I am without relations. I have always swung back and forth between alienation and relatedness. As a child, I would run away from the beatings, from the obscene words, and always knew that if I could run far enough, then any leaf, any insect, any bird, any breeze could bring me to my true home. I knew I did not belong among people. Whatever they hated about me was a human thing; the nonhuman world has always loved me. I can't remember when it was otherwise. But I have been emotionally crippled by this. There is nothing romantic about being young and angry, or even about turning that anger into art. I go through the motions of living in society, but never feel a part of it. When my family threw me away, every human on earth did likewise.

I have been alone too much. I have been bitter too long. This part of me is not in balance. It has made me alien. This is something to pray about.

There is only one recent immigrant in my family. Sidney, my mother's father, came from England around the turn of the century. I don't know his father's name, but his mother was Christine. Early pictures of Sidney show a serious English schoolboy intent on his economic future. What he did in America was learn photography and operate a small studio in Berkeley for the rest of his life. He took misty portraits of young girls and babies, Victorian still-lifes, and sweeping panoramas of San Francisco Bay.

I don't remember being touched by Sidney at all, but he was my brother's greatest influence. Even today there is a British clip to my brother's speech. When I was in his house, Sidney was always on the other side of some door. I have wondered, too, why his middle name was "Valdez." And how he came to be so dark and brooding as a young man, so gray when old. Why did he leave England? Where did he meet Clare, the mountain girl from Mariposa, who would give birth to my mother?

Clare was born thirty years after the Gold Rush, in Bear Valley. Bear Creek branches from the Merced River near there, just down the mountain from Yosemite, rippling through oak-wooded grassy hills and bull-pines. Her mother and father were born there also; he was raised in a house that had belonged to John C. Fremont. Their people had ridden wagons west across the plains or had sailed around the Horn to find prosperity in a land newly claimed from Mexico. Clare's father, Maurice, was the son of German immigrants who had traveled from Missouri in a wagon train; there is a story told by his mother, Margaret, of how one night Indians came to steal the babies. Clare's mother, Elizabeth, had a noble and well-documented lineage. Her people were known by name all the way back to the eighth century on the Scottish side and to the Crusades on the Irish. The dominant thread in her ancestry crossed into Britain with William the Conqueror, part of the family rumored to have been related to him through one of his brothers. The Normans of my mother's background are very well documented and include the modern Lord Dunboyne, although our branch of the Dunboynes split from his during the seventeenth century. This Norman part of the family included Butlers and Massys, Barretts and Percys, Le Petits and de Berminghams— names that fiercely colonized Ireland and settled on stolen land. Among the parts of Ireland that they stole were certain women: O'Brien of Thomond, McCarthy Reagh, Carthach of Muskerry, all representing royal native Irish families. Another thread can be followed to the Scottish Highlands and to royal Celtic and Pictish families via the Clans MacInnes and Drummond.

By the time Clare was born in the 1880s, the family had included an Indian man, most probably Miwok. Clare's blond hair and transparently blue eyes belied that less well-known (and possibly involuntary) heritage, but the native blood reappeared in my mother. How many almost-comic photographs do I have of the sharp-faced blond and delicate lady who sits before the long-faced mustached Englishman and, between them, holds the chubby little girl with the dark round face, that little Indian baby?

Late in the summer of 1984, I received a package from my mother's cousin Joe, who is also my godfather, although I had not seen him for more than thirty years. He was both black sheep and bachelor in the family, a mystery man of whom I have no clear memories. Now I am laughing at myself. I have always searched for my place and my people, focusing that search on my father. His Hopi people have been sympathetic but silent; they trace their lineage through the mother and I could never be more than the daughter of a Hopi man. How ironic and unexpected Joe's package was! It contained diary excerpts, lists of names and dates, and newspaper clippings about my mother's family. She had always refused to answer my questions about ancestry, citing the melting pot as her excuse. My interest in our heritage was, in her eyes, just an aberration which—like slipping away from the Church—would someday be fixed. Yet the package with its precious communication came to me.

Now why didn't Joe send it to my brother? My brother is what they wanted. He is white-looking, with brown hair and green eyes; he has maintained his ties to home and hearth, even while in the Army. He has expressed great interest in his European blood, has dabbled in Druidic and neo-pagan rites, and looks like them. His hair and beard are long, his clothing covered with mystic symbols. The package did not go to him. I gave him and my mother copies of everything; they were as surprised as I that Joe chose me.

I learned that the Normans who stole Irish land went bankrupt, lost their land, and booked passage in 1830 for Quebec. The MacInnes clan, near that time, was forbidden to wear the tartan and fled Scotland to preserve their heritage. The weekend after Joe's package arrived, Highland Games were held in Fresno. In no other year would it have occurred to me to attend, but Arthur and I walked onto the grounds to search for my roots, he Japanese and I wearing all my turquoise for courage. It may have looked funny to all those Scots to see an Indian looking for a booth with her clan's name on it. The first booth was Irish; I showed my list of ancestral names to the man there, and he pointed to certain ones and said they had stolen his castle. I apologized to all of Ireland on behalf of John Bull and returned his castle to him; I suspect it would not hold up in Parliament and, anyway, they were the ancestors who had gone bankrupt. This is not the heritage I would have picked–to be the daughter of the invaders. It is not where my sympathies lie. Searching the grounds, I found my clan.

Great-great-grandmother, Henrietta MacInnes, who came to California for gold from Quebec, you have given me what my own father could not. I learned that I am entitled to wear your tartan, your symbol of a strong arm pointing to the sky with a bow in its hand. I also learned that you were the natives of Scotland, descended from the Pictish king, Onnus, and lent strength to my apology for Ireland. The colonizer and the colonized meet in my blood. It is so much more complex than just white and just Indian. I will pray about this, too.

This year Sidney and Clare, Grandad and Nana, are turning real for me. They have been dead twenty-five years, but my thoughts go to them as I continue to listen to my mother's jokes about their embarrassment. Clare got so angry sometimes! like when people would ask what racial mixture her little girl, my mother, was. Or when that little girl shared a room with a Jew in college. Or when that little girl, who had bobbed her hair and hung out with flappers, married a man with Indian blood and rural background. Clare knew who to blame. My mother told me of her mother's peculiar habit of taking my brother into her home when he was sick to nurse him back to health and, when I was sick, of taking my brother into her home so he wouldn't catch what I had. She was amused by this.

Nana! I'm afraid you'll see me cry! I have never been able to cry in front of you, of anyone. Any strong emotion is dangerous, as people are dangerous. Poetry has been the safest way to cry in public. I bristle when people say I'm cold and unfriendly, but they're right. I can't tell you straight out how I feel without putting it into a poem. And I have written some for you, safely cloaked in metaphor or masked by a persona. I hope you understand that the poetry is the only way I can love you. I *do* love. But you are dangerous. Does mom know how much it hurts when she tells me about the way you turned from me? Does she know how much it hurts for me to know that it could have gone unsaid?

I am turning numb. I have been educated to put a name to the things that my parents did, but the child within has no such knowledge. I recall that every dirty word I ever knew was first heard from my father's lips, from the man who raised me as he struck over and over. As an adult, I take this apart and study it. I suppose it was a kind of rape for him to talk like that in the middle of his violence, to name the parts of my body he intended to mutilate or cut away. I recall lying in my bed, hearing him scream at my mother that he wanted to kill me; and I recall that he tried, more than once. Symbolic of what he wanted to do to me, he smashed my toys. My mother's memories float in and out of those scenes; at times she denies everything, but I remember it was she who pulled him away as he tried to choke me on my bed. There was no media hype about abuse in those days, no public awareness; I begged the police to put me in a foster home, but I was always sent back. Eventually I learned that I was to blame for all of this, just as I was to blame for my parents' unhappiness.

I embarrassed them. They tell me their marriage began to go bad when I was born, although they never divorced. He lives in one room, she in another. How much it must embarrass them now for me to say these things to strangers! I would say something else, be someone else, act some other way—but there is no way I can twist my genes around. There is no sugar sweet enough to smear on the story of our household. These are ghosts that will never leave, the ghosts of knowing how I destroyed their lives. They sent me to social workers and psychiatrists, to priests, to people whose roles or professions I never knew. They told me I was sick and must try to get better so that my family could mend. Everything, they said, depended on me. I just wanted to get out so that the beatings, the obscene language about my body, and the constant knowledge of his hatred would be far away. Didn't they believe what I told them? Couldn't they see the scars? I didn't know that such scars never heal up. It's probably lucky that my nature is a fighting one; otherwise I would have died.

I will just talk about being different, as if I were talking about someone else. My mother said I was born different.

Her mother said she was born different. No one ever said what that difference was all about, but everyone knew it when they saw it. They avoided it as if it burned them. And so she was always alone and not just alone, but thrown away. They made sure she knew she was being thrown away. They told her so, over and over, through action and word, until she could see it in no other way. And so she knew she was rejected and she knew she was rejectable. She learned to worship her difference, whatever it was, and this empowered her. She rejected them.

Or, I could try this. I'll make up a story about my childhood and see if anyone believes it. I will tell about happy summer days with all my friends. Us girls are trying on makeup, combing each other's hair, comparing lies about boyfriends. The boys all want to date me, but I can only choose one at a time. I hate to hurt the others. I have been riding my beautiful stallion on the mountain; alongside is my healthy young collie. I know that when I go home, my parents will be glad to see me; they'll hug me and kiss me and hold me. Uncles and aunts and cousins will be there, too, and they will hug me. They know all about me, what my interests are, what I did that day. I have been placed in the gifted program at school and will be high school valedictorian. I have been skipping grades because everyone thinks I'm so smart. I'm pretty, too. I will enter college at seventeen with an enormous scholarship. I will receive gold jewelry or a diamond for my graduation. My father will kiss me on the cheek and take my picture.

I don't want to lie to you, but I don't want to tell the truth. The dirty laundry flaps in the wind, yet the alternative is to go on wearing it. How do you admit in public that you were abused, that the only time your parents ever touched you—that you can remember—was in anger, that your cousins probably don't know you exist, that your own grandparents had no use for you? How do you acknowledge that you were left so alone you never learned to brush your teeth or fix your food? How do you reveal that you were a bag lady at fourteen, having been turned out of the house, or that when you ran away no one looked for you? How do you expect anyone to believe how hungry you were at times, how you nearly died from starvation twice—when they can plainly see how fat you are now? How do you explain that you dropped out of high school, were classified as retarded but educable, and were not allowed to take college-prep classes? How do you reconcile being an "Indian writer" with such a non-Indian upbringing? It is not the Indian way to be left so alone, to be alienated, to be friendless, to be forced to live on the street like a rat, to be unacquainted with your cousins.

It would certainly be better for my image as an Indian poet to manufacture something and let you believe in my traditional, loving, spiritual childhood where every winter evening was spent immersed in storytelling and ceremony, where the actions of every day continually told me I was valued.

Today I live about fifty miles from Bear Valley. As I write, it is early August and the days are valley-hot, the nights thickly warm and filled with crickets. Although last winter was dry, this summer has found an explosion of toads in my yard. To uncover the memories, I have peeled back layers of scar tissue. I have invoked the ghosts and made them work for me. Is that the answer? To keep them busy? There is nothing authentic or nice about my past; I am sure that I would be a great disappointment to anthropologists. But then, you know—now—why I write poetry; being Indian was never the reason. I have agonized for months about writing this essay, and now that it is finished I am afraid of it. I am mortified and embarrassed. I am certain I said too much, whined perhaps, made someone squirm. But there is no way I can change the past and the literal fact is that I have tried to forget what is unforgettable; there are few happy moments that I recall—or perhaps, as I have succeeded in forgetting the bad, the good has also been forgotten. Perhaps the editor and the readers will forgive me for using them in an exorcism.

My father told me, when I took Arthur down to Hopi to meet him, that Hopi earth does contain my roots and I am, indeed, from that land. Because the roots are there, I will find them. But when I find them, he said, I must rebuild myself as a Hopi. I am not merely a conduit, but a participant. I am not a victim, but a woman.

I am building myself.
There are many roots.
I plant, I pick, I prune.
I consume.

JOY HARJO

Ordinary Spirit

Joy Harjo, born in Tulsa, Oklahoma, in 1951, belongs to the Muskogee Nation and is a member
of the Tallahassee Wakokaye Grounds. Besides her
status as an award-winning writer, she also plays saxophone, performing solo and with her band, Poetic
Justice. Her many books of poetry include *In Mad
Love and War* (Wesleyan University Press, 1990),
which won an American Book Award and also the
Delmore Schwartz Memorial Award; *The Woman
Who Fell from the Sky* (W. W. Norton, 1994); and
How We Became Human (W. W. Norton, 2002). She
edited, with Gloria Bird, *Reinventing the Enemy's
Language: Contemporary Native Women's Writing
of North America* (W. W. Norton, 1997). Her CD,
Letter from the End of the Twentieth Century (Red
Horses Records) was released in 1997 and won a
1998 Outstanding Musical Achievement Award.
Her most recent CD, *Native Joy for Real* (2003), is
available on her own label, Mekko Records. She lives
in Honolulu and teaches at the University of Hawaii
and at UCLA.

• ; : ; "

I was born in Tulsa, Oklahoma, on May 9, 1951, after a long hard labor that occurred sporadically for over a week. My mother didn't know it was labor because I wasn't due until mid-July. I also surprised her because I was a single birth; she had been told to possibly expect twins. The birth was hard on both of us. I was kept alive on a machine for the first few days of my life until I made a decision to live. When I looked around I saw my mother, only nineteen, of mixed Cherokee and French blood, who had already worked hard for her short life. And my father, a few years older, a tall, good-looking Creek man who was then working as a mechanic for American Airlines. I don't think I was ever what they expected, but I am grateful that they made my life possible and honor them for it.

I was the first of four children who were born evenly spaced over the next eight years or so. And much later had my own children, Phil and Rainy Dawn. We are descended from a long line of tribal speakers and leaders from my father's side. Menawa, who led the Red Stick War against Andrew Jackson, is our great-great (and possibly another great) grandfather. I don't know much about the family on my mother's side except there were many rebels and other characters. They are all part of who I am, the root from which I write, even though I may not always name them.

I began writing around the time I was twenty-two years old. I am now thirty-four and feel that after all this time I am just beginning to learn to write. I am only now beginning to comprehend what poetry is, and what it can mean. Each time I write I am in a different and wild place, and travel toward something I do not know the name of. Each poem is a jumping-off edge and I am not safe, but I take more risks and understand better now how to take them. They do not always work, but when they do it is worth it. I could not live without writing and/or thinking about it. In fact, I don't have to think about it; it's there, some word, concept always being born or, just as easily, dying.

I walk in and out of many worlds. I used to see being born of this mixed-blood/mixed-vision a curse, and hated myself for it. It was too confusing and destructive when I saw the world through that focus. The only message I got was not belonging anywhere, not to any side. I have since decided that being familiar with more than one world, more than one vision, is a blessing, and know that I make my own choices. I also know that it is only an illusion that any of the worlds are separate.

It is around midnight. I often write at this time in my workroom near the front of an old Victorian-style house near downtown Denver. Tonight a thick snow has muffled the sounds of traffic. The world is quiet except for the sound of this typewriter humming, the sometimes dash of metallic keys, and the deep breathing of my dog who is asleep nearby. And then, in the middle of working, the world gives way and I see the old, old Creek one who comes in here and watches over me. He tries to make sense of this world in which his granddaughter has come to live. And often teases me about my occupation of putting words on paper.

I tell him that it is writing these words down, and entering the world through the structure they make, that has allowed me to see him more clearly, and to speak. And he answers that maybe his prayers, songs, and his belief in them has allowed him to create me.

We both laugh, and continue our work through many seasons.

This summer, during one of those sultry summer evenings when the air hums with a chorus of insects and there's the sound of children playing in the street, I sat, writing. Not actually writing but staring into that space above the typewriter where vision telescopes. I began remembering the way the world was before speech in childhood. A time when I was totally conscious of sound, and conscious of being in a world in which the webbed connections between us all were translucent yet apparent. I remember what it felt like to live within that space, where every live thing had a voice, and each voice/sound an aurora of color. It was sometime during that reminiscence that I began this poem:

SUMMER NIGHT

The moon is nearly full,
                the humid air sweet like melon.
Flowers that have cupped the sun all day
                        dream of irridescent wings

under the long dark sleep.
                               Children's invisible voices call out
in the glimmering moonlight.
                                 Their parents play wornout records
of the *cumbia*. Behind the screendoor
                                      their soft laughter swells
into the rhythm of a smooth guitar.
                                 I watch the world shimmer
inside this globe of a summer night,
                              listen to the wobble of her
spin and dive. It happens all the time, waiting for you
                                          to come home.
There is an ache that begins
                         in the sound of an old blues song.
It becomes a house where all the lights have gone out
                                      but one.
And it burns and burns
                    until there is only the blue smoke of dawn
and everyone is sleeping in someone's arms
                              even the flowers
even the sound of a thousand silences.
                         And the arms of night
in the arms of day.
                Everyone except me.
But then the smell of damp honeysuckle twisted on the vine.
And the turn of the shoulder
                    of the ordinary spirit who keeps watch
over this ordinary street.
                And there you are, the secret
of your own flower of light
                    blooming in the miraculous dark.

(from *Furious Light*, Watershed Foundation cassette, 1986)

For years I have wanted to capture that ache of a summer night. This summer in Denver was especially humid, reminded me of Oklahoma. I wanted that feel, in the poem, of a thick, sweet air. And I wanted the voices I remembered, my parents' talking and scratchy, faint music of the radio. In the poem it is my neighbors I hear, and their old records of the *cumbia*. I also wanted to sustain a blues mood, pay homage to the blues because I love the blues. There was the sound of a sensuous tenor saxophone beneath the whole poem. I also added the part of everyone being in someone else's arms, "everyone except me," for the blues effect.

But I did not want to leave the poem there, in the center of the ache; I wanted to resolve it. I looked out the front door into the night and caught a glimpse of someone standing near the streetlight, a protecting spirit who was keeping watch over the street. I could have made that up, but I believe it is true. And I knew the spirit belonged in the poem and, because the spirit lives in the poem, too, helps turn the poem around to a place of tender realization. Hence, "And there you are, the secret / of your own flower of light / blooming in the miraculous dark."

When I first began writing, poetry was simply a way for me to speak. I was amazed that I could write anything down and have it come out a little more than coherently. Over the years the process has grown more complicated, more intricate, and the world within the poem more immense. In another recent poem the process is especially important:

TRANSFORMATIONS

This poem is a letter to tell you that I
have smelled the hatred you have tried
to find me with; you would like to destroy me.
Bone splintered in the eye of one you choose
to name your enemy won't make it better for you
to see. It could take a thousand years if you name it
that way, but then, to see after all that time, never
could anything be so clear. Memory has many forms.
When I think of early winter I think of a blackbird
laughing in the frozen air; guards a piece of light. I
saw the whole world caught in that sound. The sun
stopped for a moment because of tough belief. I don't
know what that has to do with what I am trying to tell you
except that I know you can turn a poem into something
else. This poem could be a bear treading the far northern
tundra, smelling the air for sweet alive meat. Or a piece
of seaweed stumbling in the sea. Or a blackbird, laughing.
What I mean is that hatred can be turned into something
else, if you have the right words, the right meanings
buried in that tender place in your heart where
the most precious animals live. Down the street
an ambulance has come to rescue an old man who is slowly
losing his life. Not many can see that he is already

becoming the backyard tree he has tendered for years,
before he moves on. He is not sad, but compassionate
for the fears moving around him.
That's what I mean to tell you. On the other side
of the place you live stands a dark woman.
She has been trying to talk to you for years.
You have called the same name in the middle of a nightmare,
from the center of miracles. She is beautiful.
This is your hatred back. She loves you.

When I began writing the poem, I knew I wanted an actual transformation to be enacted within it. I began with someone's hatred, which
was a tangible thing, and wanted to turn it into love by the end of the
poem. I was also interested in the process of becoming. I tried to include
several states of becoming. The "process of the poem" becoming was one.
I entered the poem very consciously with lines such as, "I don't know
what that has to do with what I am trying to tell you," and "What I
mean is . . ." I also consciously switched tenses partly for that reason,
and others. I often change tense within a poem and do so knowing what
I am doing. It isn't by accident that it happens. Time doesn't realisti-
cally work in a linear fashion.

Within the poem is also the process of the "hater" becoming one
who is loved, and who ultimately loves. The "I" is also involved in the
process.

Earlier in the day an ambulance came into the neighborhood to pick
up an elderly neighbor who had suffered a stroke and was near death.
It was a major event. All who witnessed it walked carefully through the
rest of the day. I was still thinking of him when I wrote the poem and
knew that somehow he, too, belonged in the poem, for he was also part
of the transformation.

I was not sure how the poem would end when I began writing it,
but looking back I realize the ending must have originated in one of two
places. One was a story I heard from a woman who during times of deep
emotional troubles would be visited by a woman who looked just like
her. She herself would never see her, but anyone passing by her room
while she was asleep would see this imaginary woman, standing next to
her bed. I always considered the "imaginary" woman as her other self,
the denied self who wanted back in.

And I was reminded, too, of the woman who had followed me

around at an all-night party in Santa Fe a few years before. We had all drifted around the house, talking, dancing, filled with music and whatever else we had tasted. She finally caught up with me around dawn and told me that she was sorry she was white, and then told me that she believed white people had no souls. I was shocked and sad. And I saw her soul, starved but thinly beautiful, knocking hard on the wall of cocaine and self-hatred she was hiding behind.

So the poem becomes a way of speaking to her.

It is now very late and I will let someone else take over this story. Maybe the cricket who likes to come in here and sing and who probably knows a better way to write a poem than me.

It is not the last song, but to name anything that, only means that I would continue to be amazed at the creation of any new music.

IN THE AMERICAN INDIAN LIVES SERIES

CPSIA information can be obtained
at www.ICGtesting.com
Printed in the USA
LVHW08s1132290818
588505LV00025B/671/P